D0639503

TOUCHSTONE

ALSO BY SUZANNE GORDON

Black Mesa: The Angel of Death

Lonely in America

Suzanne Gordon

 A Touchstone Book Published by
Simon and Schuster

Copyright © 1976 by Suzanne Gordon
All rights reserved
including the right of reproduction
in whole or in part in any form
A Touchstone Book
Published by Simon and Schuster
A Division of Gulf & Western Corporation
Simon & Schuster Building
Rockefeller Center
1230 Avenue of the Americas
New York, New York 10020

Designed by Irving Perkins
Manufactured in the United States of America

1 2 3 4 5 6 7 8 9 10

Library of Congress Cataloging in Publication Data

Gordon, Suzanne.
  Lonely in America.
  Bibliography: p. 311
  1. Loneliness.   2. Social isolation.
3. United States–Social conditions–1960–
I. Title.
HM132.G66   301.6'2   75-28318
ISBN 0-671-22143-4
ISBN 0-671-22754-8 pbk.

Permission to reprint from the following is gratefully acknowledged:
    Attachment and Loss, Vol. I: Attachment, from Chapter 2, "Observations to Be Explained," by John Bowlby, © 1969 by The Tavistock Institute of Human Relations, Basic Books, Inc., Publishers, New York.
    Corporate Wives, Corporate Casualties, by Robert Seidenbert, M.D., © 1973 by AMACOM, a division of American Management Associations, reprinted by permission of the publisher.
    Culture Against Man, by Jules Henry, © 1963 by Random House, Inc.
    Future Shock, by Alvin Toffler, Random House, Inc., © 1970 by Alvin Toffler.
    On Encounter Groups, by Carl Rogers, Harper & Row, Publishers, Inc.
    The Self and Others, by R. D. Laing, Tavistock Publications, Ltd., and Pantheon Books, a division of Random House, Inc., © 1961, 1969 by R. D. Laing.
    Untitled poem by Karen Shattuck, © 1975 by Karen Shattuck.

Acknowledgments

This is not an upbeat book. I offer no quick measures to end loneliness. It would be easy to proffer illusory and simplistic solutions for very complex problems, but my intention is rather to present the problem of loneliness, not only its theoretical aspects but also the feelings it engenders, in the hope that this will lead to a better understanding of what is wrong, and that change will grow from this understanding.

The writing of this book was not, for me, a simple exercise in "objective" journalism. And loneliness is not something that I view from without. I have spent the better part of my thirty years grappling with loneliness. And although I have not personally spoken of my loneliness because I do not want to intrude on the eloquence of the people who allowed me, at least for a moment, into their lives, these people speak for me also, and my reflection stands behind their words.

I have throughout substituted fictional names and, where it was necessary in order to protect anonymity, have disguised home towns, occupations, family relationships and, in certain instances, other significant characteristics. However, the essential facts of their loneliness have been accurately reported.

I would like to thank those interviewed and the following for giving me a chance, however small, to help end this dilemma of ours.

I would like first and foremost to thank my friend Isabel Marcus Pritchard for her inexhaustible help. She was constantly available for the comment and support without which this book could never have been completed. It is her book almost as much as it is mine, and there will never be an adequate way to thank her. I give unending thanks as well to Lloyd Linford for his editorial assistance, his enthusiasm, and his steadfast moral support. To Christine Joy, my wonderful friend, I give thanks for her support and for having accompanied me on many of the excursions necessary for the research of this book. I am grateful to my friend Bob Fitch for his ideas about encounter and gurus, and to my friend Judith Klein for the use of her paper "Hello in There," and for her insights into the problems of the elderly. I am also grateful to Dr. Richard Budson, Director of the Community Residence Program for the Commonwealth of Massachusetts. I am indebted to Ursula Caspar and Martha Shattuck for their aid in my project. Many thanks also to Naomi and Ed Rovner and again, to Wilma and Stan Keller. I am eternally grateful to Nancy Keller for her last-minute help with the completion of the book. And a titular thanks to Richard Margolis.

To the following people I also owe acknowledgment and gratitude: Carlos Hagen of KPFK Radio Los Angeles, Peter Osnos of the *Washington Post*, Cecile Goodman, Barbara Lazlett, Sherry Clark, Michael Schatz, and Barbara Epstein of the Jewish Family Services, Co-Op City branch, and Helen Breuner, Paul Baum, and John Atkisson.

Last, but of course not least, I would like to thank my agent, David Obst, who has held my hand, at long distance, from the beginning of this project, and to my editor, Alice Mayhew, whose enthusiasm and suggestions carried me through. And finally, many many thanks to my mother, Blanche Gordon, for her unending confidence in me and my ideas.

For Peter

Contents

A collective problem, if not recognized as such, always appears as a personal problem, and in individual cases may give the impression that something is out of order in the realm of the personal psyche. The personal sphere is indeed disturbed, but such disturbances need not be primary; they may well be secondary, the consequence of an insupportable change in the social atmosphere. The cause of the disturbance is, therefore, not to be sought in the personal surroundings, but rather in the collective situation. Psychology has hitherto taken this matter far too little into account.

C. G. JUNG, *Memories, Dreams, Reflections*

Except for saints, life can be polarized between love and death only if there is no intensity in between; only if everything else has dropped out of life; only if there is nothing else on which to bestow meaning. Thus we can say that man thinks only of love and death when he has nothing else left to him. Put another way, when life is empty man flies from death into love; and when he cannot love he is frightened of death and so turns to love obsessively. Obsession with love and death fills the void left by the departure of significance from life, and significance is driven out of life, paradoxically, when the effort to survive becomes too much for us.

JULES HENRY, *Jungle People*

Part One
Introduction

Chapter One

The Geography of Loneliness

To be alone is to be different, to be different is to be alone, and to be in the interior of this fatal circle is to be lonely. To be lonely is to have failed. There is no excuse for that. It is clear to the teenager that he or she should have a date after school, and it is clear to the average man or woman that he or she should have a mate, family, a circle of friends. Or a consciousness-raising group—intimacy. There are maps to follow to get you there: grade school, high school, perhaps college, church, company, promotion. Or the People's Yellow Pages. We live in an era of openness and possibility. Never has there been so much talk of sharing, so many books and courses to facilitate smooth relating, explaining both how to begin and, in case of a mix-up, how to end. The tight boundaries of rural, neighborhood, family-centered America have burst, breaking the bonds of exclusiveness and duty, freeing people for alternatives that seem to have no end, so much do they promise. And yet—the problem of loneliness. When it is mentioned, even the eyes of those who tend to deny its existence flicker inward for a moment.

Life in America has exploded, and loneliness is one main ingredient in the fallout. What was once a philosophical problem, spoken of mainly by poets and prophets, has now become an almost permanent condition for millions of Americans, not only for the old or divorced but also for the men and women filling singles bars and encounter groups, the adolescents running away from home or refusing to go to school, the corporate transients who move every two or three years, and the people calling suicide and crisis hot-lines in search of someone to talk to. Knowing no limits of class, race, or age, loneliness is today a great leveler, a new American tradition.

To begin to understand the origins of the problem, one need only look at New York's high-rises, Los Angeles' pedestrianless streets, suburbia's front-porchless houses. The halls of large apartment buildings do not encourage conversation, nor do the aisles of supermarkets, the noise of factory assembly lines and factory-like offices, or the forbidding streets of the metropolitan areas that house 69 percent of the American population. Despite all the recently voiced desire for contact, there are few places where it can be made, spontaneously or otherwise. In the great rush for freedom we have lost the ability to be free together. And since personal identity seems to require the validation of another person's confirmation, many people feel faceless—empty, lonely.

In small towns or urban neighborhoods people had more than one strong relationship to affirm who they were. In their daily lives they reinforced and created networks of contacts. Doing daily chores, for instance, meant more than just purchasing the makings of the evening meal, cleaning the front stoop, or mailing a letter. These were more than just burdensome responsibilities, they were social events through which people gave each other mutual recognition. Today's American marvels at the "quaint" Europeans who still shop daily for groceries, visiting three or four small shops and taking as much time to buy food for a meal or two as an American in a supermarket might take to buy all the week's groceries. It's more than a question of pace; it's a question of people. It's pleasant to chat with your butcher or baker, to be handed a can rather than to take it off the rack in a store where efficiency has replaced humanity.

In rural settings people might, as the cliché goes, have known everybody else's business; but they were also there to help during a crisis, and one did not have to worry about calling for help in such a situation. Not so in contemporary America, as one California suburban resident vividly commented. When her husband had a stroke she hesitated before picking up the phone to call a neighbor for help. It could have been an imposition. In small towns or extended families, not to have called would have been the insult. A woman rancher living alone in Montana explained that during the winter she calls her closest neighbors, who live miles away, to tell them when she leaves to feed her cows and when she returns. "If I don't call," she said, "my neighbors are furious. They'll have to come looking for me and take care of me if I should fall from my horse or have an accident. It saves them worry. They know something is really wrong if they don't hear the phone ring." Among the most rugged of America's rugged individualists such concern is second-sense. There is an aura of community that leaves the most physically isolated people with the feeling that they *belong*.

In the past, rural areas and urban neighborhoods also provided a center where people of all ages could meet. The old could maintain contact with the young, and youth had some familiarity with aging and death. Although generational conflict has always been present, old people and young were not as radically separated, with the old set aside and doomed to loneliness in euphemistically characterized "senior citizens' communities." Today age segregation has passed all sane limits. Not only are fifteen-year-olds isolated from seventy-year-olds but social groups divide those in high school from those in junior high, and those who are twenty from those who are twenty-five. There are middle-middle-age groups, late-middle-age groups, and old-age groups— as though people with five years between them could not possibly have anything in common. Like white light going through a prism, America divides into its component parts.

Mobility has a great deal to do with this erosion of American life. People move with such astounding frequency (40 million Americans change their residence once a year, and the average person will move fourteen times in his or her lifetime) that they lose family ties, friends, and themselves. There is a myth among the most highly mobile (corporate transients, academics, and those in the armed services) that those who have met in the past will, at one point or another, meet again. They will not entirely lose touch. There are also the mails, phone lines, and air routes. Just because we live three thousand miles apart doesn't mean it's over. You can call after six o'clock, visit regularly. Technology, however, is unable to completely vanquish distance. And distance undoes the ties formed by frequent contact—the thing that makes friends friends. People do indeed lose each other, and the pain of that loss, renewed every two or three years, makes people withdraw from further contact. "I sometimes feel that I don't ever want to make friends again," the wife of a university professor said. "You find people to get close to, and then they leave or you leave. At first it seems this will happen only every once in a while. But it happens over and over again. I sometimes wish I lived in a Chinese village where nothing changes and you know everyone from birth till they die."

Mobility does more than affect close friendships; it changes the whole tone of a neighborhood. When people lived in the same place for years, residents in a community knew one another. When someone moved onto the block you brought cake or candy. Today it is not unusual for people not to know their neighbors at all. Why should one make the effort of a welcome when the new arrivals will be leaving in a year? No sense wasting the energy. I knocked on the doors of a residence hall at the New York Hospital–Cornell Medical Center in Manhattan to ask the residents if they knew their neighbors or socialized with people living near them. All the residents in the building are doctors, nurses, or technicians; all are interested in the same things, presumably having strong interconnections. Yet very few even knew the names of the people living directly next door, and almost none met socially. Only the women with children met—and the children made much of the effort. It seems that even where we are the closest we can neither reach nor touch.

This communal apathy is also fertile soil for crime, since

people have no idea which face goes with which front door. If someone walks out of the house with a TV set, a neighbor has no idea if it is the owner taking it to the repair shop or a burglar making off with an easy haul. And crime has never been noted for its healthy effect on human relationships. You are not likely to enter into a spontaneous conversation on the street if you think the person addressing you is a potential mugger, or open your door at night to help someone in trouble if you think that person might pull a knife. In a circular swing, more distrust and more loneliness. We feel like strangers on our own streets. Where we should feel the safest, we rather feel that no one would help us if we were in trouble, that what happens to us, whether good or bad, makes no difference to the world around us—that *we* make no difference. And because we tolerate such antihuman life-styles, the encounters we have with others are more likely to be hostile than pleasant. It is not only the muggers that are frightening but the faces of shoppers waiting on lines that are too long, and the ferociousness with which commuters honk their horns and curse in heavy traffic.

Another disturbing effect of the isolation from family, friends, and community is the added difficulty it imposes on the average marriage. Besides socially inherited communication problems and increasing dissatisfaction with our work, modern marriages have to cope with the added burdens of high mobility. In the past, husband and wife were to be "the one" for each other, the perfect companion. Now a woman or man must be not only confidant and lover, but family, community, friends—all things to one other man or woman.

In the past, relationships founded on large families and close communities gave people some options if things weren't going well at home. Today, when family bonds are weaker, more and more is being asked of the nuclear unit. It is as though one loaded a table with heavier and heavier weights while shrinking the circumference of the tabletop and chopping at its legs. The table will eventually collapse—just as the nuclear family is collapsing.

Change, mobility, freedom from burdensome commitments—all these can be exciting and enriching. Apologists for discontinuity in American life are fond of drawing upon an analogy between trees and people to support their positions. It is true, they admit, that some trees, in order to grow strong and healthy, need a great deal of time in one place so that they can send down solid, deep roots. Other varieties, however, can grow healthy despite frequent transplants and shallow roots. But the problem is that people are simply not trees. Trees, whether shallowly or deeply rooted, do not, as far as we know, need communication with other trees in order to flourish. Standing alone, they do not feel lonely.

What began as a great adventure may be turning into just another fetter. In retrospect, it is not clear from what exactly we have been running. Were small towns, for instance, suffocating or idyllic? Were ethnic, urban neighborhoods prisons or protectors? But whatever complicated reasons are behind the constant push for change and movement in urban and suburban America, people have a vision of where they are heading: toward technical and social progress—by definition a better state. What *will be* in America has generally been taken to be inherently superior to what *was*.

Our present, however, makes it abundantly clear that the price for such passionate optimism is the shattering of both personal and community life. It is a process that can only destroy much of the potential the future may hold and that is certainly demolishing any hope we may have in the present. We are paving the road forward with psychological wreckage, obstacles that make it impossible for many to make the journey and that provide a bumpy ride for those still able to travel.

Though there has been some attempt to treat the causes of the problem of "future shock," much of the emphasis has been toward disguising it—patching up the cuts, passing out the Valium,* and hoping that the patient won't cause too much trouble

* According to a *New York Times* article of May 19, 1974, Valium is the most widely prescribed drug in the U.S., with one in ten Americans of

in the future. For the most part, however, people are left alone to deal with the traumatic loneliness in modern life. And so for many Americans life becomes a bit like playing the stock market in a time of recession: one is less concerned with maximizing one's gains than with minimizing one's losses. To borrow from Karen Horney's description of the major preoccupation of neurotics, we are forced to seek safety rather than satisfaction, despite all our claims to the contrary.

It's obvious that loneliness is a human emotion common to all people in all eras. But at certain points in history, because of specific social changes, what were inevitable moments in life become, sometimes overnight, life-styles for millions of people. Mass loneliness is not just a problem that can be coped with by the particular individuals involved; it is an indication that things are drastically amiss on a societal level.

When the societal is distinguished from the psychological, as Jung has noted, an individual experience becomes a collective disturbance—a "social problem" in the sense in which Michel Philibert, the French gerontologist, uses the phrase. A social problem, says Philibert, is one that affects a category or group of people in a society, provided that the problem carries the following three qualifications:

1. It must be considered as deriving, at least in part, from the functioning of the structure of society itself.

2. It must be considered as affecting not only the category or group of people primarily involved but in some way having a pervasive influence on the rest of society, so that other people who do not face that specific difficulty are concerned about it; and it is seen as jeopardizing the whole fabric of society and endangering the development of the health of the society, so that those not directly affected are made uneasy and think something should be done about this problem.

3. It must be considered as being susceptible to some sort of

---

eighteen years or over having used it at some time for various problems. Women, the article states, use the drug more frequently than men. And Valium is only one of many tranquilizers used.

treatment through the action of society itself—that is, social action, and in the long run through political action.*

People have always had to deal with hate and love, anxiety, aggression, violence, and loneliness. In certain epochs, however, these universals become the simultaneously held *preoccupation* of a major segment of the population. And the intensity of this concern is such that even those who do not feel it directly are disturbed.

To understand and begin to deal with loneliness as it exists today in America we must therefore consider more than the personal history of the particular lonely person and his or her emotional background. We cannot interpret the present problem exclusively in terms of childhood traumas: lack of affection from parents, for example, lack of openness, and thus loneliness. For present difficulties, while they encompass the problems of the past, are not simply mere reflections of it. The lonely person is not, as is commonly thought by many psychologists, lonely because he or she *needs to be lonely*, and is thus somehow enjoying it. People are lonely today because of both the psychological baggage they carry with them and the peculiar way American society alienates the potentially closest of friends, colleagues, lovers, and workmates.†

In this investigation into loneliness, therefore, I will be discussing not only individual stories but also such topics as political apathy and disillusionment, the character of work in America,

* From a lecture, "The Third Age," at the University of California, San Francisco, August 1973.

† Throughout this book I will be accusing American society of various significant failings, and considering loneliness in the light of these. This is not to say that other countries do not share the same shortcomings or have the same problems. We are, however, Americans, and our major concern is with America. To excuse our problems by pointing out that things are no better elsewhere is irrelevant to any attempt at social change at home. America is, furthermore, one of the most industrially advanced countries, and the problems that result from mobility and disintegration of the family and community dominate life. Thus if we see loneliness as being inherently related to these aspects of modern life, we must admit that loneliness is more of a problem in a more advanced country such as America than in less industrially advanced societies.

and other elements in the social climate. In Part Three, "The Loneliness Business," we'll look at a new, billion-dollar industry that has arisen supposedly to relieve, but in any event to profit from, extensive misery.

I have limited the scope of this investigation in several ways. I will not discuss the loneliness of those isolated from others by such physical disabilities as mental retardation or crippling diseases (except in the case of the elderly for whom illness is an essential component of loneliness and may, in part, be a result of that very loneliness). This is in no way intended to differentiate the loneliness of the physically disabled from that of the "normal" person. I have decided not to include this aspect mainly because I have found that the majority of people who are lonely are not disabled, at least not physically. And because loneliness is something to which most people do not like to admit—to themselves or to anyone else—comparing their loneliness with that of people who are isolated because of physical problems allows the "healthy" person to dismiss any similarities between his or her situation and that of the "abnormal" person. If that is how you define loneliness, the "normal" person will respond, "Then of course I am not lonely." It is too easy to hide behind the mask of "normalcy," and it is my hope that when confronted with the loneliness inherent in "normalcy" we can see the problem for what it is.

I have also decided not to touch on the problem of loneliness in minority communities. Again, not because that problem doesn't exist.* It is simply beyond my scope. For understanding the signs of loneliness involves more than speaking the same language; it involves a profound and considerable knowledge of

---

* Some black psychologists have stated that loneliness in black or minority communities is not, perhaps, as severe as that of white middle-class communities. There is a certain sense of closeness that comes from being a member of a visible minority: blacks are linked together, for instance, by their shared blackness. These same psychologists predict that that identification will be lost when and if minority groups are assimilated into the larger society. And thus they may then be susceptible to the same loneliness that plagues that society.

the culture in question. I prefer to be silent rather than risk misinterpretation.

Finally, I do not take up the subject of loneliness in rural communities. The main concentration of this book will therefore be on loneliness as a mass social problem in urban and suburban America, as it is experienced by the white middle class, in the context of the institutions and environment of contemporary urban life.

Furthermore, in talking about experiences of loneliness I shall try to distinguish between the quality of those experiences as they are felt by both sexes. There is some pressure these days to make quantitative as well as qualitative distinctions when dealing with female versus male loneliness, and some would insist that more women suffer from loneliness than do men. I find that such quantitative concerns are fruitless and do not help our understanding of the subject. I believe that men and women do suffer loneliness differently, that their different experiences of loneliness follow from society's definition of the characteristics assigned to each sex, and that these differences tend to present barriers to mutual understanding of loneliness. I do not, however, believe we can say that one sex suffers more loneliness than the other. Although women cannot as easily submerge their loneliness in activity, they often, for example, have more freedom to expose their emotions to others. Men, on the other hand, can try to forget their feelings in work-related activities, yet they are more inhibited about expressing emotion to either men or women. Can one say, then, that women are lonelier than men, or men lonelier than women? I believe not; and I think it is more appropriate to describe, as I have attempted to do, how men and women experience loneliness and explain the variations than to turn those variations into assertions of greater or less suffering depending on one's sex.

Before going further, however, we must define what this emotion called loneliness is. There is not only a good deal of confusion concerning the origins of the problem of loneliness today, but also a significant tendency to misunderstand what exactly we mean when we speak of "being lonely."

It's an empty feeling, loneliness. Empty and desolate. The dictionary is not much help in providing a comprehensive definition. Webster's says, rather sparsely, that loneliness is: (1) a standing apart, (2) being alone, or (3) unhappy at being alone. The last characterization comes closest; for one can be alone without feeling lonely. Common as well as literary and psychological usage is equally imprecise: loneliness is often equated with solitude; depression and loneliness are confused, as are alienation and isolation. In a well-known article, "On Loneliness," which appeared in *Psychiatry* in 1960, the psychiatrist Frieda Fromm-Reichman wrote:

Very little is known among scientists about its [loneliness'] genetics and psycho-dynamics and various experiences which are descriptively and dynamically as different from one another as aloneness, isolation, loneliness in cultural groups, self-imposed aloneness, compulsory solitude, and real loneliness are all thrown into the one terminological basket of "loneliness." (p. 6)

Because it shares characteristics with other emotional states, it is difficult to determine the borders of loneliness.

Yet if we look closely at our own feelings of loneliness, or those expressed by people near to us, we distinguish a certain dynamic. There is almost always, for instance, a physical account of the symptoms of loneliness. That feeling of emptiness. Some find it in the pit of their stomachs, others experience it as a kind of vertigo, or as the disappearance of brightness from life—that sense that everything is colorless.

These feelings come because something is missing in our lives. A friend may have gone away, a divorce or death may have shattered a marriage and a way of life, a move may have separated us from a whole network of friends, family, community. We feel lonely, apart, alone. Or we have been taught that to be happy and successful we should be part of a couple, and we cannot find a mate. Again, we feel lonely because something promised has apparently been denied us. We feel this absence; to be in a room by oneself is not to be alone with oneself, but *alone without others*. It is this constant reminder of absence that makes people feel alone whether in a crowd or when they are actually solitary. You are with a group of friends but they are not "the friend," you are with a mate but do not have a wider community to relate to. You are with and simultaneously without.

We can begin, then, to define loneliness as a feeling of deprivation caused by the lack of certain kinds of human contact: the feeling that someone is missing. And since one has to have had some expectation of what it was that would be in this empty space, loneliness can further be characterized as the sense of deprivation that comes when certain *expected* human relationships are absent.

We all count on the presence of various human relationships in our lives. An infant is supposed to have a parent to supply not only food and protection but tenderness and love. It is only natural. A child is supposed to have loving parents and playmates, and later friends. And finally, as adults, we are supposed to complete the social cycle, having children and a family in our turn.

Whether we have actually experienced these relationships does not alter the fact that most of us have learned that they are the norm. We may never have had parents who loved us, or friends, or a mate, but we still have a notion of what friendship is or what it would be like to have a lover. We can mourn the absence of something that is only a concept rather than a lived reality. We feel any of these relationships as a sort of negative presence, a phantom possibility.

We also expect other, less intimate relationships to accompany us through life, those with neighbors, acquaintances, distant relations, co-workers, shopkeepers—the people with whom we come in contact in our daily life, where we live, where we work, where we relax.

Thus we experience loneliness both as a lack of intimate relationships and a lack of less profound but nonetheless important and supportive social relationships. Psychologists and sociologists have categorized these two types of loneliness as emotional and social isolation.*

* See Weiss, *Loneliness*, pp. 9–27.

Still, there is something missing. To say that loneliness is the deprivation of either social context or intimate relationships doesn't capture the emotions that accompany the experience of loneliness. For there is a crucial qualitative dimension to this emotional and social isolation—the incredible intensity and pain that obliterate the memory of past relationships and spill over into the future. Because of it we feel desperate and hopeless about the possibility of recouping those losses in time to come. As Fromm-Reichmann says in "On Loneliness":

More severe developments include unconstructive, desolate phases of isolation and real loneliness which are beyond the state of feeling sorry for oneself, the states of mind in which the fact that there were people in one's past life is more or less forgotten and the hope that there may be interpersonal relationships in one's future life is out of the realm of expectation or imagination. (p. 9)

Thomas Wolfe describes it in an essay, "God's Lonely Man":

The huge, dark wall of loneliness is around him now. It encloses and presses in upon him, and he cannot escape. And the cancerous plant of memory is feeding at his entrails, recalling hundreds of forgotten faces and ten thousand vanished days, until all life seems as strange and insubstantial as a dream. Time flows by him like a river, and he waits in his little room like a creature held captive by an evil spell. And he will hear, far off, the murmurous drone of the great earth, and feel that he has been forgotten, that his powers are wasting from him while the river flows, and that all his life has come to nothing.*

Although this definition clarifies the parameters of the emotional state we are discussing, it does not seem to encompass many of the characteristics we observe in the conduct of lonely people. For even the most insightful definition of loneliness cannot totally explain the various processes involved in such experiences. Thus we must now look at the components of the dynamic of loneliness to understand how this emotion manifests itself in the real world.

* *The Hills Beyond*, p. 159.

The dynamic of loneliness seems to universally include the following major components: feelings of hopelessness, as we have mentioned, which lead people to escape into relationships that might appear solidly grounded but that in reality are only a means to an end rather than an end in themselves; fear of experiencing feelings of loneliness; the desire to deny that one is actually lonely; and feelings of worthlessness and failure generated by the experience of loneliness.

Hopelessness is part of the vicious cycle of loneliness. And it is often difficult to detect because it may masquerade as its opposite. Lonely people may appear to be obsessed by blind hope. In their constant search for someone to solve their sense of isolation they will attach themselves to anyone or any group in order to assuage their suffering. We have all observed, in ourselves or in others, this tendency to accept terrible self-compromise, this grasping of any hope of companionship.

The motivation behind this search for a "relationship" is simply the desire to end the awful feeling of loneliness. The group or person who is employed to achieve this end is an instrument, an object rather than a subject appreciated for his, her or their personal qualities. Rollo May calls love relationships formed on this basis "unfree love." "The hallmark of such unfree love," he says in *Man's Search for Himself*, "is that it does not distinguish the 'loved person's' qualities or his being from the next person's. In such a relationship you are not really 'seen' by the one who purports to love you—you might just as well be someone else." "Unfree" love is not limited to what are typically love relationships. This characteristic applies equally to any relationship formed where the basis of the connection is the desire to escape loneliness. And the result of such a relationship is often not the wished-for escape but further entanglement in the dilemma of loneliness.

Jane is lonely. She feels that if *anyone* were there she would no longer suffer from that emotion, and so she sets out to banish loneliness. Tom presents himself as a solution to Jane's problem. He is that "anyone," and it is as solution rather than as person

that Jane sees him. Tom feels vaguely uneasy about this relationship. He does not, perhaps, recognize the precise reason for his
uneasiness—but it is there. He is not quite sure Jane likes him for
himself. And Jane too is not as happy as she thought she would
be. Underneath she feels she is accepting a substitute rather than
the "real thing." She clings to Tom because she is afraid to be
alone, and the knowledge of her desperation affects the quality
of the relationship.

It is not only the existence of a relationship that is important
but the quality of that relationship. Any warm body will not do.
Although we may accept a second or third choice, we are still
aware that it is not first choice. Although we may have many
acquaintances or friends, we may still feel lonely because they
are not *exactly* what we had in mind. And this dissatisfaction and
doubt will in turn affect the person who is used as the instrument
to combat loneliness. Whoever is sought out of desperation will
feel degraded by the sense that he or she is being used. Because
of this realization such a person too will feel lonely. Loneliness
is contagious.

Paradoxically, then, people can feel at times more hopelessly
alone with others than they feel when they are all by themselves.
When you are completely alone, there is that hope that someone
will soon be there and you will no longer be lonely. In solitude
we can fantasize another who will be all that we want and need.
With actual confrontation, however, comes the possibility of disappointment if that person doesn't coincide with the fantasy. This
only increases the panic of loneliness, which can result either in
further attempts to lose oneself in a relationship (no matter what
price to the self) or in total withdrawal from others. Pushed to its
limits, loneliness can propel its captives between extraordinary
self-deception and equally extreme cynicism.

In relation to self-deception one might mention Rennie Davis,
onetime leader of the antiwar movement, currently an apostle of
the teenaged guru/god Maharaj Ji. Abandoning his belief
in the possibility of radical change in America through the direct
action of citizens protesting government policies, Davis is now

preaching the coming of God, the millennium, through the person of a rich kid from India whose claims to spirituality seem undercut by his adoration of fast cars, electrical appliances, and money. There is something comic in Davis' antics, but it is the comedy of despair, as described by Davis' friend former *Ramparts* editor Robert Scheer:

Here was someone [Rennie Davis] so scared and alone that he was willing to appear totally ridiculous, that he had suspended all restraints of logic and friendship to find some peace. It didn't matter whether he was a new left heavy, a professional athlete, or a Houston businessman, the individualist fantasy that one could, through personal heroics, alone transcend the social environment, and alter the facts of life and death on this planet was doomed from the onset. It is to be expected that one who lives the American dream so fully as Rennie Davis did should end up dependent for his salvation upon a god who has an ulcer.*

In seeking examples of cynical withdrawal as a reaction to loneliness we need look no further than the local singles bars. A thirty-two-year-old San Francisco lawyer described the singles scene:

For the most part the eminently respectable sons-of-bitches walking around the financial district of San Francisco know how to get laid. The question is "Is that what they want to accomplish?" and the answer is "no." But that's what they'll settle for. They want, however, more than that. They want to accomplish "it," of course, the ultimate, mind-blowing experience, make the ultimate human connection, the ultimate emotional experience. What it boils down to is falling in love.

So a typical thirtyish divorced or single man sets out on a Friday evening with all the normal sex drives and that wish for "it." He sets off with the desire to meet "her," "the one." He stops off at the local pub to drink with his friends. And during the evening he gets drunker. And here comes the role of alcohol, 'cause as he gets drunker, his philosophical order of priorities falls apart. His judgment is impaired, his purely sexual horniness just zooms. He never loses the

* "Death of the Salesman," p. 240.

desire for that ultimate completion, it's just that everything is reduced to a very gut level. Hence the many heartaches on waking up the next morning. Two people in bed who would probably hate each other under any other circumstances.

And then it begins again the next Friday night. The difference between people is perhaps just in their level of cynicism and in the degrees to which they continue because they are afraid to be alone.

An essential component of the dynamic of loneliness is fear; over and over again people express their fear of being alone and lonely. Americans today often tend, mistakenly, to equate solitude with loneliness. Over and over again we see escapism and cynicism used as defenses to avoid the pain of loneliness. Why is it that we're so afraid of loneliness?

A lack of human contacts is always painful. People need intimacy, warmth, a sense of worth, and frequent confirmation of their identities. To illustrate the consequences of deprivation of such contact we can refer to studies that seemingly deal in extremes but that in fact tell us much about "normal" society. R. D. Laing, for example, has reported that the families of people classified as schizophrenic are often not guilty of extreme cruelty toward their children, or infliction of excessive traumas, but rather of what he terms "disconfirmation." Children later labeled "schizophrenic" are told that they do not see or hear what in fact they do see and hear. They are told they do not feel and think what in fact they do feel and think. They may not be physically assaulted, but their perceptions are constantly attacked, and soon they begin to doubt not only themselves but the world around them.

The noted anthropologist Jules Henry similarly comments on the lack of positive contact in the functioning of schizogenic families.* Henry visited the homes of families that had at least one very young child in a mental institution and one child at home. Watching the mothers and fathers in these families as they cared for their "normal" children, he found that mental distur-

* *Pathways to Madness* and *Culture Against Man.*

bance could result from parental disregard of a child's need for simple human contact rather than from outright physical abuse. These are extreme examples but they substantiate a human being's need for caring and connection with others. Although most people do not suffer to the extent of becoming schizoid when deprived of human contact, they generally exhibit some adverse reaction to this lack.

The reluctance with which people approach the topic of loneliness, their hesitancy to admit that they are or have ever in their lives been lonely, the desire to flee loneliness—all testify to the pain associated with that emotion.

But while fear of pain is indeed one of the most important reasons why people do run from loneliness, it's not enough to explain the obsessive and often contradictory flight of lonely people, who will often put themselves in situations that would seem to add to their discomfort rather than alleviate it. Most of us have had occasion to observe the punishment humans inflict upon one another in the name of intimacy. Wouldn't it be better, we may wonder, to be alone than to be with a husband who beats you or a wife who subjects you to various psychological tortures? Wouldn't it be better to be alone than to submerge your identity in a group whose beliefs are patently ridiculous or even inimical to human life? Wouldn't it be preferable to admit to loneliness rather than deny what you know to be the case, and what is also evident to those around you? While the answers are all logically "Yes!" they are frequently, empirically "No!" People consistently prefer a situation that would appear to be more painful than being alone. It cannot be only the desire to escape pain that makes people so afraid of loneliness. To satisfactorily explain the fear of loneliness we must understand the need for human contact and also the value placed on that contact, or its lack, in our society.

One might stereotype America as a competitive, success-oriented society where there is supposed to be abundant opportunity for financial enrichment and for personal and emotional expansion. Because there is supposed to be plenty for everyone and then some, if we don't succeed in either business or our personal lives, it's not the fault of anyone but ourselves. We have no one else to blame if we fail. And to fail is one of the worst things that can happen to us. Because, again, if there is so much opportunity for success, failure indicates a terrible individual flaw, one that may not be noticeable but that is certainly there.

Success is measured, furthermore, not only in terms of how much money we have in the bank, or what title is attached to our names, or how well we care for our children. It is also measured by the kinds of relationships we have. The more friends, the better you must be; the happier your marriage, the nicer you must be; the wittier your mate, the more it reflects on you. Relationships are important not only for the pleasure they may bring the individual but as a mark of his or her status as a functioning and valuable member of society. Not to have the requisite relationships is to lose that status or to abandon all hope of achieving it. In a society whose financial and social coffers are always supposed to be full, loneliness or emotional emptiness is more than emotionally distressing—it's socially stigmatic.

Loneliness equals failure; having people around equals success. Solitude is lonely; everyone should choose to have people around and be a success. Thus the reasoning runs, and the deduction is inevitable: Do anything to avoid being alone. If you are not truly likable, get a gimmick. Play bridge, then you'll have friends. Learn to play an instrument—as my mother told me when I was a child—then people will have to gather around you at a party, even though you may be a social washout. Be rich, then people will need you. And make sure you're not alone at such special times of year as holidays, which you are supposed to share with loved ones.

The association between failure, loneliness, and solitude is so strong in our culture that people often find it difficult to believe that there are some who like being by themselves. When we see someone eating alone in a restaurant, our first thought is generally: He/she must be so lonely. So difficult is it for us to imagine that a person could be content with his or her own company.

Such a desire may even be interpreted as a sign of illness. There must be something wrong with a child who wants to be alone. There must be something wrong when someone withdraws from group membership—when, as Herbert Porter said during the Watergate hearings, you refuse to be a team player.

There is an excellent passage in Kate Chopin's book *The Awakening* that illustrates this point. The book, written in the nineteenth century, tells the story of a woman's withdrawal from a conventional marriage and her attempts to find an identity for herself. Edna Pontellier, the heroine, begins this quest by abandoning her social obligations, luxuriating for the first time in her life in her own presence. Although she is quite content, the fact that she seems to enjoy solitude disturbs her husband, who consults, in this passage, with the family physician.

One morning on his way into town Mr. Pontellier stopped at the house of his old friend and family physician Dr. Mandelet.

"Ah Pontellier. Not sick I hope. Come have a seat. What news do you bring this morning?"

"Oh, I'm never sick, Doctor . . . I came to consult, no, not precisely to consult—to talk to you about Edna. I don't know what ails her."

"Madame Pontellier not well?" marveled the doctor. "Why I saw her—I think it was a week ago—walking along Canal Street, the picture of health it seemed to me."

"Yes she seems quite well. It isn't easy to explain."

"Has she," asked the Doctor with a smile, "has she been associating of late with a circle of pseudo-intellectual women—superspiritual superior beings? My wife has been telling me about them."

"That's the trouble," broke in Pontellier, "she hasn't been associating with anyone. She has abandoned her Tuesdays at home, has thrown over all her acquaintances and goes tramping about by herself, moping in the street cars, getting in after dark. I tell you, she's peculiar. I don't like it, I feel a little worried over it." (pp. 108–109)

It is inconceivable to Pontellier that anyone could voluntarily withdraw from society. He takes such withdrawal as a sign not of strength but of weakness. In this he follows a well-trodden path, equally as accepted today as it was when Chopin wrote. As Paul Tillich wrote in *The Eternal Now,* there is an education leading us away from solitude, and thus assuring that solitude and loneliness become almost interchangeable:

Today, more intensely than in preceding periods, man is so lonely that he cannot bear solitude and he tries desperately to become part of a crowd. Everything in our world supports him. It is a symptom of our disease that teachers and parents and the managers of public communications do everything possible to deprive us of the external conditions for solitude, the simplest aids to privacy. (p. 22)

It has not always been the case. In the middle ages, solitude was the interval in which man communed with God, the silence necessary to hear the divine voice. And still, for those who commune with God or their inner selves today, solitude is an emptying-out not only of the distractions of the world but also of the self, so that either God or an inner voice can be heard. As the Trappist monk Thomas Merton wrote of communion in *The Seven Storey Mountain,* silence is a bountiful place.

What wonderful happiness there was, then, in the world! There were still men on this miserable, noisy, cruel earth, who tasted the marvelous joy of silence and solitude, who dwelt in forgotten mountain cells, in secluded monasteries, where the news and desires and appetites and conflicts of the world no longer reached them. . . .
And the Poor Brothers of God, in their cells, they tasted within them the secret glory, the hidden manna, the infinite nourishment and strength of the Presence of God. They tasted the sweet exultancy of the fear of God, which is the first intimate touch of the reality of God, known and experienced on earth, the beginning of heaven. The fear of the Lord is the beginning of heaven. And all day long, God spoke to them, the clean voice of God. (pp. 309, 310)

Most of us, however, no longer hear a divine voice, and as our own voices so often carry ambivalent or contradictory messages, solitude seems a space for confusion rather than for security. It is not surprising that people express such terror at being alone for either extended or short periods of time. Nor is it surprising, given our national preoccupation with success, that a sense of failure and worthlessness is also part of the dynamic of loneliness.

Perhaps this feeling of worthlessness is most evident in people's unwillingness to admit to feelings of loneliness. Among "normal" people it is hard to believe that there are those who have never, ever felt lonely, just as it is hard to believe that there are those who have never felt pain or joy, at least at some point in their lives. Yet there are people who will insist that they never feel lonely. Perhaps once when he was twelve, one young man told me—but now, at nineteen? No, absolutely not. Or consider the man I met at a conference on loneliness. I asked him why he was attending the conference, and he said it was just out of curiosity. Was he ever lonely, I asked. No, certainly not, was the reply. But, I continued, this was after all a lecture on loneliness—not the most cheerful topic. Why, if it has nothing to do with you, listen to such depressing stuff? Still he insisted it was just curiosity. After more prodding he admitted that, well, yes, perhaps, he did feel a little lonely at times. He moved around a lot, as did his friends.

This unwillingness to express lonely feelings may be more exaggerated in the male, who is always reluctant to discuss weakness. But what of the woman who would talk to me, a stranger, an interviewer, but who would never express such feelings to those close to her? Or the middle-aged woman who attended a San Francisco women's consciousness-raising meeting to pour out an excruciating tale of a lonely and tortured marriage? When asked if she did not have friends to whom she could confide, she answered that, yes, she had friends, but friends were not to be told such depressing tales. She was truly alone. Although younger people today seem more willing to discuss with others the lonelier aspects of their lives, there is still, among many, a terrific reluctance to broach the subject. I asked a young man in a singles bar if the singles scene was lonely. His response was that the singles scene was rife with loneliness—it was just that he himself was, of course, never lonely.

This denial of loneliness is symptomatic of a society that does not deal lightly with what it identifies as weakness. As we have seen, to be lonely means to be a failure, to be a failure means to be unworthy of occasions for success, and to be unworthy is to be weak. We all see what happens to the weak in our society. The businessman who can't compete is swallowed up by the conglomerate; the members of the "weaker sex" are subject to constant attack, either physically or on magazine centerfolds; the elderly are mugged on their way from picking up their social security checks; and adolescent runaways are turned into prostitutes on the streets of large cities.

The feelings of worthlessness that accompany loneliness are not emotions we want to share. We do not want others to see such feelings for fear that they will take advantage of our weakness, or worse still, confirm our own low self-estimation. We engage in a hiding process. We try to conceal our low opinion of ourselves, keeping our real, tarnished selves in reserve, as it were, and proffering an image of a false, more confident self. But still we feel lonely and valueless. For we cannot hope to make contact with someone we feel cannot "really" know us. Similarly, we may continue our loneliness by withdrawing from others. We do not want others to have the occasion to see what we "really" are. We shut ourselves into the circle of our dilemma.

People feel lonely for two types of relationships: intimate contact and a social network of less intense associations. But what about two other kinds of loneliness commonly included in the literature on the subject: artistic and existential loneliness? Much current usage would apply the term "loneliness" to the human being's existential situation in the world and also to the solitude in which artistic creation occurs. Although there are parallels between these states and loneliness, a closer look uncovers a tendency to confuse loneliness and aloneness.

Existential loneliness, the argument runs, is inherent in the human condition. We are all inevitably alone because we are all separate from one another. We are born alone and we die alone. We are enclosed by our bodies in a unique space that can never be completely penetrated by another. Although we may try to delude ourselves that connection with another is possible, that delusion will be abruptly and violently shattered at the moment of death, when we realize that nothing and no one can share our fate. This inevitable condition of humanity is, to the advocates of the existential argument, the root and essence of loneliness. We feel lonely because we cannot truly connect with others, because it is in the nature of things that people are distinct from one another, because there is no way to break through the natural barriers separating people.

The existential interpretation of loneliness is a convincing one. We all recognize our own separateness. We all experience moments when we realize our true distance from others, even from those to whom we are the closest. There are times of death or decision when no one can help, when we are alone with our own contingencies and weaknesses. And no matter how hard we try, how much we share ourselves with others, these moments come again and again in our lives. But this momentariness demonstrates the flaw in equating existential aloneness with loneliness. For most people the sense of existential aloneness is not felt as a constant state, but rather comes in disconnected flashes—moments when one feels totally alone. But these moments do not necessarily compromise the totality of one's existence or the meaning of one's contacts with others. The moments pass and one returns to whatever connections one has with others.

We can accept our own separateness and still have important and close relationships with others. To insist on the contrary is to ignore our duality, to refuse to recognize that our separateness does not negate our need for others or deny the possibility of meaningful interpersonal relationships. Indeed, our existential situation is tolerable precisely because we have the possibility of forming such relationships with others.

A similar confusion exists in relation to artistic solitude and loneliness. The myth of the "lonely" artist is strong in our culture. Its substance is the equating of the solitude necessary for most artistic creation with loneliness. The fact that an artist retires from the world for hours or days in order to paint, write, or compose means (according to the mythic interpretation) that during that time he or she is lonely.* Thus one of the occupational hazards an artist must deal with is the problem of loneliness during the process of creation as well as the problems of inspiration and just plain work.

Like most false generalizations, "the lonely artist" involves much projection and confusion. Artistic creation is generally a solitary endeavor, but solitude and loneliness are two different things. Although a lonely person is so afraid of solitude that he or she would never consciously choose to be alone, this does not necessarily mean that one cannot delight in solitude and choose to spend much of one's time alone. The artist does spend much time alone because that space and time is productive, positive, and hopeful.

To clarify the nature of artistic aloneness we must make a distinction between the personal life of the artist and his or her experience during the process of creation. Although an artist may be personally lonely, and although that loneliness may be expressed in his or her art, the time and space of creation is characterized by the absence of loneliness rather than by its presence. Loneliness may present an insoluble problem to the artist as a private person, but that problem is resolved in the work of art—in the world of the artist as creator. It is as though art were a sanctuary from loneliness; for the process of giving form to emotion transforms it. In those moments of artistic solitude the feelings are something the artist controls rather than something that controls him. Because of this they are used as part of a positive, productive process; they cease to be negative, destructive forces. This distinction between the loneliness of an artist's life and the solitude of artistic creation is eloquently

* This confusion between artistic solitude and loneliness is very apparent in Clark Moustakis' book *Loneliness*.

formulated by the poet and novelist May Sarton in her account of a year passed alone in her home in New Hampshire:

I have felt that the work of art (I am thinking especially of poetry), a kind of dialogue between me and God, must present resolution rather than conflict. The conflict is there, all right, but it is worked through by means of writing the poem. Angry prayers, and screaming prayers are unfit for God's ears. So there is Hell in my life but I have kept it out of the work. Now it threatens to wreck what I care for most, to drive me back into a solitude that has, since I have been in love for a year and a half, ceased to be fruitful, become loneliness instead. And now, I am trying to master the Hell in my life, to bring all the darkness into the light.°

If we accept, as Sarton does, that art is the resolution—through work—of conflict, we can see to what extent loneliness and artistic solitude differ. Loneliness sets one in the midst of chaos, negativity, hopelessness. And overwhelmed by those feelings, the lonely person submits to the pressures of his or her personal world. The work of art, however, is the ordering of chaos. It is not that the artist does not feel the painful emotions to which we are all subject. It is simply that creation is a different mode of experiencing those emotions.

In creation the artist feels that pain, uses that pain, while at the same time establishing a distance from that suffering that is necessary to allow art to grow. In the solitude of creation the artist establishes a tension that balances the emotional openness necessary to experience the pain of life and the emotional distance necessary to order that experience. It is a difficult balance to hold; like a photographer looking through a viewfinder, the artist must find exactly that point where there is no distortion of the image, where the balance between depth and surface, light and dark, is maintained. Just one flicker, just one tiny turn to the left or the right, and the balance will be lost. The image will lose its precision. The artist will fall from productive solitude into lone-

° *Journal of a Solitude,* p. 31.

liness, from order into chaos. When this occurs, the artistic process must cease for the time, and the artist suffers from the same loneliness that afflicts the lawyer or the laundrywoman. But when the balance is re-established—through whatever devices the artist has developed to place things again on an even keel— the artist reopens the self-confrontation from which the work of art grows.

The solitude in which the artist creates is also self-imposed. And this presents a vital distinction between artistic solitude and loneliness. The artist chooses to be alone. The artist may suffer in his solitude, but he knows the problems involved in that withdrawal. And because he has chosen solitude, he can end that solitude whenever he pleases and return to society.

The lonely person does not have a choice. He or she does not choose to be lonely; rather that loneliness is felt as an imposition from outside, over whose comings and goings there is no control. When I sit in front of this typewriter and close the door to my room I know that I can walk outside and be among people. I can pick up the phone and call a friend; I can, at will, end my solitude. When I feel lonely, even if I walk down the street, I feel alone. Even if I talk to a friend I feel locked into myself.

In both existential and artistic solitude we are not dealing with loneliness but with *aloneness*. While aloneness is part of the ordering of the human condition, loneliness is a pathology inimical to that condition. Loneliness is something we can understand. And to best grasp the dynamic of loneliness today in America, we must explore its presence in the lives of those individuals whose existences are confined within its borders.

Part Two
Experiences of Loneliness

Chapter Two
Childhood and Adolescence

What gives loneliness its shifting appearance is our experience of it, and how those experiences make us behave. In the psychological literature on loneliness an excellent discussion of the various stages of people's need for contact is found in psychiatrist Harry Stack Sullivan's *The Interpersonal Theory of Psychiatry*. Sullivan traces the developmental stages* of life and their concomitant needs for intimacy. Loneliness will arise, he argues, when the needs described aren't satisfied.

The first stage of development is infancy, during which the infant requires tenderness, protective caring, and simple human connection. As the infant grows into a small child, the need for adult participation in play is added to these needs. From this participation the child learns to take pleasure in another's sharing of his or her accomplishments. During what Sullivan calls the juvenile era another interpersonal need for intimacy is added—the need for peers, whose presence helps the child learn and gives him or her a sense of acceptance. And finally, during preadolescence and early and late adolescence, a person continues to require those things previously described, but adds to them the need for intimacy with another person—most often a member of the opposite sex. Loneliness, then, can begin in childhood and adolescence.

* These stages are not determined by age but by emotional development.

45

It is a commonplace that the family unit seems to be in more trouble today than it has been in its very long history. Although the family may never have provided the ideals of contact presented in Sullivan's developmental scheme, the current instabilities in the nuclear family make it especially difficult for today's infants to get the kinds of warmth and protection they need to satisfy their interpersonal needs. Divorce, parental role confusion, and an individual growth ethic increasingly provide an atmosphere that fosters loneliness in the very young. Those factors shake the family from within. And from without, mobility threatens a child's ability to create a group of friends and peers.

Jennifer is twelve. At night, while she sleeps, she picks at a spot on her leg until it bleeds. It hurts when she wakes up the next day, but still, that night, and the next, she picks at it again, unable to stop. When Jennifer was ten her mother and father divorced. Her mother had difficulties in dealing with a small child as well as with herself. When she finally met another man she did not really want to be bothered with Jennifer. So she sent the child to her sister's house to live. She promised Jennifer that she would come back for her. She did come to visit once, with her boyfriend, and took her daughter home. But the child was again too much for her. She wanted to be alone with her boyfriend, and so one day she locked Jennifer out of the house and refused to answer the child's repeated knocks. That was a year ago, and Jennifer hasn't seen her mother since.

I get lonely because I miss my mom. I live with my aunt. My mom left me there while she was looking for a job. And then she got this boyfriend and she never came for me. She's only written to me once in that time—six months ago with no return address. I like my aunt but sometimes I'm afraid of her. When I try to explain things to her, I think she'll get mad like my mom did. I guess I could never talk to my mom when I was lonely cause she was lonely too.

Peter, thirteen, was an only child until about three years ago, when his sister was born. He says of his life:

I've been alone most of my life. The worst time came after my father died. But now sometimes too I feel lonely. I come home from school and stay all alone until around seven o'clock when my mother comes home from work. I watch TV but it gets pretty boring. So I imagine things. Like that I have house full of friends. Or that I get into trouble.

At times I like being alone. But it's a strange feeling. You're there all by yourself. You've got nobody to talk to. When my mother comes home it's just as bad because when she comes in she's tired and she goes to sleep. I'm still stuck. When I try to tell her what I'm feeling, she'll get mad or something.

Diana's parents divorced two years ago. There were four children: Diana, an older sister, a younger sister, and a younger brother. In the two years since their parents' divorce the four children have been split up in several different ways—living at different times with either their mother or their father. When they are with their father they are together, but are lonely for their mother; and when they live with their mother the children can never be all together, so they miss one another.

Me and my sister are living with my dad right now. We were living with my mom but we got in trouble. We took the car one night and so my mom kicked us out. My younger brother and sister are still with my mom. We live with my dad. But I never did like my dad. None of us kids like him. When my parents were in the process of getting a divorce, he gave my mom all sorts of trouble. He used to beat her up and stuff, and sometimes us too. We were always there when that happened. He'd do it right in front of my little sister. We never have forgiven him. We miss our mom. But she's had a lot of trouble. But now she says she feels better. She says she's going to try to take us back, me and my sister at the end of this year.

Children of the divorced, like two of these three, used to be relatively rare; divorce did not threaten one out of three marriages as it does today. Today, however, there are an estimated seven million children under eighteen who are the products of divorce. Although Diana and Peter and Jennifer have, perhaps, more difficulties than many children, the problems they react to are fairly typical. Parents who remarry often resent the presence of children who are reminders of a painful marriage and separation. In turn, the children resent the presence of a new father or mother. The new couple is often so enmeshed in its own difficulties that neither parent can deal intelligently with the troubled children or even have the time and energy to try to understand what the children are going through. Or if they do understand, they often react to their children's complaints with the anger that comes from guilt. The children then react to this anger or neglect like Diana and her sister did. They get into trouble, and the parents send them back and forth between father and mother. Or, like Jennifer, they are shunted off to relatives.

Dealing with the problems of divorce is extremely difficult for parents who do remarry, but these difficulties are multiplied for the single parent. If the mother or father must work to support the family, he or she often has neither the time nor the inclination to give the children the attention they require. Nor is the parent able to make sure the children have playmates, since our large cities and widespread suburbs make constant chauffeuring necessary. The single working parent does not have time for such things. Parents, like Peter's mother, may feel guilty about their failings. And so they rebuff a child's attempts to be close. When children complain, parents get angry, thus pushing their children further into a world that they may understand well enough but with which they are ill equipped to deal.

For these children loneliness comes as an overwhelming awareness that there is no support anywhere—that the people upon whom they depend for survival, warmth, affection, and interest, can provide only the most meager attention to their needs. In this situation children also feel helpless. They have nowhere else to go, there is no one else to turn to, and no one, including themselves, can meet their needs.

The child's response to this overwhelming sense of loneliness is anxiety. In the case of small children, anxiety and fear cause them to cling to the mothering figure. As the English psychiatrists R. D. Laing and John Bowlby report, children often cling to the mothering figure even if she is the source of this anxiety.

Bowlby explains this behavior as a sort of instinctual seeking for comfort from the mother, a behavior that does not distinguish between the mother as protector and the mother as anxiety-creator.

Laing, in *The Self and Others*, notes the same clinging to the parent-as-source-of-discomfort-and-protection in schizophrenics. And in the dynamic of loneliness we can see a similar desire for protection from a relationship that is in fact the source of the distress. This clinging behavior begins as an instinct in infancy, and we can speculate that it is carried over into adulthood as an unconscious reaction to the anxiety and fear of loneliness.

It may be that there is an instinctual tropism to the mother which does not meet with adequate terminating response in the mother. If Bowlby (1958) and others are correct, when an instinctual response system in the human being does not meet an appropriate terminating response in the other, then anxiety arises. If, however, the instinctual response to anxiety at some stage is to cling to the mother, then the more anxiety is generated by the failure of an adequate terminating response in the mother, such as a highly "confusing" reaction, a smile with tense facial muscles, soft arms, tight hands, and a harsh voice, the more the need for the mother is stimulated.

There may be something wrong with the "fit," with the interaction between mother and baby, so that within this context each starts to "double-bind" the other. It is possible that an instinctual response is genetically set not to end itself, even when the terminating response is given, but goes on like a Sorcerer's Apprentice, unable to break its own spell. Prolonged intense clinging may begin to evoke a "double-bind" like behaviour on the mother's part. Stimulated by it and exhausted, wanting the infant to continue and to give it up, she acts ambivalently. This in turn may contribute to the infant's developing a second level of disturbance, in that it may cease to respond to the mother at all, or begin to respond in simultaneously inconsistent ways, or in one stereotyped way. But speculation can go too far ahead of information. This field of research lies open, but curiously uncultivated except by a few. (p. 150)

This pattern that Bowlby and Laing describe is certainly not limited to the children of the divorced. But the complications of many divorces are an added burden to both parents and children. "For many children," says Barbara Lazlett, a counselor of runaways and troubled youth in Berkeley, California, "growing up today is like free-fall. There is just no one there to help."

Even when there is no divorce, children may feel abandoned, because the energies of many mothers and fathers are absorbed by confusion over their roles within the family. In the past, generational conflict in the family most often concerned children's turning away from tradition and from responsibility to the family. Parents represented a stable, all too rigid and unchanging force, for even if parents questioned their roles, they did not have the freedom, as they do currently, to act out their confusion. The task of growth, therefore, was to break away from this seemingly inflexible domination of the parents.

Today, however, it is often the parents who are the focus of change within the family—questioning marriage, fidelity, the role of motherhood, the duties of fatherhood. The rapidity of social change in America is reflected in the family structure. A man and woman will marry thinking that marriage is a lifetime contract, that a woman should stay home and take care of the children, that a man should work at getting ahead, and that both partners should practice sexual fidelity. After six or seven years this same family, responding to the times and their changes, will decide to experiment on many fronts. They may split up for a time. They may stay together and experiment sexually. The mother may go to work, the father may come home to take care of the kids. Or both parents may work and leave the child with baby-sitters. Suddenly the children are a burden. The issue for kids, on a very simple level, may be to find someone at home.

Psychologists believe that this increasing stress in the family may be one of the factors responsible for the growing rates both of alcoholism and of suicide among young people. There are currently 450,000 teenage alcoholics in our country, and suicide is the second leading cause of death for people between the ages of fifteen and twenty-four. What we see developing in white middle-class America is the kind of instability that used to be peculiar to poor and black families. As a counselor in suburban Connecticut says:

Some of the young children of the very rich suffer from a total lack of stimulation at home. It's hard to get children to come over and play in a spread-out suburban community, particularly little kids, so they tend to spend time, when they're not in school, in front of the TV. I know of many kids who spend 30 hours a week in front of the television. And then they are not good in English-speaking skills because they are raised by non-English-speaking maids. They are not well taken care of and don't dress well, so that sometimes you can't tell the difference between a poor and rich kid.

All this is complicated for young and teenage children by the mobility so prevalent in our society. Talking to groups of young people in cities and suburbs around the nation, one is struck by the effect of mobility on the formation of friendships and larger peer groups. Families move so often that children have little chance to form stable friendships with those of their own age and are deprived of the support children can give one another—support that can help them deal with their family problems.

More studies are needed to determine the effects of such constant change on children and how it will influence their adult personalities. But studies conducted on very young children who are torn away from parents seem to indicate that mobility, especially combined with family instability (as it frequently is), will breed many problems. A rather long but very important passage from John Bowlby's studies of mother-deprived children, *Attachment and Loss*, illustrates some of these difficulties:

During the phase of despair which succeeds protest [at the absence of the mother], the child's preoccupation with his missing mother is still evident, though his behaviour suggests increasing hopelessness. The active physical movements diminish, or come to an end, and he may cry monotonously or intermittently. He is withdrawn and inactive, makes no demands on people in the environment, and appears to be in a state of deep mourning. This is a quiet stage and sometimes, clearly erroneously, is presumed to indicate a diminution of distress.

Because the child shows more interest in his surroundings, the phase of *detachment* which sooner or later succeeds protest and despair is often welcomed as a sign of recovery. The child no longer rejects the nurses; he accepts their care and the food and toys they bring and may even smile and be sociable. To some this change seems satisfactory. When his mother visits, however, it can be seen that all is not well, for there is a striking absence of the behaviour of the strong attachment normal at this age. So far from greeting his mother, he may remain remote and apathetic; instead of tears there is a listless turning away. He seems to have lost all interest in her.

Should his stay in hospital or residential nursery be prolonged and should he, as is usual, have the experience of becoming transiently attached to a series of nurses each of whom leaves and so repeats for him the experience of the original loss of his mother, he will in time act as if neither mothering nor contact with humans has much significance for him. After a series of upsets at losing several mother-figures to whom in turn he has given some trust and affection, he will gradually commit himself less and less to succeeding figures and in time will stop altogether attaching himself to anyone. He will become increasingly self-centered, and instead of directing his desires and feelings toward people, will become preoccupied with material things such as sweets, toys, and food.* A child living in an institution or hospital who has reached this state will no longer be upset when nurses change or leave. He will cease to show feelings when his parents come and go on visiting day; and it may cause them pain when they realize that, although he has an avid interest in the presents they bring, he has little interest in them as special people. He will *appear* cheerful and adapted to his unusual situation. *But this sociability is superficial; he appears no longer to care for anyone.* (I, 50–51; my italics)

A Texas housewife with an only child, who has moved at least five times in her fourteen-year marriage, remarked:

My daughter was very unhappy when we first moved away from Texas. It was very difficult to deal with. But I don't know what you

---

* As we shall see later, this syndrome of increasing detachment from people and increasing attachment to goods not only applies to children but to many of the wives of transients and to others who experience high mobility in society.

can do about it. You can sympathize with her. But it's ridiculous. People move all the time. Sometimes you have to move. And we can't just say we won't do it because the child isn't happy with it. I sympathize with her, and I spent about $200 on clothes the first six weeks trying to cheer her up.

But despite the child's reluctance and the problems she has had with moving, her parents say they will move again in six months and at any other time if need be.

This attitude leaves children in a very contradictory and lonely position. To their parents they are simultaneously all and nothing. Theoretically, we will make any sacrifice for our children. They are our little gods and goddesses and nothing is too good for them. We want them to be healthy when they grow up, and we have never voiced as much concern for their psychological well-being as we do today. We also fancy that we are not only parents but our children's friends. Consequently children today have very high expectations concerning parental treatment. The discrepancy between expectation and reality is much of the cause of loneliness and a sense of injustice in the young.

These high expectations are a recent problem and distinguish our age from the past. In previous generations the idea that parents would also be friends simply did not exist. My mother, for instance, an immigrant from Poland, did not expect her parents also to be her pals. It would not have occurred to her to confide in them. They were "her parents." They provided shelter, food, and as much stability as they could until she married. And had she not married, she would have lived with them for the rest of her life, or at least for the rest of their lives. She, in turn, had certain responsibilities toward them. She earned her keep, helped clean the house and cook, helped in their business, and helped take care of them when they were old. There was a certain unwritten contract, which, for the most part, was adhered to by all parties involved.

That contract contained no clauses concerning sharing and friendship. And indeed, most families did not attempt such familiarities. So when there was no expectation of sharing and friendship, no one was disappointed. Nothing had been promised that had not been granted. Today there is much talk about friendship and "communication" between parents and children, and the agreed-upon contract includes such demands. When parents act only as parents, or when they are not even available for parenthood, much less for friendship, children feel not only lonely but ripped off. Something has been stolen from them. The contract has been broken, yet there is no court of law that can right the matter—fine the thief and give restitution to the victims. In such a situation the child is without recourse. The parents implicitly promise much more than they can give, and children are expected to be able to handle insecurity and mobility and bounce back without a complaint.

Much rationalization comes from an expanding concept of individual fulfillment. The individualist ethic has always been the backbone of America. In the past, however, the individual unit included the family—either extended or nuclear. What was good for the individual was good for the family, and what was good for the family was good for the individual. Whether or not this was the case, people believed in it.

Today the ethic of personal growth and fulfillment includes the idea that everyone—mother, father, sister, brother—should do his or her own thing, seek individual fulfillment while simultaneously maintaining the cohesion of the nuclear unit. Today's American Dream is a TV in every room, a set for every member. This creates a world of one—me and the tube, me and my fantasy. The other becomes unnecessary. I don't need her (him) to fulfill myself. In fact, consideration of somebody else's needs often puts a limit on my freedom. This attitude is exemplified in the philosophy presented in Frederick Perls's Gestalt precept, which says that while "I do my thing, and you do your thing/I am not in this world to live up to your expectations." Thus children are a limitation, and we develop the concept that they are infinitely elastic and can be put in almost any situation and come out unscarred. Or, when they are scarred, we develop the psychological notion that a person gets what he or she neurotically wants. If a person is miserable, it is because he or she wants to be miserable.

The nuclear family is isolated against the world; and now, within the family, its members are isolated against one another. People feel empty and seek individual solutions, which only separate them further from each other. And the society in turn fosters the delusion that such solutions are possible within the complex whole of the family. You can, we seem to think, be a parent without being a parent. You can shuttle your children between all sorts of untenable alternatives. You can have a family and still be independent.

On the surface, the struggle for independence within the family would seem to indicate that many people today have developed a greater capacity both for self-love and for self-fulfillment within the structure of the family. This self-love, as Freud (and common sense before him) recognized, would be manifest in unambivalent attitudes toward one's children. Yet a deeper investigation into the dynamic of contemporary family life reveals a profound ambivalence. Real independence presupposes an equilibrium between freedom and commitment. Where this balance is missing we have no independence but rather a struggle of spiraling entanglements in which our love for our children is undercut by our resentment; and our love for ourselves, from which true independence is born, proves to be rather disguised apathy toward ourselves at best and self-hate at worst. From such contradictory attitudes toward the self can come only the most ambivalent and confused experiments in living. And these negative experiments complicate the problems of both parents and children rather than resolve them.

Experimentation in itself is not a bad thing, but it is destructive when its aims are so muddled.* If there were a larger com-

* I am by no means advocating that we halt change, hold onto bad marriages, and preserve the status quo. But I am, however, against the kinds of unconscious irresponsibility we find today. As we see over and over again today, people seem to be entering marriage and having families with the expectation of failure. If it doesn't work, young couples say, we can always get a divorce. If we don't stick to the contract, we can always cancel it. If we stay married and move around, that's okay, because children can

munity or family grouping to which children and parents could relate, even such confused experiments would be less damaging. There would be others to fall back on for support when necessary. For if we are going to abandon our children, either physically or emotionally, we have to at least make sure there is someone there to pick them up when we do so.

We can see this most clearly in the problem of runaways. Running away is no longer the adventure it was for Tom Sawyer and Huck Finn. It is rather a matter of survival for many young people. "Most of the population we deal with," says Robert Meltzer, director of the Educational Alliance, a New York City group that attempts to help runaways, "are runaways or throwaways. The difference between the two is technical. The kid runs away with or without just cause from a home that basically wasn't there for him. Or he may never have had a home and be in adoptive or foster care. In general the response of the parents is that they don't want to be bothered."

These kids usually have a long history of trouble at home before they decide to leave. Their parents are often divorced, or if married, simply cannot handle their children. There is a typical pattern: parents try to deal with their children and fail. They then send the kids to the juvenile court or child-welfare system, perhaps to a foster home. The child returns home to more of the same. And gets into trouble again. The parents increasingly see the child as incorrigible and delinquent. So again they have recourse to the system. This time the child runs away. If found, he or she is sent to juvenile hall, and perhaps to an honor farm— a reform school with a bit more freedom. The child runs away again, is caught, sent back—and so the treadmill goes.

Ken is such an example. At twenty, his history includes seven flights from his northern California home. Until he was about seven he and his mother were alone together; his father had left them when he was a baby. His mother then remarried, to a man

---

handle anything. They might be unhappy for a time, but that will pass. Most frequently, however, this unhappiness does not pass, and when things do finally fall apart—as they have been unconsciously scheduled to do—it is the children who suffer most.

with whom Ken has never gotten along. After several years of marriage Ken's parents adopted a young boy and girl.

Ken was never very much motivated in school, although he did well in those subjects that interested him. To his stepfather, an engineer, this was not enough. He was pressured to do better, did not, and incurred further displeasure from his parents. He tried, vaguely, to explain his feelings to his parents. But they were problem drinkers and seemed unwilling to listen. They sent Ken to a psychiatrist, while refusing to undergo therapy themselves. Ken was the trouble, they agreed, and what went wrong in the family was all his fault.

He ran away once. But his parents found him and gave him a second chance. For a while things were all right at home. But then things slipped back to what was, for that family, "normal." He then ran away again. This time, when he was picked up by the police, he was sent to juvenile hall, and then to a foster home. But he ran away from the foster home, so he was sent to an honor farm, with white boys like himself, and poor black and Chicano boys sent up for petty theft.

I didn't do well on the farm. I guess I'm not much into fighting and things like that. They wanted us to do things like learn to box, and I said I didn't want to learn to fight, that I didn't come there to learn to fight. So they thought I wasn't institutionalized. If you're institutionalized, well then you do what they tell you. It was pretty rough there because I just wasn't into all that macho shit. I guess I stayed about four months and then came out.

But I kept running away anyway. My parents never once felt that there was anything wrong with them, or how they handled us kids. And then the people in juvenile hall never once thought there was anything wrong with my parents. They have a nice house, my father has a nice job. So how could anything be wrong? It was all my fault, I was the one blowing it. Here I had everything I could possibly want. I was so fortunate, so why couldn't I make it?

Ken finally landed in Berkeley and became part of the Berkeley street scene. He got into drugs, speed, grass—anything he could get. Slept in doorways, avoided the police. After too many doses of speed and not enough sleep he got sick and found himself in the hospital. By then he was old enough to stay away from home without being sent to juvenile hall. So when he was released he decided to stay in Berkeley.

Things are better for him now. It's his younger brother and sister he worries about. Both runaways and in trouble, one is in a foster home and the other in a group home for girls. He would like to help them out, but his parents won't let him near the two; it was his fault, they say, that the family has disintegrated to such an extent. Ken knows that isn't true, but it is depressing not to be able to go home, even to such a home as his. He's getting it together, little by little, working here and there, trying to play his guitar. But he still gets depressed easily, and at those times life seems an unremitting battle, with few victories.

Among runaways Ken is a lucky one. For a twenty-year-old, he has gone through some pretty heavy scenes. But they are lightweight compared to what happens to many runaways when they hit the streets of big cities. Girls and boys come to Berkeley or New York and are met at bus stops or youth gathering places by helpful people—that is, people who want the kids to help them. Their loneliness is frequently exploited by people who profit from their misery. And they may become even more alienated from the adult world.

The runaway may not be the typical adolescent, but the difference is one of degree and not kind. Many adolescents suffer from the same sense of helplessness and abandonment that plagues the boys and girls we have just described.

Adolescence is by definition a lonely time. You are not a child and not an adult. You no longer want to depend on your parents, but there is little sense of self to cling to. This creates a diffused sense of loneliness. One cannot pin it to a specific relationship— all relationships are somehow unsatisfactory. Your girl- or boyfriend does not really help, your parents do not really understand —there is no one, really, to rely on. As one fifteen-year-old boy puts it, there comes a time when growing up doesn't seem to provide the utopia he imagined when he was small:

It was just a couple of days ago when I started thinking about when I stopped wanting to grow up and when I started wanting to go back. And I think I finally figured it out. That the change came when I started acting interested in girls, in the opposite sex. Because prior to that time everything was really secure; any problem I had I could go to my mother and I could always get an answer. But for some reason you can't really talk about your failures with a girl, or ask for advice about that. So from then on I couldn't go to my mother anymore so I had to start making my own decisions.

Failure, love, and loneliness. Growing up, as Freddie describes it, is learning to make those connections—connections that are carried over into adulthood. This educational process begins, as we have seen, in the family, and it is continued in secondary schools. As Jules Henry reports in his studies of high school students in *Culture Against Man,* American secondary educators often give more attention to teaching students to relate to the opposite sex than to teaching them to develop their intellects.

In the nineteen-sixties, it has become so obvious that para-courtship is a necessary, rigid ceremonial which one must not offend, that work and obligation become subordinate to it. How explain, otherwise, the students' complaints at the trifling homework assignments? In a broader context we might say that the development of the pattern of fun, of which para-courtship is but a part, has intruded so far into the orthodox procedures, obligations and austerities of school that it has received recognition by the school authorities. (p. 204)

After such socialization it is not surprising that we have an adult population obsessed with love and uninterested in most everything else. There is no self but the loved self, no world but the world of love, and to be left by the loved one is to be demolished. Since our lovers outrank our friends, and we will leave a friend for the possibility of romance, we have indeed little support when we lose the one-in-whom-we-placed-all-our-hopes. Rhonda, aged sixteen, explains it this way:

I think the reason why I feel very lonely is because—well you can't have friends if you feel badly about yourself. And I guess I don't like myself very much. When I first meet someone I'm always afraid that I'll put my foot in my mouth, or say the wrong thing. And so I just don't talk and make friends, and that's why I think I'm very lonely. See, I was going with this guy for two and a half years. And while I was seeing him I didn't really have any other friends. But then I broke up with him and it was really hard to open up and meet other people. I couldn't go back to my old group because they took it personally when I wasn't with them so much because I had a boyfriend. And if I tried to be friends with them again, they would have just said "so you're coming back 'cause you broke up with Louie."

There are, of course, adolescent friendships, but they are, like those of adulthood, often superficial—easily formed and easily dissolved.

Adolescents themselves, however, turn upon one another viciously in sexual matters, and let one another down in interpersonal relations. On the other hand, there is much long-standing friendship among them. Much of this friendship is expressed in bumming and messing around, by both boys and girls, for the adult world has not provided anything more significant for them to do. Magazines, movies, TV, radio, and Home Ec engulf the adolescent in inducements to self-indulgence, to the degree that it is largely through mutual participation in impulse release that the friendships of adolescents reach their fullest expression; much more time is spent just "having fun" or talking about "fun" than anything else. Since friendship and love have no meaning unless cemented by some agony, adolescent friendships often tend to evaporate without pain.*

Although teenagers today are purportedly more deeply involved with one another, on more profound levels than they were in the late fifties and early sixties (when Henry wrote), there is still a tremendous fluidity and inability to share among them. This easy come-and-go of relationships causes much loneliness. It is especially difficult to share this loneliness with peers because adolescents generally lack confidence in their own abilities and, by extension, in the helping capacity of others their own age. "I just wouldn't tell my problems to my friends," a seventeen-year-

* Henry, *Culture Against Man*, p. 281.

old boy commented. "It would be like talking to a brick wall. They just wouldn't understand."

And just as these kids often lack confidence in the ability of their peers to help them, so they feel sorry that they cannot help each other. "I feel worse when I'm lonely and someone comes to me and I know they feel bad and I just withdraw," says John, aged twenty, a former runaway from a broken home. "I know that if I just held out my hand or did something really simple like that, that would be all the person would need. But I just can't. Something selfish inside says 'No, don't do that.' I really would like to work through that."

All these problems are exacerbated for the adolescent today by the instability of the world around them. It is a frightening enough feeling for the teenager to realize that he or she cannot hold his or her act together. But in the past that feeling was mediated by the sense that the adult world offered the possibility of security. Growing up today, kids not only feel that their parents are too involved in their own changes to bother with their problems, they also feel that the adult world offers them no models they would like to imitate, that being an adult means only more of the same—more insecurity, more instability, more unhappiness. John, the ex-runaway, comments again:

It really bothers me to see myself and other kids today. They are just floating. They see their parents are alcoholics, or divorced, or unhappy in their jobs. They don't want to copy that. But they need some direction. And there's no one to help. Kids today just can't believe in anything—personally, politically, everything is fucked up. I mean it really is an ugly dance. I think that's one reason that kids take drugs. It eases the tension. °

The political ambiance in the country—Watergate, economic instability, disillusionment on the part of the whole country with the functioning of the political process—affects young people too. And on a personal level, it is easy to understand their disillusion-

° Drugs may not be as popular now as in the sixties, but today many more kids are taking alcohol at earlier ages as a replacement. There are an estimated 450,000 child alcoholics.

ment with marriage and family life. Perhaps we do not understand the dangers that this inability to form models presents. For, as Jules Henry explains, it is the entire processes of our culture, and culture in general, that are being called into question:

[There is a widespread] *erosion of the capacity for emulation,* loss of the ability to model one's self consciously after another person. . . . What I have in mind when I speak of the erosion of the capacity for emulation is not emulating a person in respect to his property, but rather emulating his *properties.* Culture depends on this latter potentiality, for it is to a great degree through *Homo Sapiens'* strong inherent potential for the emulation of properties that the moral questions of culture have been maintained, and *Homo Sapiens* has relied heavily on this mechanism to educate the rising generations. But when cynicism, resignation, and passivity enter life the first makes all emulative choice of properties seem vain, and passivity and resignation sap the will necessary to the emulative decision. But positively, in order for a morally sound emulative choice to be made there must be present some faith in one's self; a certain amount of naive optimism and a certain quantity of will. When these are lacking, life readily becomes a series of moment-to-moment choices dominated, especially in adolescence, by the Id and status cravings.*

Although kids have always had problems and difficulty seeking advice from their parents, there were usually other outlets to turn to. Family, neighbors, teachers—and for those fortunate enough to afford college, professors—have acted as surrogate parents and models without parental complications. Today, however, fewer kids want to go to college, and dropouts have a hard time finding a responsive and responsible adult from whom to gain some shelter. A dropout's parents often reject him or her for refusing to go the traditional route, and there are only other dropouts, equally confused, from whom to get advice.

Even in college it is hard to find help. A confused adolescent is lost in America's huge colleges and universities. Classes are too

* *Culture Against Man,* pp. 228–229.

large for many kids to get to know and be able to adopt a willing professor or instructor. Large universities prevent even students from getting to know one another. Dorms are no longer popular, and more students live in their own apartments. Unless they try very hard, it is conceivable that students could go to college for four years and meet very few people. For students coming from high school and families to an apartment near campus, in the context of mass, uncaring education, there is little support and no one to care if they are in trouble. The family may be there in case of emergencies, but kids are loath to run back to mom and dad and admit they couldn't make it on their own. There is certainly more "freedom," but for people who have never been taught to use it, freedom is a worthless gift.

In the face of all this free-fall, one could advise a young person to think of the future—of the possibilities of fulfillment in a career. But increasingly it's hard to find an answer to floating and loneliness in the hope of good and meaningful work. Even if there is a great desire on the part of a young man or woman to find a good job, it is often undermined by the rapidity of flux in the job market. In contemporary America whole professional categories are wiped out almost overnight. Teachers are no longer in demand, engineers are out of jobs, there are too many writers, to become a doctor is too expensive, working people are subject to constant layoffs and injuries, lawyers are plentiful. Where can one tell an adolescent to look?

In this context, life does indeed become the moment-to-moment affair of which Henry speaks. Why bother taking up a career if that career is apt to be no longer in demand when you finish your training? Why commit yourself to marriage or love, since the former seems to have lost its meaning and the latter is only a fleeting experience? There is among many young people a terrific sense of loneliness and aloneness in a world that no longer seems to have rhyme or reason. In growing up and gaining a new awareness, they feel that the world is lost both to them and to everyone else. It is the loneliness spoken of in this poem by sixteen-year-old Karen Shattuck of Wilton, Connecticut:

Alone in a
huge house with no
one in it, I waited for
nothing to happen to me.
Surprisingly enough, it
didn't.
For as I sat, I sudden-
ly wanted to dance
down the road and collect
people like a magnet.
Then a dog barked, tell-
ing me the sun had gone
down, leaving a starless,
muddy sky. And I sat,
dying to
bring cookies
        to the
          crowds.

Growing up has never been an easy affair. It is hard to say
that kids today are more lonely than kids a hundred or five hundred years ago. There is no doubt, however, that the problems
of loneliness, why and how it occurs, are different today, and
there is some reason to believe that the compensations formerly
available to adolescents have eroded. Thus the legacy of adolescence is frequently a lonely one: the association of love with
failure, the inability to form close relationships, the overde-
pendence on romantic fulfillment, and a sense of insecurity in
the face of the family and the world. Rather than disappearing
with age, these problems will shape the themes of loneliness in
adults.

Chapter Three
Singlehood

Emotional isolation is hard for anyone to endure; it becomes a calamity, however, if it coincides with apprehensions and uncertainties about one's self.

It is this situation which provokes, in the normal individual of our time, an intensified need for affection as a remedy. Obtaining affection makes him feel less isolated, less threatened by hostility and less uncertain of himself. Because it corresponds to a vital need, love is overvalued in our culture. It becomes a phantom—like success—carrying with it the illusion that it is a solution for all problems.

KAREN HORNEY, *The Neurotic Personality of Our Time*

Our society exhibits an extraordinary preoccupation with love. Every other song on the radio laments love lost, praises love found, and makes it clear that you're nothing until some *one* loves you. It's not surprising, given this bombardment, that love (or its lack) occupies so central a place in our minds. For single adults it's almost an obsession.

Harry Stack Sullivan in *The Interpersonal Theory of Psychiatry* sees things differently from the rock-and-roll writers. He identifies love, along with intimacy, as one of the primary "integrating tendencies" in development. When the child reaches early adolescence, Sullivan says, he or she feels the need for intimate companionship with one other person:

There comes in pre-adolescence the need for intimate exchange, for friendship, or for—in its highest *refinement*—the love of another person, with its enormous facilitation of consensual validation, of action patterns, of valuation judgments and so on. This becomes, in early adolescence, the same need for intimacy, friendship, acceptance, intimate exchange, and in its more *refined* form the need for a loving relationship with the other sex. Now this is the great structure which is finally consolidated, made meaningful, as the need for intimacy, as it characterizes late adolescence and the rest of life. (p. 291; my italics)

What we have, according to Sullivan, is a constellation of relationships in which love is a "refinement" of the others. *It is not the culmination of all relationships. It does not negate the other interpersonal needs, nor does it discard previously important relationships after intimacy has been achieved.* As Sullivan says in a later discussion:

The last of these great developments is the appearance and growth of the need for intimacy. For collaboration with at least one other, *preferably more others.* . . . Another thing which can quite certainly be extrapolated is that, whether it be by eternally widening interests, deepening interest or both, the life of the mature—far from becoming monotonous and a bore—is always increasing in shall I say, importance. (p. 310)

Such growth is an expansion of contacts and interests, to be arrested, presumably, only by the inevitability of death.

In contrast to this healthy pattern, growing up in our society often involves a process of reducing down. We pass through the stage relationships, and on reaching adolescence and adulthood achieve our one intimate relationship. But it is at this point that the reduction process occurs. Love becomes the only thing of real importance, and people make or break other alliances in its interests—forgetting friends, family, and community—because the bond of all-encompassing love is so strong that we believe we really don't need anything or anyone else. Although we admit that an adult needs various kinds of contact—sexual, protective, friendly, approving, participatory, affectionate, career-oriented— the loved one is expected to satisfy the interpersonal needs that previously required a whole array of others.

There may be recognition that an adult needs others—workmates, some friends, family—but the importance of these others is vastly underestimated and clearly secondary to the love bond. In many of the new primers on how to achieve intimacy, for instance, it is clear that friends are cultivated not for the enjoyment they bring, or because intimacy is something one can share with people who are friends rather than lovers, but because they will help keep the love relationship together. To illustrate we have a passage from *Pairing:*

> Isolated, and exclusive pairings can generate hostility against the outside world and become psychiatrically dangerous. Besides, the overlapping of two social circles provides stimulating grist for the conversational mill.
>
> To keep running off to the woods (or the Bahamas) alone with a partner can kill a pairing. To have a social circle that recognizes the pairing as an entity lends social sanction, and makes the relationship feel more real.*

This attitude assures that only lip service is paid to the need to have other than one primary relationship, and that all peripheral relationships will have little value and be superficial at best. As in the case of a person walking into a dark room after leaving the sun, the image of romantic love shines so brightly that we see other relationships only as outlines—things we bump into rather than things we actively seek.

Not only is the loved one supposed to fulfill the interpersonal needs of his or her partner, he or she is also the major extra-occupational interest in life. What one finds when talking to people in America is a population that lacks meaningful interests

---

* Bach and Deutsch, p. 106. Interestingly, Bach and Deutsch are against objectifying (or "thinging," as they call it) a loved one, but don't seem to mind objectifying, as they do here, friends or acquaintances.

outside of work with which they might occupy themselves in their time alone. We are not, as is commonly remarked, a speculative or intellectual people: we do not read much, we are not much interested in "higher" culture; we are active, always doing something. And most frequently we do not even enjoy the work with which we earn our keep and spend most of our waking hours. Love becomes very literally all—the major hobby, occupation, and recreation of many people's lives.

Hence, if and when we do have friends, there are strict limitations placed on the quality and quantity of contact. Nonmate relationships are considered unimportant—fillers with which to occupy the time before the main feature. A thirty-two-year-old architect in New York explained that he is tired of palling around with boys, going to different bars to pick up women. He wants to meet a woman and settle down. One gets the distinct impression that he will not see much of his friends when he finds his mate. She will be the center of his life, and that life will not begin until he finds "her." No sense fixing up a house for himself, he says, until she comes along. No use developing other interests: he must look for "her." No sense sticking with his friends after he finds "her."

In marriage the same qualitative limitations exist concerning friendship, but added to those are quantitative concerns. The time in which one is free to see one's friends, if married, is severely limited. There are mutually exclusive time allocations for friendship and for the "couple." Thus women who do not work and whose husbands do are free to see their friends while their spouses are away from home. Similarly, men and women who work may see colleagues during working hours. But for many the evening is the couple's time. And friends are expected to respect the privacy of these sacred hours.

An illustration of this time consciousness came in a conversation between two elderly women, both admittedly lonely, at a senior citizens center. One woman, an Italian widow, and another, a married woman, discovered that they lived quite near each other. And as both had voiced a need for companionship, they agreed to meet. They were delighted at this arrangement until they tried to agree on the time. The widow explained that she felt most lonely at night, when there was no one for her to talk to, and the married woman said that although she felt lonely most of the time, she couldn't possibly leave her husband in the evenings. That was their time together, even though he spent most of "their" time watching TV. Sadly, the friendship ended as quickly as it had begun.

There is one exception to this time rule: work. Encroachments on the couple's time are allowed if they have to do with the work of either spouse. A man or woman is free to have dinner in town without his or her mate if it is with a colleague. Both are free to go out of town alone if it is to attend a convention or work-related meeting.* Superficial social acquaintances are also formed in the interests of a career. Couples will meet socially, but such relationships most often avoid personal matters and keep "strictly to the facts."

And of course there are goal-oriented social relationships—golf partners, tennis partners, even, among swingers, new sexual partners. But all this is directed toward the achievement of a certain aim, whether it be a better tennis score or a bigger and better orgasm. These are not truly interpersonal relationships, as the mask (and not the person) is what's involved.

While this dependency on a single relationship may satisfy us for a time, it leaves us terribly vulnerable to loneliness should anything at all threaten the solidity of the couple bond. At that point we realize how important and necessary are peripheral and supportive relationships.

Most single people still believe in the myth of the one, despite all the current evidence of the instability of such exclusive bonds. They also believe that the lack of the "one" is the primary cause of their loneliness.

---

* This has largely been a male pattern, as women do not often have jobs that require out-of-town excursions and meetings, after work, with colleagues.

The single man or woman, particularly the woman, is on the outside. The burden of singlehood has always weighed more heavily on women, given the role of "homemaker and wife" that women are encouraged to accept. But even too much bachelorhood is not a good thing, as people begin to look askance at a man who is still unmarried when he reaches his late forties and fifties. It is simply incomprehensible that someone would actually choose to live alone. A solitary person must, by definition, be lonely. And indeed, given the ethic of the society, many single people do not remain so out of choice, and they are lonely. But how not be lonely in a society that places you in exile because you do not have a mate?

We are a "couple culture." Even in the various types of new awareness promulgated in books, encounter groups, and the growth movement, the emphasis is on the couple—this time the open, honest, communicative dyad rather than the closed, uncommunicative one. If you are not in a couple you are missing out on something truly great or potentially truly great. If you are not part of a couple, whether that couple be sanctified by marriage or not, you are a failure. So when are you going to get married, the Jewish-Italian-Polish-Irish-Wasp mother asks her daughter or son. And despite the offspring's terse reminder that mother should tend to her own business, the daughter or son repeats incessantly the same question to herself or himself: So when am I going to find someone to love?

I don't know what it is, it's really very neurotic I suppose, but I just get terrifically insecure if I don't have a woman. I get restless and so lonely that I just can't do anything. I know I should read, or develop myself, but I sit home at night with a book for an hour and then I start to go stir-crazy. I have to go out to a bar or something.

Sometimes I just want someone to hug. I'm a very physical person, and very warm and I just want to be physical with someone. It's not a sexual thing—although I am into sex. But just emotional warmth, to hug a woman. You can't exactly go around hugging your men friends.

I just broke up with a girl recently. I had been going with her for three months or so. I wanted to live with her, but she wanted to have other lovers. It was very cozy the way we had it. We cooked to-

*gether, and spent four or five nights a week together. We were be-
ginning to fix up her place and I suppose I had hoped that we would
live there together. It was nice just to fall asleep next to someone.
But it didn't work out. It was all very demeaning really. I really let
her step all over me for a while. I didn't want it to end. I wasn't in
love with her, and when you get right down to it, we weren't even
that close. But it was very cozy. I know it will take me a while to find
another woman and I wanted to hang onto her. To see her once in a
while until I found someone else. But it was too hard to do that, so
we don't see each other at all now.*

Alan is a carpenter in Boston. He is twenty-seven years old
and spends most of his nights roaming around with his other unattached friends, going to bars to find women. He is no more or
less neurotic than anybody else. In fact, he is quite aware of his
problems—that he should do something with his nights other
than go from bar to bar. But he feels unable to stop himself. He
is not particularly fond of the bar scene. But for a man who
works with other men it is difficult to find women. There is of
course the possibility that his friends could introduce him to
women. But most of Alan's friends are also unattached and looking for available women, and his friends who are married aren't
much help in his search.

Adrienne has a horror of being alone on a Saturday night. For
most single people Saturday's the worst night of the week.
"Everyone else is out having fun while I'm the only one sitting
home alone," Adrienne and others lament. When Adrienne
doesn't have a date she feels awful—despite the fact that she has
spent several years in a consciousness-raising group and realizes
how stupid such feelings are. She will do ridiculous things, she
admits, in order not to be alone on that particular weekend
evening. She arranges, weeks in advance, things to keep her
occupied. She invites a friend over, or invites herself away
for the weekend. She cannot, however, keep this up indefinitely,
and there are moments of panic when she realizes she will, indeed, be alone on a Saturday night.

Adrienne has a problem with men. She doesn't trust them.

Too much brutality in her own home when she was a child, too many difficulties being the only girl among three boys in a family where men were the ones who got everything and girls were the ones who got pregnant. If she were really to take a look at herself she would probably realize that she is not happy with men at all. It's not that she's a homosexual, but rather that she has never completely overcome certain unpleasant childhood memories.

Adrienne spends much of her energy worrying about men and how to find one. She has a tendency, despite her insistences that she would love to have a man, to tighten up when she's with a man. She smiles at the wrong moments, her body stiffens at his touch. She goes to encounter groups and therapy sessions to try to overcome her rigidity. It is a contradictory situation, trying to love someone whose essence you essentially dislike, wanting something you do not really want.

Thomas Taylor, twenty-eight, has spent four of the last six years in the army and the past two years training to be a stockbroker in Washington, D.C. His social needs were to a certain extent satisfied by army life, where there was a lot of moving around in a distinct, ready-made community. He was not then a lonely man. Today, in a more diffuse world, things have changed for him.

I really would like to find someone—a girl, you know. And if I have to marry her to keep her I will. I'm willing to sacrifice a lot at this point. I used to have a certain idea of a girl, Miss Right, you know. She had to be rich, and beautiful, and intelligent and good in bed and cook like a platoon of French chefs, and not make too many demands, and take care of my home and me. But now I'll settle for a lot less. This dating business is just such a hassle. How do you approach her, do you approach her, how do you know she's interested, when do you come on, do you come on, when can you cut the bullshit and just take up your normal, gross, nose-scratching behavior?

Before, I didn't want to get attached because I felt I hadn't done everything I wanted to do. But it's getting pretty close now and I have done just about everything. Sometimes I lie in bed and get frightened. I think that there's nobody in the world who really cares about me and what happens to me. Friends . . . ? Yes, I have some friends, but I've moved around a lot and haven't really kept up as much as I should. And then I have a distinct and definite need for sex. If I don't get physical affection, you know, just the huggy, cuddly stuff, I get peculiar.

I get so goddamned lonely. It never used to bother me, but it gets worse and worse. If I sit home and read a book and there's a woman there, I can concentrate. But if I spend an hour reading alone, I feel lost. And I like to spend time at home. But I rarely do. It seems at the end of a week that I have hardly spent any time at home. If a woman is with me, I'll feel that I've been there all year. It's a relative time theory.

I just want someone who cares about me. If I have that, I can mesh my human and career goals. But I can't do the one without the other. I have certain things I want to accomplish through my work—like get loaded. But I can't do that just for myself. Like right now I have a lot of hassles at work and I really need some positive reinforcement at home.

What can I do for a woman? Well, I'm polite and considerate and charming. And good in bed. And I'd care about her, and give her ego a boost and give her a reason by giving her someone to care about.

For Judy, a twenty-five-year-old secretary working at the Baltimore *Sun*, the worst thing about living alone is eating alone.

Just to stop eating alone, I would move in with a man right away. But there is no way for me to meet men. I work alone in an office. Outside my office is a large room with a clerical staff composed only of women. There are male supervisors but they are older and all married. The only chance to meet men is in the cafeteria, and the only available men are the reporters. But at the Sun, and I think most newspapers, there's a kind of class prejudice. The reporters are college-educated and they don't have much to do with clerical staff. I'm college-educated also and so are some other girls, but there is just this prejudice against us meeting. The only men who are "our types" are maybe pressmen but there aren't many of them. It's really quite hard. I don't even meet that many women. Every time you begin to talk to someone, a supervisor walks up and tells you to get back to work.

You may meet on the lunch hour but it's hard to get on the same lunchtime as someone you are friends with.

I find it very difficult to meet people here in Baltimore. There's not even a coffeehouse where you can just sit. Sometimes I get terribly depressed, you get tired of working and going home and watching TV. I don't like going to bars. I feel like a piece of meat. You have to strike up a conversation with a complete stranger. My God, he could be a rapist or murderer or something. This isn't the safest city, you know. I wouldn't want to go out with someone I had never seen before, or whom no one I know knows. I mean when I was in college, I'd go out with someone I had just met. But that was different. I could see him at the library, I could watch him for a while, see how he acted. I might have known someone he knew. So when I finally met him I felt safe. I would never feel safe going out with a man I had met at a bar.

This harking back to college or high school days is a common theme in American literature, film, and conversation. Collegiate or high school days were the time of easy friendship, when a setting was provided as background for one's social life. The hero of *Rabbit Run,* the characters in the Broadway hit play *That Championship Season,* the single woman above—all nostalgically compare their present loneliness with the ease of meeting people then. They may also have been lonely in college or high school, as nostalgia has a way of favorably reinterpreting the past. But the important thing is that they claim that these institutional experiences provided them with opportunities for creating interpersonal relationships. Now, they all say, now they are grown and in the adult world, these opportunities are lost. The friendships of single adulthood are not the same.

And for the single person friendship is very important. There is no man or woman to keep one constant company, and frequently there is no close community to which to relate. Single people rarely buy their own homes in the suburbs and so do not benefit from whatever small communal feelings suburbia offers. They most often live in anonymous urban settings.* They do

* This trend is changing and more single people are moving to the suburbs. But life there is only slightly less anonymous than in cities.

not know their neighbors or the storekeepers, and often do not socialize with people at work.

If single people do have friends, they are almost invariably other singles. Couples in America are very reluctant to have single men or women as close friends. The unattached party is almost always considered a threat to one of the partners in the marriage. As one young woman in Chicago explains:

I had a really upsetting experience with a married couple I was very close to. I had been going with a guy for over a year. He and I were very close to this couple I mentioned. We saw them all the time. We were all close. While I was going with my boyfriend, I used to see the husband alone. We would talk, and he helped me a lot with my problems. He was very insightful, more so than his wife.

After my boyfriend and I broke up, I continued to see them, and he and I would talk. I guess I had a lot of problems and so I needed his help. There was absolutely nothing but friendship between us. In fact, he was more like a therapist. Finally he began to act cold to me, and I couldn't understand it. I got up the courage to ask him what the matter was. He told me that his wife, also my friend, was feeling very threatened by his relationship with me and asked him not to talk with me anymore. He said he felt very bad but that he had to go along with her. After that, I stopped seeing both of them. I felt very bitter about the whole thing. Everytime I think about it I feel that way. There were the closest friends I had.

So singles rely on each other for friendship, and such relationships can be very solid. But where the search for a mate is of paramount interest to either friend, problems develop. In such a context the friend of the same sex is often considered a second-class citizen. The friend is important when there isn't someone of the opposite sex around. But when the possibility of a date arises, out goes the friend, as this single woman in New York explains:

It's very hard to be friends with women who are only interested in men. I had one friend who was typical. She was my roommate. We did a lot of things together. But she was really into having a man.

One day we had planned to go out to do something together. It was a lovely day, and just before we were to go the phone rang. It was some guy she vaguely knew asking her to go to a picnic. She accepted and told me. She said she couldn't refuse, and because it was a man I was supposed to understand. The thing was that she didn't even like the guy. It really made me feel bad, to know that I was being deserted like that, as though I and my needs didn't exist at all.

This pattern of male priority over female friendships is part of the socialization of women, as women's liberation has so well pointed out. But even "liberated" women fall easily into such patterns. Opposite-sex priority over same-sex friendships is, moreover, not restricted to women. If you see love as the answer to loneliness, then any opportunity for love, however ephemeral, will automatically override alliances with friends.

All this does no good for either person involved in the friendship. When people abandon close friends for a member of the opposite sex, they are not only devaluing their friends but also subconsciously devaluing themselves. Their actions invite similar treatment from the friends. Thus the price of romance becomes one's own self-esteem; and the purchase is left in doubt. If you're not valued by your friends, how can you possibly be valued by a lover? This realization makes friends feel that they cannot depend upon one another. Thus, together, they are alone.

Friends who find mates do not always drop mateless friends. Often they will continue to see one another, but the friend who has the mate will present her- or himself not as an individual but as part of a unit. One woman explained that her best friend had found a boyfriend, and each time she called this woman about a problem, the friend would appear on her doorstep with her boyfriend tagging along. "I felt really terrible," she recounts, "when that happened. He was a stranger to me, and had I wanted to talk to him, I would have told her to bring him along. I wanted to talk to her and did not feel close enough with him to confide in him. She really put me in the middle: either I had to talk with him there or I had to ask him to go. So I just stopped calling her."

Single friendships where the priority is not the welfare of the other but the finding of a mate have a tendency to self-destruct once this goal is achieved, as these stories illustrate. Perhaps it's because the cement that holds the friendship together is precisely the common search for love. A great deal of time is spent talking about how to find a mate, going out and looking for a mate together. The two friends share the hunt, but once it is over, and the lover found, there is no longer any link between the friends. The success of the struggle leads to the destruction of the friendship.

The effects of our increasingly anonymous culture weigh heavily on the single person. Being single in contemporary America places one in a particularly contradictory situation. Single people can theoretically do what they like, live where they like, work where they want at what they want without having to worry about the financial restrictions a family may impose. They can also frequently enjoy more sexual freedom with fewer complications than can the married man or woman. People can and do remain single longer or even permanently because of, among other things, increased mobility, birth-control pills and the sexual revolution, and increasing affluence. But the technological advances that have allowed people to remain single longer have also helped create a cold and impersonal world that the single person especially finds unfriendly. Thus the single person is tantalized by the life-styles idealized in *Playboy* and *Cosmopolitan*, and yet may have little idea how to make the well-publicized dream of singlehood come true.

Michael, a man of thirty-two, is astonishingly cynical. He has been through the singles scene—bars, dances, apartments—and he has seen and experienced the effects of the "action circuit." He began going to singles bars in the late sixties. That was the only sort of place where he could easily meet women.

There's no way you're going to kill the action circuit. The days when knighthood was in flower, when married couples or unmarried couples put their favorite eligible woman and their favorable eligible bachelor together at a dinner party are gone. There are no dinner parties, they don't exist, in fact parties are very rare—for reasons I don't understand, they've been supplanted to an incredible extent by the action circuit, and this is true for every ethnic group and class. Given that there isn't that additional social vehicle where people can meet each other—and they're not going to meet at Laundromats or photo classes, or Esalen, or Werner Erhard's rip-off est. They're not doing it. And they're as a last resort going to Perry's, a high-class singles bar in San Francisco. And what they're finding is that they are spending enormous amounts of money getting very drunk, hurting their professional lives and their physical lives playing this muddy game.

For the last several years the singles bar has become a mainstay in Michael's life, as has the drinking that is typical of the singles scene. And it is in singles bars that he has met most of the women with whom he goes out. Despite the fact that he is a successful "swinger" and often ends up going home with a woman he meets at a bar, these quick affairs don't satisfy his cravings for closeness.

I think men can tolerate being alone less than women. I know many women who enjoy being by themselves. I respect that. I seem to need to be with somebody all the time. I would love to find a woman to whom I could commit myself. But bachelors these days don't seem to be able to commit. It seems a particular disease of the American male not to be able to commit. To women or to work. We seem to need a woman all the time, and we're constantly on a quest for new flesh. One woman, five women, ten women.

I haven't asked a woman out on a date in a long time. Of the women I've gone out with this year, I've only called maybe three to ask for a date. I think that's a bit unhealthy. I should probably call a girl up and ask her to go to the symphony or out to dinner but I never do. It's too easy to just pick someone up. That way there's no commitment involved. It's just a casual thing.

Women are not all Michael can't commit himself to. In recent years he has also begun to feel disillusioned with his work. He had hoped, when he set out to be an attorney, that he would both make money and do a certain amount of social good. Except for those hopes he might have followed his dreams. When he was in college he played in a band and sailed in the school sailing club. Sailing and music are still his greatest loves. In fact, he could have become a professional at either. But he turned down offers to do both because he felt the law would allow him to better satisfy his rather expensive tastes.

For several years he worked for law firms, and then he and four other lawyers opened their own office. What better way to have freedom, Michael thought, than to work for himself? The practice did not do as well as expected, however, and the money did not come in as fast as the bills. After a year the office was closed; Michael had lost $10,000. He couldn't help thinking during those last months that had he become a musician, he'd have gotten all the free drinks he wanted, thus saving the $200 or more a month he now spends on booze. Or if he'd gone into sailing, he would have saved all the money he now spends to go out to sea.

Now Michael is in practice with men who have more moderate ambitions. He spends his lunchtimes chasing down lawyer friends who work for large firms, trying to get them to refer small cases to him. Promising referral fees that cut severely into his profits, he hustles business for himself. After a day at this he has only the energy to go to a local bar and ease the strains of the day with a few drinks, or he may use his hustling talent to find women. When he is sober enough to consider it, he finds this a rather undignified way to spend his time.

The effects of the seventies have also changed June's attitude about being single. When she first moved to Boston the town was friendly. After finishing work on Friday night she'd go to a small bar where she would be sure to find friends with whom to drink and chat. Someone would discover where the party was that night, and the whole crew would go *en masse*. If a man asked you out, he would pay for you, which June feels is only right, since the men she likes—up-and-coming businessmen—make more than a secretary. There was a friendly, community feeling, which made being single rather enjoyable.

Six years later, June says that feeling has mysteriously disappeared. Men no longer offer women a drink, and they seem to expect that you will hop right into bed with them, even if they treat you rather shabbily. The singles scene has grown a bit too brutal for June's taste, so she often lacks male company when she would most enjoy it. And she also makes bargains of which she might not have approved several years back. She will go out with married men as long as they are from out of town. And she will sleep with a local married man if she knows he has some sort of arrangement with his wife. These are necessary bargains for June since she most often meets married men.

June no longer hopes to find a nice professional man to marry. Yet she cannot imagine remaining single forever—not the way things are today. After an evening with one of the men who call her when they come in from out of town she feels slightly depressed. Her situation is certainly not that of the stereotyped (back-street) woman who is exploited by married men who refuse to leave their wives. For she never allows herself to get attached to the men who travel in and out of town. But when an evening is over, June is never quite sure who won and who lost, or why she bothered in the first place.

It is rare to find people who actually like to be single and want to stay that way. What one finds more frequently are men and women who say they *adore* being single but who spend most of their nonworking time looking for some kind of sexual or romantic attachment. Tony, for example, has a certain image of life with a woman. It includes fidelity, marriage, domesticity. But until he finds the particular woman with whom he can have total communication he won't give up his freedom. He has had several almost-major involvements in the past years. But each time he started measuring the current woman against his mental image. Reality never quite matched the ideal: the woman was too thin; they didn't really have that much in common—there were always objections. And he'd begin to long for his single days again. The last time this had happened, the woman found someone else. And he continued on his rounds of the single life. After a time Tony watched the woman get more and more involved with her new man. He began to rethink his relationship with her. She was actually more intelligent, prettier, and more sexually exciting than he had realized. She would not have been a bad person to spend a life with. He even talked to her about that prospect, but she was too attached to her new beau and they were thinking of living together.

This kind of ambivalence about attachment is common. Despite criticism of their parents' relationships, because they were too all-inclusive, many men and women today seem to have a vision of love that is even more inclusive than the preceding generation's. Their's will be a total commitment—total communication, total trust, total honesty, total freedom. And this will all take place in a world without any larger community in which the couple shares. These limitations are so overpowering that should love miraculously appear, those who seek it would either quickly destroy its potential or flee. Thus life becomes a fluctuation between two equally untenable alternatives. You want your freedom, but that freedom is very lonely, haunted as it is by this phantom love. There is no warmth within, so you search for warmth elsewhere, but without too much involvement. For involvement would mean total entrapment.

This kind of ambivalence has been traditionally attributed to men, although I believe women are increasingly identifying liberation with this attitude. For men this ambivalence is exacerbated by the physical limitations put on relationships between men. Men cannot touch each other or share their personal fears and weaknesses. Their emotional needs, at least those they are willing to express, are met by women. The "weaker" sex is not appalled to hear of similar weaknesses in men. In fact, such confidences make a man seem more attractive. Aside from sexual contact, a man is allowed to touch and be touched by a woman and get affection from her. Men, therefore, have the contradictory problem of not being emotionally prepared for involvement with the woman and yet needing her simple physical presence.

Among women the problem is a bit different. They have the

privilege, although they may not use it, of being physically affectionate and personally confiding in one another. Although things are changing, the main issue for women concerning relationships with the opposite sex has traditionally been the assumption of a positively valued identity. She finds a man and she assumes a new life, molded by the man and his personal and career interests. In many cases she gets attention and affection from the man, but her commitment to him is more total than his to her. For the man, as we have seen, it is not a question of a woman giving him an identity but of bestowing worth on whatever identity he has forged for himself. She is the confirmation of who he is. She gives form to the content of his existence, while he gives her both form and content.

The absence of such a relationship is consequently more serious for a woman than for a man, as the negative image of the spinster compared with the bachelor suggests. The woman who does not eventually find a man, who lingers on into singlehood as she enters her thirties, is identityless, or saddled with a very uncomfortable identity. As a result, a certain kind of woman forms one category of lonely person in the single population—those who live *resigned* to living alone, who have given up hope of ever finding a mate.

Elaine is an example. There is a kind of desperateness about her. Nothing specific, just a feeling one gets when with her that her balance is not firmly established, that she has not truly made peace with her life, and that the most minor occurrence could tip it one way or another. She is in her middle thirties and wears her age like a blush. She lives alone in a large, high-ceilinged flat in Boston. Although she has lived in the flat for five years, there is a rented-room feeling to it. The walls are gloomy green and barren except for a wall hanging above a narrow, monastic bed.

It is perhaps her incessant efforts to be cheerful that make you realize her pain. She is in school now, she recounts, trying to get a bachelor's degree. When she was young she went to college for only a year, "majoring in boys." Then she left and became a professional ice skater, traveling in North and South America with an ice show. Despite the purported glamour, she says those years were a lonely time, and she began to drink to escape her feelings of emptiness. After she came home from South America she worked at various jobs, none of which she liked.

And there was no one I could really talk to. I stopped eating and would begin to cry for no reason. And I couldn't confide in anyone because my feelings were so intense that I was ashamed. I guess I had sort of a mental breakdown then.

She has recovered from that episode in her life and has established a delicate equilibrium—one that includes neither men nor marriage. "I think people have given up on me as far as getting married. And I've pretty much given up on men. They're always trying to psychoanalyze me, and I don't like that."

Elaine justifies this decision rather defensively. Living without any kind of relationship with a man, either permanent or merely sexual, is in our day a double failure: you are a failure because you don't have a man to love you and because you are a sexual oddity. It was bad enough being a spinster in the past. But there was a certain dignity in that choice. You could not get a man to marry you and so sex was out of the question. Today if you don't have somebody to love, you should at least have someone to have sex with. If you don't, there's *really* something wrong with you.

This feeling of inferiority results from the myth that ours is an age of easy sex. This myth has it that you do not have to be married, or go to a whore, or be involved with one person, to have sex. All you have to do is have the right attitude and step outside your door and there it is—sex. But according to hundreds of people I have interviewed, "easy sex" is painfully at odds with reality. As one young man in Berkeley succinctly put it, "Everyone I know is horny. You can't just go out and find a lady and get laid as much as you want. It's not so easy to get laid if you aren't living with someone or if you aren't married."

It is not at all simple to find that one-night stand. It is commonly said, for instance, that most people who begin an evening alone in a singles bar end up going home without a companion for the night. Whether the arena is the singles bar, the office, the encounter group, or the street where one lives, the story is similar. The notion, propagated by the media, that sex is available on almost every street corner is demonstrably false. But the idea does make those who are unable to find sex feel that there is something terribly wrong with them. If sex is so available, they ask themselves, what's wrong with me?

Thus the new sexuality is used not only to liberate but to compel. It may be second best to live alone or with a roommate, it says, if you redeem yourself with some kind of sexual encounter (extra credit will be given for a bisexual, group, or homosexual encounter). This makes the loneliness of singleness all the more difficult to tolerate. You haven't found anyone to love you, your friends are all in search of that special someone to whom you are an inferior second best, and you—you can't even find someone who will use you as a simple sex object.

"You want to know what it's like being single?" a twenty-six-year-old businessman asked me. "Well, I guess in college you don't really think about it. You have friends and roommates, so you don't worry. But after college, that's when it hits you. At first it's okay. But after a while you get tired of taking night school classes just to meet people. I guess you get bummed out and kind of lonely. I'm getting married soon. It certainly will be a relief."

Chapter Four

Leonard Davidson

The shops stay open late the month before Christmas. After work Leonard Davidson comes home and showers, watches the news, and eats dinner in the breakfast nook of the kitchen. A slice of meat fried quickly and some frozen vegetables. Perhaps, although rarely, a glass of beer. Jews, he is proud to think, are not drinkers. After dinner he leaves by the back door. He has cut a route across the rooms in his mother's large house, the house in which he grew up. Bypassing the large living room, he moves up the stairs to his bedroom and the bath, then downstairs once again to the television room and kitchen. And finally out the back door. Charted thus, the house seems smaller, the rooms left closed seem content without people filling them. He can ignore the empty space.

He drives out of the garage, and going two streets out of his way, he passes a smaller house, the one in which he spent the last ten years of his forty-four years. Seven-thirty. His family will have finished dinner, his wife will be doing the dishes, the kids their homework, the littlest will be watching television. He hopes the program is not a violent one. He could invent a reason to drop in, something to tell the kids, to see how they're doing. It would be better not to. His brother-in-law keeps telling him that it's really not the kids he wants to see but his wife. That he hasn't untied the cord yet. But twenty years of marriage gives one a lot of cord to untangle. How would his brother-in-law, with his happy family and big house on Long Island, understand the complexities of undoing such diligently tied knots?

The shopping center sits in the middle of a maze of overpasses, underpasses, and construction that seems never completed. When he was a child all this land was open—trees and fields. To his parents, immigrants from eastern Europe, it was The Country—the final escape. Now Harrison has become another extension of New York City. Black people have moved onto the block where his mother's house sits. They are nice people, clean and neat. He has nothing against them. But he would never have imagined that such a thing could happen. Just as he would never have thought that he would be going shopping before Christmas without his wife or one of their four children, with nothing to buy, just to escape an empty house, just to wander through rows of people jostling one another, just to hear the saleswomen ask if they can help him.

At nine-thirty the lights in the store flash closing time. He drives home, going out of his way again to pass the small wooden house on the corner. When he and his wife were courting they used to pass the empty lot, years before the house was built. He had never expected to live on that piece of land, in the same town where he had grown up. Back then, when he was first out of college, he had expected to do other, more exciting things, which would take him to other, more exciting places. Maybe he would be a writer; his family had always praised his long, detailed letters. Or maybe art—become a curator—or radio. He had once been a guest usher for NBC. Before the networks had training programs they hired college-educated boys, offering them prospects to work on the staff, get a feel for the business, work their way up. When he hears their voices on the radio or television he smiles, thinking of these now famous personalities as they were years ago, holding flashlights and helping people to find their seats. He could have been one of them if he had only stuck with it. His family wasn't really against it. But then again, they weren't exactly for it. His father had simply said, "Well, if you want to go into radio, and that's what you really want, then go into radio." After Leonard had begun his career and discovered that the pay was much lower than he had expected, too low to allow him to have the things his family had given him, his father had extended an offer to put his son into business. When he quit radio it wasn't entirely his father's doing. Radio was a career in which you had to move around a lot, be ready to pull up your roots any time, be willing never even to plant them. And Leonard wanted roots, a family, to stay in one place. Radio was not really for him. Besides, he remembers the feeling of discomfort he had working with those men who have since gone on to be so famous. He never did believe he was as good as they. He never quite felt adequate. Sure, he could talk easily and his voice was deep enough, but compared with their expansiveness, he seemed shy and rather reticent.

So he married Ruthie and went into business.

He worked in clothing, and in Ruthie's family's business until her brother kicked him out, after ten years. And then he went into the restaurant business. For a while things went well and he had a number of successful restaurants. But one bad location and some business errors and the whole thing collapsed into bankruptcy. He had hoped to do well, like his father, a true Horatio Alger, a man who had raised himself by his own bootstraps and become a millionaire. But Leonard was too nice. His father had once told him that to succeed in business one had to be ruthless, not unnecessarily so, but when required. Leonard, however, seemed unable to be ruthless when necessary. So now he is a schlepper. In Yiddish that means an odd-job man or a gofor, someone who carries and drives, does whatever has to be done. It is quite a comedown for him. He knows he could begin again. Go into restaurant management, use his potential. But he promised his mother he would stick with this job for a while. She wanted him to have a job in work that would not require the investment of large sums of money. His mother had said she would help him financially if he did not earn enough. He does not like the arrangement, but he had accepted. So now, really, he is not his own man, he is a ward of his family. Things won't go on this way for a long time, his mother assures him, just until he gets his family situation straightened out.

He had always believed that that was the one thing in his life that was completely secure. He had tried to make it that way. Ruthie was a secure woman—quiet, not too bright, relaxing—a woman who would listen. Without quite knowing it, he can see now, he married a woman whom he could dominate. Not in any overt way. Quietly. "Don't you think we should do things this way, dear?" he would say. He never gave an order, he didn't have to. She always agreed. It was the same with the children. He rarely yelled. He liked the feeling that it was his house, his family, that he was the important one, the one who made all the arrangements.

He had never realized that Ruthie resented those arrangements.

But quite suddenly, about two years ago, Ruthie began to hear noises in her head. They went to the family physician and then a neurologist, who were both of the opinion that the cause wasn't physical. Perhaps what Ruthie needed was some kind of counseling. In fact, the doctors said, it might not be a bad idea if the two went for counseling together. Leonard would never have agreed if it weren't for Ruthie's noises. He had already been to a psychiatrist years ago when he was in college, and after that he felt no need for further help. For Ruthie, though, he would go. He had assumed that counseling would help solidify their marriage. It had never occurred to him that it would help Ruthie decide to leave him. Things seemed to be going so well in therapy. After the therapist warmed to them, he felt he was learning so much about himself and how to improve.

Ruthie, on the other hand, did not seem quite so positive about things. Those voices, which, they discovered, were the sounds of her anger and resentment, were no longer turned against her, but thrown at him, over and over again, in one accusation after another. He was not trustworthy, he did not trust her, he was unresponsive. He did not care about her. All these charges seemed incredible to him. Had he not trusted her so much, cared about her so much that everything—the car, the house—was in her name? Was that not a sign of trust? But no, she argued, that was not enough. She wanted more—a share in the daily decisions of his life; that was real trust. Still he could not understand. How could he consult Ruthie about business matters that she could not possibly understand? How could a woman who spent all her time at home comprehend the complexities of a world she knew nothing about? Perhaps, the counselor suggested, Leonard could have explained things in such a way that she would have been able to help more. Perhaps . . .

But he had been proud that Ruthie did not have to help, proud that his wife did not have to work, did not have to be burdened with such things. Just as he had been happy to leave the housework and daily details of raising the family to her. Men and women, he had always believed, had different things to do in life. When he came home from the factory, in the early years of his marriage, he did not want to do the dishes. He had his arms up to the elbow in water and dirt all day, and at night he just wanted to relax. Besides, it was not entirely true that he never encouraged Ruthie to do things. There was her stamp collection—one of the finest to be found of stamps of musical instruments. She had been a pianist before they married, and when he had thought about her love for music, he had shown her all the various stamps he thought might interest her. She had continued on her own.

Again, that was not enough, Ruthie said. If he were completely honest, he had to admit that she was right. That had been his biggest mistake, he could see now, now when the knowledge was almost useless. He had not encouraged her to develop herself. In fact, he had actively discouraged her. He does not quite know why he felt so threatened when Ruthie said she wanted to do more with her life. She was never one of those women's libbers. By no means. She just wanted to become more of a person. He remembers those discussions. Those were the days when he really did yell and scream. Somehow he had just felt intuitively that all those liberal ideas would tear him and his family apart.

He can see that it would have done only good. They might still be together. But at that time he couldn't imagine what it would do to their lives if she went to school or got a job or helped more in his business.

And then, of course, there were other problems that came out in counseling. Sexual problems. Ruthie accused him of being cold, of not desiring her. When she said those things he was flabbergasted, astonished. How could she believe that of him? Then he began to think, she was right, he had been avoiding her, holding back. He seemed not to have had any drive. Was there something wrong with him—was he sick? Maybe they had just gotten into bad habits that kept them apart. He, for instance, was a night person. He could stay up all night and still be wide awake the next morning. Ruthie was a slow-metabolism kind of person, who needed lots of sleep and had to get to bed early. Well, if she went to bed at ten and he at twelve, how would they meet? She had begun to think he was staying up late deliberately, in order to avoid her. Perhaps if they had talked sooner, if they hadn't let it go on so long. But sex was something one didn't talk about. Even in therapy it had taken a year and a half to discuss those things. And then, just when they had got around to it, the tragedy happened. The counselor, a lovely, birdlike woman—a true professional, a woman who did not need to work but chose to work—died of cancer. Right in the middle of therapy.

He can't help blaming their next therapist for the separation. She never did warm to him, and finally he realized that she was not very professional. Or maybe she thought the marriage simply wasn't worth saving. Whatever it was, when Ruthie told her that she intended to ask Leonard to leave, she should have called him, asked Ruthie to wait till the three of them could meet together and discuss it further. But no, she did nothing, except approve, he supposed, Ruthie's decision.

He and Ruthie went away that weekend—for Labor Day. Before he left for work on the day after they returned home Ruthie told him she wanted him to move out of the house. He cannot help resenting the way in which she arranged it all—sending their eldest daughter to her sister's and refusing to tell him where she was if he didn't leave. Telling him in the morning, when she knew he always tried to keep his mornings smooth and uncluttered with family worries. Leaving him just when things financially were the worst for him, after she had stayed with him through all the good years. And involving the children. He will never forgive her for the look on his daughter's face when he finally saw her. "Daddy, will you hug me?" she had asked hesitantly. She thought her father no longer loved her and wanted her sent away. He understands his wife's bitterness, and that her family does not approve of him—but a seventeen-year-old girl cannot be expected to comprehend all the subtleties of destruction that go on between a man and wife when they rip out the stitches that held their marriage together.

After that morning he and his wife talked mainly through their lawyers, and Leonard moved to his mother's house. His father had died four years earlier, and his mother had remarried —a nice elderly man, a companion. Leonard has the house to himself, since his mother and her new husband have gone to Florida for three months to escape the winter. To some it probably seemed strange for a forty-four-year-old man to go back to Momma's. A grown man, they would probably say, should just go out and find a place of his own. But it was all a matter of survival, and to accept the terms of survival was something he had learned early in life. Being a Jewish kid outnumbered by Christians meant not fighting, running away. If you ran quickly enough, you could always return to fight some other time. He was taught not to be ashamed of cowardice. Not a pleasant lesson—but a necessary one. So he is not ashamed of living in his mother's house. There is safety in that house and its familiar spaces: the old grandfather clock still keeping time in the corner of the living room, as it had when he was a child, ignorant of all the changes that have gone on between its tones; the rugs worn down by him and his sisters and all their children. Without that house he cannot imagine how he could have made the transition from husband and father to . . . something he has yet to define.

Perhaps it is that sense of loss—the psychologists, he read in one of the many books he has recently devoured on divorce, call it loss of identity—that disturbs him most. All of his life he has had a certain plan, a reason for living. Before his marriage his goal was to make a good living, be something he and his family could be proud of. That goal was the same after marriage. Successes, failures—he shared everything with his family, people to whom he could cry, "Look, look what I've done." These days there is no one at night to come home to, no one to whom he can read something he finds interesting, who will ask his opinion about this or that. He finds himself still cutting out items from the paper, articles he thinks his kids should read. And as quickly, he throws them into the wastebasket. Before, his children were a captive audience. They had to listen and appreciate. He does not know how they would take the same attention today. He no longer quite knows how to approach them. Before he left the house his rabbi asked him whether he wanted to stay home and see his children arranging their lives in the moments of peace that came in between hours of tension. Would he rather remain at home and watch his children suffer or leave and know that they were happy? Of course he could desire only his children's happiness. That is what frightens him, the idea that his children could be happy without him. If that were true, then he would be useless. No one likes to think that he is dispensable. People have assured him that he can maintain a relationship with his children even though he no longer lives with them. But that seems impossible. How can you be a father when you do not see your children every day, when you do not watch them grow from week to week, let alone from minute to minute?

And then there are other worries that assail him—financial worries. He had always hoped to save enough some day to really relax—do whatever he wanted. It was as though he were sacrificing all sorts of momentary pleasures for a little pot of gold. The way you save all the calories for one very special thing. Divorce completely changes everything. Even if he did get back on his feet, recover from bankruptcy, there would be child support and alimony. If he remarried he would have to support two families.

During the day he hides these fears behind his thick glasses and the calm smile he learned in business. It is at night that his anxieties disturb his stomach as a constant reminder. To quiet them he tries to keep away from the house and be near people, activity. He spends at least two nights a week and Saturday and part of Sunday occupied with some sort of synagogue business. Then there is his family. Thank God, when he begins to talk back to the TV he can always call his sisters or his brother and invite himself to dinner. His younger sister has learned to anticipate his needs, and he laughs when the older one—the rich one on the Island—asks him to hold on while she checks her social calendar. "Mildred," he tells her, "I don't care if you're in or out, I'm coming over. If you're not home, I'll baby-sit." That's at least three, sometimes four nights taken care of. But after that, there are still the others to fill.

When he and Ruthie were together, there was always something to do. He never quite knew how, but the time was filled either with the kids or with friends. Empty evenings seemed a relief rather than a burden. Now there are no friends whom he can call. The morning he left home, after Ruthie announced her decision to separate, Leonard realized that loss. On the sidewalk, feeling dizzy, frightened, he realized that he did not have one single friend. All his friends had come into his life because Ruthie and other women had pulled their men together. True, there was still one couple he knew, a couple who were also Ruthie's friends. To go to them with his troubles would be out of the question. It would mean putting them in the middle, asking them to choose between him and his wife. Ruthie might do that, but to be a friend, he has always believed, means never putting someone in that position. Like the property, friends would be split as well, and Ruthie would get the major share. He would have to start from the beginning.

With women too he would have to begin again. He cannot,

nor would he want to, spend the rest of his life alone. He is, after all, still a young man. He can have another wife, not perhaps another family—but who knows? He has learned a lot from all that he has been through. He could find a good wife, a better wife than Ruthie, and he would not make the same mistakes. He would be a better husband, encourage his wife to develop herself, do more things with her, be more aggressive sexually. But, my God, how do you find a woman—and if you find her, how do you act with her? For twenty years, more, he has been with the same woman. In fact, he has never in his life had another woman. He and Ruthie were both virgins when they married. Everything they knew about love and sex they learned together. With Ruthie, when it happened, it was so easy. You just turned over in bed and touched, suggested. But with another woman, a grown woman. . . .

He feels scared and a bit ridiculous, as if he were in high school again. And then it astonishes him, the things that happen once people find that he is no longer with his wife. Divorced or widowed women that he has known for years, whom he likes and admires as friends, suddenly act differently toward him. He almost feels the victim of predators, not knowing how to turn himself on, or them off. It is all happening so quickly, all these changes. He must slow it down. No fantasies, no quick affairs. Even when he was young he never felt too confident about his attractiveness. He was perhaps a bit too short, a bit too nervous. Now, after twenty years. . . .

He must take it all slowly. A friend told him about Parents Without Partners, a group in which you can share an interest in children and in which there are various kinds of activities. And you don't have to commit yourself too quickly. Not like a singles bar. He's never been to one, but he's heard stories. If you don't ask for her name and phone number as soon as you meet a girl, you may never see her again. At Parents Without Partners you can take your time. You may see a woman over and over again, see how she acts, be able to talk quietly. At the first meeting he was impressed with the cross section of people, from a bus driver to a wealthy woman from Scarsdale. She was an attractive woman and he would have liked to talk to her. But intuitively he could sense her anger against men. He would not even approach a woman like that, who would attack him with her pain. But there are other women—at dances, parties.

A friend and he are driving to a dance in Connecticut given by a woman who is trying to start a group for older, Jewish singles. On the phone she warned him not to be in a hurry to find someone. Men, she said, often remarry too fast and then end up in the same sort of situation they shared with their first wives. Waiting makes more sense. If you learn to be by yourself; make it past the first two years. Two years is a long time, but he has done other difficult things in his life.

Soon he'll have to leave his mother's. She'll be coming back from Florida in a couple of months and he'll have to find a place of his own. When he thinks of going out and looking, his stomach does flip-flops. He'll really be alone then. He remembers when his wife used to go on vacations or to see her parents. Being alone for a couple of weeks was almost fun. There was frozen food in the freezer, and he was given instructions on how to do this and that. It was like camping out. But now . . . he hasn't done his laundry since he was in college. Maybe it won't be so bad. There are always surprises, unexpected things. He has always believed in staying alive and just seeing what comes next. And smiling, always having a smile on his face. Lennie the tummler, his family always calls him—the one who's always laughing.

Chapter Five

Marriage

When marriage is used as the solution to loneliness it becomes a negative bond whose reason for existence is not the unity of two people who desire each other but a common defense against that oppressively empty feeling of being alone. It may seem at first that loneliness has been defeated. But in reality it has been implanted at the core of whatever relationship is formed. Because of this many marital relationships exist with an absence of personal contact rather than providing the basis for such contact. And loneliness is more severely felt because it occurs where least expected.

Our cultural tradition and our personal needs lead us to believe that marriage is the answer to all, or almost all, of our problems. We join together in matrimony, and as a couple we are welcomed into a community of family, friends, neighbors. We get, as it were, twice what we had expected for our effort— an intimate relationship and a place in society. Our identity is assured and confirmed. There will be someone there to share our life, to fight for us, to love us, to care for us. With enough goodwill and effort we can win.

Encouraged by social values and our own illusions, we have staggering expectations of our marital relationships. From the beginning we believe that our unity as a couple will banish our individual emptinesses. Tom and Jane, individually, feel they cannot make it alone. So they decide to undertake life in concert. If I can't do it alone, each thinks, we can surely do it together.

Such an admission of the individual's defeat subtly affects the whole tenor of the marriage relationship. The union established is not a reflection of each person's wholeness but rather a reflection of each partner's loneliness. And every positive gesture toward the other is also a negative gesture away—from loneliness and fear.

This dilemma is particularly difficult in our era, when people are no longer supposed to do things because of external pressures. Forty or a hundred years ago Tom and Jane could marry because of such pressures, and that would have been perfectly normal. People in those days were swayed by religious, financial, community, and family considerations. Today Tom and Jane are reportedly unhampered by such considerations. They chose each other freely.

But should they actually manage to overcome all social and parental influence, they may still be pushed by the pressure of loneliness. While supposedly making a choice of their own free wills, they are in fact motivated to act and to choose because of their own bondage. The consequences of such choices are profound. Many modern marriages become the arena of conflict rather than development. The two partners realize the role loneliness has played in the creation of their relationship and they are therefore ambivalent about each other. Much of their time together is spent discussing whether they ought to be together. They are rather like people who want to build a house and yet spend most of their energy and time worrying about whether to buy the land on which to build, and how much they should spend on materials. The house does not get constructed.

Of course, not all marriages are motivated by loneliness. Many men and women marry for the most positive of reasons. They actually like each other. But because of the social context in which most contemporary marriages unfold, loneliness can nevertheless become one of the major problems even in the most solid of marriages. Increased mobility, the isolation of the woman and the family in suburbia, sexual confusion, and the general lack of stability in our society—these issues are threats to the best relationships. And for those relationships whose underpinnings are shaky or whose origins are confused the effects can be catastrophic.

As we trace the experiences of loneliness in marriage—both in solid and troubled relationships—we must distinguish between the way different social and personal dilemmas affect the husband and wife involved. Because men traditionally leave home to work and women do not, the loneliness of a man will be influenced not only by his socialization and his relationship to his wife and community but also by what happens in his daily work away from home. The loneliness of a woman who does not work will be determined by her socialization, her relationship to her husband, and her position at home and in the community. We can begin to elaborate this distinction by considering one of the primary experiences in family life, pregnancy.

Pregnancy and childbirth can shatter the unity of a married couple. The sense of loneliness it generates is often due to the isolation in which today's nuclear family unit exists. Far from family, isolated in the suburbs or the anonymity of large cities, a woman is shut in with her child and shut out of the workings of the world. It is an incredible shock to a woman who feels that she should be content just to be with a new-born infant to find that infant a fetter chaining her to an empty existence.

Sarah was twenty-nine when she had her first child. She and her husband had recently moved from Chicago to Cleveland, where her husband was pursuing postdoctoral studies. In Chicago Sarah had been a successful book reviewer for magazines and newspapers, and her days were filled with interesting contacts with exciting people. She had very much wanted to have a child, although she did have certain insecurities about her future. But all her friends had told her such insecurities were natural and she shouldn't worry too much. She could always resume work after her child was born, especially since her field allowed her to work at home.

The child was born about four months after the move to Cleveland. Perhaps, Sarah thought at first, the trouble was the lack of culture and sophistication in Cleveland compared to Chicago. Or the child, or three years of marriage. She couldn't figure it out, but something was surely wrong after her daughter was born. It extended long past postpartum depression. She could not make the adjustment. Trapped by the city, and her child, she stayed home all day remembering the time when she had spent her hours working, keeping busy, talking with intelligent people. Each time the baby cried, each time she held her, Sarah felt as if someone had added another bar to her cage. An intelligent woman, schooled in contemporary psychological concepts, she realized how important these years were for her baby. How important it was to give a baby warm, ungrudging care. So when she felt her resentment and dismay she simultaneously hated herself for feeling it. What in God's name am I doing to my baby, she asked herself, looking pityingly at this little stranger whom she could not accept into her life.

Worst of all, there was no one to help her. No friends, for she had left all her former friends in Chicago, and having to tend a baby seemed to lock her out of all but the most superficial relationships with other women who also had babies. No husband, as he was gone all day and had a difficult time relating to her constant depression. No self, for she was suddenly changed, unable to remember what she had been like.

Pregnancy for many women such as Sarah means that while they have proved their worth as women, they have lost their worth as people. The difference between "real work" and women's work is this: in our society work is generally classified as that to which we can give a monetary value. Although a woman may spend all day working in the home, she cannot attach financial value to her efforts. She feels she is merely taking up space and not really making a contribution, as her husband is. This sense of loss of value, says Cecile Goodman, a psychologist in suburban San Jose, California, makes it difficult for many women to gain the confidence necessary to venture outside the home—to make contacts that would help them allay their loneliness.

I think one of the loneliest groups of women are those in these tract developments, with one-car families where the husband takes the car.

There are no community or neighborhood centers. They don't know where to go to get what. Their husband comes home at night and they expect him to fulfill all their longings during the day. That puts an extra strain on the marriage. They're shut up with three kids, the last of which they probably didn't want anyway. And I think they are just trapped in a life they didn't expect and it simply baffles them. These women don't have any idea of what's out there as an alternative, and they have no sense of themselves as capable and competent. They do not even have the social skills to develop relationships with one another.

The purely physical impediments of getting from place to place while pregnant or with small children can also deter a woman from getting out of the house, says Connie Varmus, mother of a new-born son in San Francisco:

After I had my baby, I suddenly found that I could sympathize with the plight of old people. Old people and recent mothers have a lot in common. Having a baby makes it terribly difficult to get out. All of a sudden little things that you would never think about make you think twice about going out. Getting the diapers, putting a pack on, getting in and out of cars, things like that. You have all this extra weight, just like an old person carrying a sack of laundry or groceries. You're very encumbered. Some women just give up and stay home all day and watch soap operas.

The television-watching syndrome so often associated with the woman who stays home all day can begin with pregnancy and childbirth. A small child is not much fun to talk to, and so, for companionship, women begin to watch afternoon television or listen to radio talk shows. In many instances the television program may be their only "contact" with adults all day. And although the sound of human voices may make a woman feel that there is someone there, this is escape into illusion of almost pathological dimensions. Getting child care is a way to escape this situation. But child care is expensive, beyond the means of many mothers in today's economy.

Pregnancy and the isolation of the woman in the home can be the beginning of the intrusion of loneliness into a marital relationship. There is suddenly a huge distance between the wife and husband, and any schism that was implicit before marriage becomes explicit. Suddenly two people who apparently started off together part ways. Their concerns are no longer the same and their worlds are separated. Peg Bertolino, a woman in Mill Valley, California, recalls the gap that was widened by the children who were supposed to bring her and her husband together:

When my husband and I would go to parties, where we knew a lot of artists and other interesting people, I felt that I just didn't have a thing to say. I couldn't talk about the diapers there. So I got even more depressed. And I wouldn't talk at all, and that made me feel more lonely. I would tell my husband that I wanted to get out more and he would say that his mother—he comes from a big Italian family —always stayed home all day and never complained. I had a nice house, he would say, and wasn't that good enough for me? So I'd think that he was right and wonder what was wrong with me. There must be something wrong with me. But I don't think my husband realized how much his mother really got out of the house, and how much people would drop in and visit.

The loneliness of the new mother with her child is complicated by this kind of guilt. She should feel happy, fulfilled as a woman, the world tells her, and so she dares not admit her feelings of isolation. But the new mother's ideas about appropriate child rearing are inherited from a social situation very different from her own. Things are not the same as they were a hundred or even fifty years ago; today we are isolated in small nuclear family units, far from extended family, or exiled in anonymous suburban neighborhoods and city high-rises. Women in the past could stay home all day and still have a fairly full social life, surrounded by an interested community, with friends and family dropping in. In today's urban and suburban environments such compensations for isolation from the "real" world have largely vanished.

The move to suburbia is particularly difficult for the young or expecting mother. And as 37.6 percent of all Americans (over 76 million people) live in the suburbs, this difficulty is one many women face. In some urban neighborhoods there are parks within walking distance of residential areas, and women can get out and be among people. Suburbia, however, is largely an affair of the automobile. There are few neighborhood parks and places of communal congregation within walking distance of most homes. The young mother and housewife is supposed to be content with her back porch and back yard, but these soon become more like cells than enclaves. As Ms. Bertolino says:

When we lived in San Francisco, I never felt lonely with my baby. People dropped in all the time. And there was a lovely park nearby where I could go with the baby. Whenever I went there alone, after a few minutes there was a crowd of mothers around. But when I moved to the suburbs it was really bad. I didn't drive and I was shut in the house all day. I didn't know anyone and I guess I felt that other people should take the initiative and call me. But also it was the circumstances. There was nowhere to go to meet people, no parks to take the kids to. I got more and more depressed, only I wouldn't admit it to myself. I would just get terribly tired. I would wonder why, because I hadn't done anything all day. Then my husband worked all day and talked to people so when he came home he was tired and wouldn't want to talk to me.

Privacy is a barrier of silence raised between houses that are no longer separated by moats or high fences. And such concern for privacy makes it difficult to initiate the new contacts that a woman moving to the suburbs needs. Again Ms. Bertolino comments:

It's very hard to meet people in the suburbs. It's hard to just walk up to someone's door and knock. People are very much into privacy these days. It's just a vibration in the air. You feel that if you knocked on someone's door you would be bothering them. That they don't want to see anyone. It's not so much anything anyone says, but the only kind of friendships there are are scheduled friendships. All planned and worked out. . . . No one even just drops in. You plan things days ahead of time.

One of the underlying themes of the concern for privacy is the fear of loss of control. A woman in Scarsdale, New York, explains that she would not want people to unexpectedly show up at her front door, because if they did, she would automatically lose control of her social life. "I wouldn't want my neighbors to show up for coffee or I wouldn't want to get too involved with them, because I don't want to find myself suddenly involved in being very busy every weekend. I tend to be very cautious about choosing a friend. I don't want to be caught up in a social network, because before you know it you're busy for the next ten weekends."

Many women refuse to permit themselves or their neighbors to engage in spontaneous contact, despite the fact that the loneliness of suburban life could be significantly allayed by spontaneous encounters. They believe that should they open themselves to such contact, they would be suffocated with demands on their time and energy. This prohibition against spontaneity is primarily due to two factors—projection, and the inability to place limits on demands for friendship.

Projection characterizes those who, because they fear the dimensions of their own need, see it on every stranger's face. For example, a woman who needs contact desperately fears that were she allowed the opportunity, she would swallow her friends with limitless demands. To cope with these feelings, she projects them, fearing that others will swallow her up with the demands she has projected onto them. Many women thus prefer to get involved in social relationships only when there are very strict rules with which to regulate all social contacts. Removing limitations means unleashing overwhelming demands that know no satisfaction. So when somebody shows up on the doorstep uninvited, many people feel helpless, with no choice but to submit to what may be an unwanted intrusion. If they are busy, or feel like being alone, they are unable to express how they feel.

Since there is no way to say "no" when spontaneous contact is an intrusion and "yes" when it is welcome, privacy becomes the rule, and the desire to maintain one's privacy is used as an unwritten warning that effectively blocks people from engaging in unscheduled social relationships.

It's not surprising that a desire for control is voiced by women (and men) who have the least control over their own lives. A woman in the suburbs is outside the mainstream of life. She is concerned with privacy because she has none in precisely the areas where it counts—where her own development (as opposed to that of her husband and children) is involved. She erects barriers to those who could make her life more pleasant and less lonesome. How can one escape the boredom of daily routine if one rules out surprise encounters? How can one make meaningful relationships when one rules out the spontaneous, casual meetings from which a deeper relationship can be born?

Hence, complicated by the ethic of the suburban environment, what begins as a temporary withdrawal from the world during pregnancy can unfold throughout life in the suburbs. And we have a huge group of women who are literally exiled in suburbia. Far from their husbands, from any cultural centers and from family, they feel lonely, and desperate. Psychologists Myrna Weissman and Eugene S. Paykel of the Yale depression clinic have documented the effects of such isolation on women whose depression they have studied:

We did find some women who did not fall into any of these groups [people who have problems living in the city and who bring them to the suburbs] described as having difficulty in the suburbs. These women could not adapt even though the move was considered desirable by the family. In these cases, it seems that the depressive illness was intensified or exacerbated by the suburban life-styles. For example, the low population density, and the loss of natural daily social gatherings on the porch, the street, or the corner drug-store made sharing experiences and ventilating problems more difficult. Thus more emotional demands were put on the nuclear family, especially on the husband. If the marriage were shaky, the husband unavailable because of long hours at work or emotional disentanglement, the woman felt isolated and alone.*

Tending to one's children and home does not alleviate this depression. Young children cannot completely satisfy a woman's interpersonal needs, and older children no longer require the full attention of the mother. As one former housewife in her late thirties, whose loneliness pushed her out of the house and into a career, commented:

I always felt loneliest in the afternoon. It was when the children went out to play. I would have this vision of all these women, in their individual homes, just staring out of their windows with nothing to do while their men were in the city, where there was life and things were happening. And I would feel terribly lonely, for them and for myself.

There are several ways women handle this loneliness. One method a guidance counselor in Connecticut finds typical is the "frantic scheduling syndrome."

The loneliness I'm most familiar with in my job is that of wives and mothers of small children who are dumped in the suburbs and whose husbands are commuters, executives who had moved frequently. I see a lot of generalized loneliness, but I think that in well-to-do communities they cover it up with a wealth of frantic activity. That's the reason tennis has gotten so big. They all go out and play tennis.

Daddy leaves at five in the morning and doesn't come home till seven and these women are coping with being new in a community and new schools and so forth. One way people deal with this is by scheduling themselves and their kids to death as a means of controlling their loneliness. Mothers get into this not only because of their kids' needs but because it keeps them moving.

Some women do get job counseling and go back to school, and get jobs. This is only available to middle- or upper-middle-class women whose husbands can pay for their college. Other women will go the promiscuity route, and get involved in frantic sexual activity.

* Weiss, *Loneliness*, p. 160.

Then, of course, there is the further retreat into one's home and oneself, with the company of television and radio, like this young woman:

I hated living in a suburban situation. My husband worked and went to school and I sat home all day and felt depressed and terribly isolated. I sat and watched television and put on weight and got terrible headaches. I could never understand what was the matter with me. All the other women I knew talked about how much work they had and how busy they were. And I could never understand what it was they did. So I began dropping in on different ones of my neighbors at different times of day to see what they were doing to keep busy. They cleaned and took care of their children like I did, but that doesn't really take very much time. I still don't understand what it was they did during the day.

Many radio and television talk-show hosts say that the lonely housewife is the talk show's most active participant. In California the immense popularity of the radio show "California Girls" is in large part due to the isolated housewife. The show is on the air from 10 A.M. to 2 P.M. and is popular with women between the ages of eighteen and forty-nine. Much of this appeal rests on the solicitation of listener participation by asking women to recount their individual experiences, particularly their sexual experiences, over the air. Perhaps the most interesting theme of the show is the dissatisfaction with which listeners seem to view their lives. Another recurrent subject is the lack of the ability to control one's life. Women callers recount dreadful relationships with the men in their lives and yet say they can neither leave these men nor do anything to change the tenor of their relationships. These women see themselves, as the show's title indicates, as girls, who can do nothing to alter the course of their lives.

Why do women listen to and participate in such a program? Partly because there's nothing else available—you can't talk back to the television. But for other reasons as well. "Women call," says host Chamberlain, "because they want help. They call in because they want to relate experiences that they think might help other people. They call because they feel involvement with the show. It's their show and they're the stars. They talk to me rather than to a friend because I'm nonjudgmental and they don't have to look me in the eye." Just as "California Girls" gives women the illusion that they are important, it makes them believe, obviously erroneously, that they have not been abandoned. A stranger, in whose eyes they will never see their own reflections, will come to their rescue.

Many lonely suburban housewives who just want someone to talk to will call crisis or suicide hot-lines. Suicide hot-lines report that the majority of their calls do not come from potential or actual suicides but from lonely people, who use the hot-line as their only contact with others. Men, adolescents, old people, and the lonely housewife are consumers of this service. Diana Cohen, a volunteer at the San Jose, California, crisis center, says that women are the most frequent callers during weekday daylight hours.

Most of these women are not liberated women. They focus their lives on some member of the family, and if something happens in that relationship they are absolutely without moorings. For instance, there was a wealthy doctor's wife who called. She had no children and was totally dependent on her husband. She caught him in a very small lie. It had nothing to do with an affair or anything but it shook her confidence so that she called us.

Shame is such an essential part of the loneliness syndrome that a woman would rather call an anonymous crisis center than admit such weakness to family, friends, or her husband. Such reluctance to confide in one's spouse is engendered by the promises of the American dream. Her husband becomes the reflection of the woman's failure. A New York housewife commented:

When I have felt the loneliest I have found it the most difficult to tell my husband. He would come home from work with all sorts of stories about his day and I would hate him for it. It made me feel such a failure. Here he was going out and doing all sorts of things, and I would find it almost impossible to do the simplest thing like going to the market.

This loss of self felt by many women is often intensified by a very evident withdrawal by their husbands throughout the course of marriage. A frequent complaint of many wives is that after the initial confidences of courtship and marriage, their husbands simply stop communicating with them. The men retreat into silence, making only the most limited attempts to express their feelings and problems. As one woman put it: "My husband has a timer inside him to tell him when he should stop talking. And that timer allows him only the briefest of communications." This retreat leaves women with someone, and yet with no one, with the shell of a person whose emotional reality they are not permitted to grasp.

If loneliness is hard for a woman to admit, it is even more difficult for a man to confess to such a "weakness." Men are socialized to be strong, and fears of weakness or failure must be dealt with quickly, either by repression or by nonexpression. What often happens, therefore, is that these feelings increase so greatly in intensity that they threaten the whole structure of masculinity. Michael Brown, an actor in the San Francisco Bay Area theater group Moving Men, a group that deals with the difficulties of being a man in America, explains the problem thus:

A man's whole being is involved in not feeling pain. There's a ball of loneliness and pain inside men that just builds up. It's one ball. It's not disconnected, and if you pull on any part of it all the others start to vibrate because you're touching the whole thing off—touching off everything that has been buried. It's a loneliness ball, because you've got all these things inside that you won't let anybody see. That's why men avoid things that are depressing, like depressing movies, because they know if they feel anything negative or depressing it will kick off all these feelings that you have repressed through your whole life.

That's what loneliness is. There is no acceptable way to feel pain. You have to do it alone, because you can't share the deepest part of you with anybody. Except maybe with one woman. That's where you're allowed to express your feelings. But that objectifies the woman, because she's just a pillow to cry on.

Silence does not mean that men don't feel; it is rather an attempt to hide feelings, with the hope that they will magically disappear. But when a man feels weak and lonely and tries to hide those emotions, it isn't the feelings that disappear but part of himself. And a woman is left with a shadow, someone who is there in front of her and simultaneously somewhere else. "If my husband feels lonely or depressed," said a woman in Georgia, "he feels he can't talk about what is bothering him. And then he becomes angry. Or if he wants to just be by himself, he'll pick a fight so that he can have an excuse to go off. When he feels lonely and can't talk about it, he puts on a surface. I don't feel comfortable with that surface, because it doesn't feel like he's behind it."

Part of the role tradition has assigned women is the penetration of the façade behind which men hide their true feelings. Frequently a man will admit such feelings only to his wife or lover. Male friendships, at least in America, rarely include such confidences. Women, contrary to popular belief, do not have an easy or pleasant time trying to reach behind the façade of masculinity to get to the emotions that disturb or motivate their mates. And yet women constantly hear that this is their job, that their famous intuition was made especially to ferret out the mysteries of men. Men do not have to make the effort to reach out, because women will do all the work for them.

A recent ad in national magazines gives an excellent illustration of this syndrome. Under a picture of a man pinning a diamond brooch on his wife's dress is the copy:

She knows
I'm not clever with words.
I've always relied
on her easy warm
understanding smile.
But just once,
after ten years, just once,

I wanted to tell her I loved her
like I've never told her before.

Diamonds make a gift of love.

Not all men share such difficulties in expressing feelings and
not all women are open emotionally. There is, in fact, a recurring
marriage pattern: a woman who says she is but in fact is not
open and loving marries a man who cannot express emotion;
and the lack of openness in the relationship is pinned on the man.

Jane complains that Tom gives her little affection and rarely
talks about things that trouble either him or her. According to
Jane, the lack of communication in the relationship is Tom's
fault. She, Jane, would be expressive if only Tom did not always
sabotage her attempts to be close. It's not Jane's fault, and she is
completely free of any problems relating to closeness; the fault
is Tom's. But one wonders why Jane married Tom if she wanted
to be close and loving. Perhaps she too has trouble being close to
someone, but does not recognize her problem. So she hides her
own problems behind her husband's coldness. In our society
most people, whether male or female, have difficulties in trusting
others. The fact that these difficulties are clothed in different
costumes shouldn't obscure their similarities.

The male's inability to communicate feelings may be difficult
for women, but it is much more of a burden for the man involved. "I tend to see men as having fewer resources to deal
with loneliness and anxiety than women," says Cecile Goodman.
"A typical syndrome is that the wife will begin to complain, 'We
don't talk anymore,' and the man will say, 'Yes, we do, we just
talked about the sofa.' He no longer even has the vocabulary to
deal with such problems as real communication."

Communication is no easier for men in the work world. Things
are, in fact, often lonelier at the office than they are at home. In
the competitive world of business the man must stay on top of
his work, his feelings, and his career. If he has a problem, there
is often no one in whom he can confide, because to confess to

weakness is to risk losing whatever career gains have been made. James Clovis and Pearl Meyers of the New York consulting firm Handy Associates say that the problem of loneliness in business gets even more difficult as the man rises in the ranks.

We are shocked to see that if you look at the top ranks of corporations not only are the women lonely because they don't have their husbands, but these executive men are absolutely isolated. We know that, because consultants are used by executives as friends. The entrepreneurial types are very, very lonely. They are in a hostile environment that they are trying to control, manipulate and direct. They have good survival skills because they are extraordinarily discreet. But they really have nobody to talk to. They don't even talk to their wives until the day a decision is made to do something different, like move. They have children who feel they don't know their fathers. Often an important executive will come to a consulting firm and say he'd like to bounce an idea off us. We're the only ones he can talk to, because he can't talk to the board of directors until he's really ready. So we get very top, successful men who need someone to talk to. And they also come with personal affairs. That's one of the reasons these services like financial, tax and estate counseling are so popular, because it gives the executive a confidant, someone to work his personal life through with.

In the current recession, the problems of the man at work are even more serious, for there is more insecurity and anxiety in the work world than there has been in the past several decades. There is, moreover, an increase in the number of men out of work and on the unemployment lines. With unemployment, the problems of loneliness are complicated by those of career failure—a failure that may be intensely experienced even though unemployment may have nothing to do with the shortcomings of the individual involved. Mr. Clovis and Mrs. Meyers recount an example of what can happen to the businessman who is out of work:

One poor man we knew was out of work and didn't have the courage to tell his wife. For months he would come into the city every day, as though he were going to work. And he would look for a job.

His wife finally found out because we called him at home one day, and when she said he was at the office, we realized what was going on. We talked to him and he finally told his wife.

The unemployed executive has a big problem with loneliness because there is no place to go except some counseling service that will write him fancy letters that will do no good, saying how wonderful he is. Some men get almost suicidal. They had large, expensive houses and a high standard of living and simply aren't equipped with survival skills on a certain level. And few executives will go to a psychiatrist with personal problems. They think it's a stigma and they think they can get through difficult times and that it will be better tomorrow.

The unemployed man feels that along with his job he has lost all worth as a human being. And indeed, in a society that is built on competition and success he suffers a very real loss of value—a loss of value that in well-to-do communities means loss of status and loss of friends. Reverend Stewart M. MacColl, minister of the Wilton Presbyterian Church in Connecticut, comments:

There is a tremendous problem of loneliness in men who are unemployed. Loneliness becomes visible in a community like this once someone is not in the mainstream of the community. And the mainstream of this community is the career path. Once that has been shattered, people are afraid to communicate that fact. Men are afraid to tell their wives they have been fired. People can live in this town for months and never tell anybody that they are unemployed, although that is pressing the shape of their lives.

Usually it is the unemployed person who drops his friends. It's a projection on his part, but also other people fear him because they don't know how to deal with him. And they don't want to be reminded that this could also happen to them. But I also think a lot of it is projection on the part of the unemployed man. And when he participates in the community he is with successful people and he will feel like a failure. It is as difficult for the unemployed man to be with the successful man as it is for the successful man to be with the unemployed man.

The problems of loneliness for men and their difficulties in dealing with intense emotions can often, then, combine with the social position of women to create a lonely marriage. Individual feelings of worthlessness make the husband and wife withdraw from each other. Such dilemmas can make the couple withdraw from all but superficial social relationships, or they can retreat entirely into themselves. Thus loneliness can harm not only a particular marriage but the peripheral community that could ground the marriage in a solid, supportive social setting.

Corporations and federal, public, and academic institutions in contemporary America, taking advantage of the American tradition of mobility, have extended the ethic of mobility so that it absorbs more people for longer periods of time than ever before in our history. The pioneer made one big move and then stayed in a new location to make a new life. Today transients move not once, or even twice, but over and over again, uprooting families and whole communities in order to fulfill a dream of personal advancement that has been increasingly associated with mobility. Corporations make it clear to incoming employees that promotion is dependent on willingness to move wherever and whenever the company dictates. And indeed, moving companies report that of the forty million Americans who move each year two and a half million are corporate transfers. And even in America's universities, the best place to be and the best place to be associated with changes from year to year, so that whole academic departments may move from one university to the next, to the next.* An IBM executive explained to me: "We move people because we want to find the best man for the job. He may get to one place and then discover that he should be someplace else. So we move him there."

All this transiency creates interchangeable employees who work at interchangeable jobs. But complete interchangeability demands not only that the job performance be duplicated but

---

* High mobility in America's academic community may have a great deal to do with Europe's philosophic and literary superiority over America. European intellectuals tend to form a stable community in which the constant discussion necessary to the development of ideas may take place. In America the advancement of ideas is most frequently subordinated to the advancement of salary and career status.

that the employee's ideas, family, friends, home, and community be interchangeable too. As sociologist Lloyd Warner writes in *Big Business Leaders in America:*

They [men on the move] left their homes, and all that this implies. They have left behind a standard of living, level of income, and style of life to adopt a way of living entirely different from that into which they were born. The mobile man first of all leaves the physical setting of his birth. This includes the house he lived in, the neighborhood he knew, and in many cases, even the city, state and region in which he was born.

This physical departure is only a small part of the total process of leaving that the mobile man must go through. He must leave behind people as well as places. The friends of earlier years must be left, for acquaintances of the lower-status past are incompatible with the successful present. Often the church of his birth is left, along with the clubs and cliques of his family and of his youth. But most important of all, and this is the great problem of the man on the move, he must, to some degree, leave his father, mother, brothers, sisters, along with the other human relationships of the past. (Warner and Abegglen, p. 62)

Whole industries have grown up to support this process of interchangeability. Moving companies depend for a substantial part of their business on corporations moving employees huge distances. Real estate companies benefit too, as people who move often spend more than they can afford on a new home. Mrs. Shirley DeLima of the consulting firm Homeamerica observes:

Usually when an employee makes a move, he mentally feels that this is a move up and even if the company tells him it's only a lateral move, he automatically moves up in his mind. He wants to have that extra room he doesn't currently have, the half bath, or bath, the family room with the fireplace, the bigger lot, the newer home. Or his wife wants something that's a little special. They are not really trying to duplicate their current home when they get another house. They are moving up. That's why they will always complain to management that it's costing them more to move.

And whole new industries have cropped up to help a family

make moving easier. Homeamerica is such a company. Its purpose is to counsel both individual families and companies that are considering moving to new locations. The company has been in existence for seventeen years and moves an average of 7,000 people per year, excluding group moves in which a company will move its operations from one city to another.

Homeamerica promises to smoothe out any potential wrinkles in moving by utilizing the information from an "in-depth questionnaire," which, presumably, should reveal all a family's needs. The depth of these questionnaires is actually slight. The section "Special Family Requirements" includes one line each for the listing of educational, medical, and hobby interests. And the remainder of the questionnaire deals mainly with financial considerations and superficial community concerns such as religious affiliation, maximum and minimum commuting time desired, and so forth. The family must fit its concerns and problems into a one-page sheet that is supposed to encompass the complex needs of a family uprooting all its members.

Homeamerica offers special service to women, who, Ms. De-Lima says, are the ones who worry most about moving.

We try to help families make the emotional adjustment to the new location by trying to learn what their day-to-day interests are, making them aware of facilities available in the new location. If the woman is a big Junior Leaguer, or active in Multiple Sclerosis, we will tell her where that is available. Even if it is not in a community that she can afford, we will tell her what other town it's in.

Most of the fear of a move is beforehand rather than after. Women are always concerned, obviously, with making new friends, finding people with whom they will be compatible, making sure they will not be a chauffeur to the children all the time. Men are concerned with commuting and financial impact. They are worried about performing well in the new location or new job function or both. The children are the most adaptable, particularly the younger ones.

We find that if people are given enough information in advance of the move, we are able to reduce the misapprehension and fears that they may have. Most people blow these things up way out of proportion. They listen to rumors.

In fact, however, there is a great deal of anxiety associated with moves, especially long-distance ones—anxiety that is compounded by role expectations. If the wife-mother does not get herself together and move without a second thought she is scorned for her weakness, says sociologist Diane Margolis, who has studied the effects of transiency on a group of executive families in Connecticut:

A lot of transients are just good trooper sort of people. If you ask them what they think of a woman who becomes dysfunctional because of moving, they will react angrily. "She shouldn't have acted that way," they will say, "because her job is to keep the family happy." As long as transient wives can keep the family happy and together, they can keep off the pain of moving about. As long as nobody recognizes the pain and they're all doing what they ought to do, it works, at least on the level of awareness.

The wife will say to herself, if she feels lonely or down in the dumps, "Look. Everyone else is doing it. And no one is complaining about it, so I must be a little bit crazy. I should be shaping up."

The woman is thus left to bear the brunt of the loneliness of transiency. Her husband moves from one location in a company to another, from one university to another, or from one army post to another. He is presented with a job to be done and a ready-made world in which to do it. The woman is left to find the schools, the playmates for the children, the doctor and dentist and supermarket and a society into which to fit herself. That is not easy in most suburbs, as we have seen. She does not have the excuse of work interests to give her permission to approach people, and she must muster the courage herself. Repeated moves, however, often shake her confidence in herself and her social abilities.

Ms. Margolis found that wives of executive transients registered the pain and loneliness of transiency only after repeated moves, and when the woman was in her forties. For many women under forty, she says, moving is still an adventure. After consistent mobility, however, the woman realizes that mobility has become a pattern of life and that this move will not be the last or the next to the last. At this point disillusionment and desperate loneliness appear.

Frequently it's something that happens to their children that makes them [women] start wondering about this kind of life more often than something that happens to themselves. For instance, one example was a woman who moved to Connecticut from Massachusetts. Her son was in his senior year and decided to finish high school in Massachusetts. Then her husband was transferred again and the woman refused to go with him. She said "he separated me from my son and it's not going to happen again." She was willing to have her son leave her to go to college, but she was not willing to be separated from him a year early while he was in high school.

According to Myrna Weissman and Eugene Paykel's studies of women, the effects of transiency can result in severe depression.

During the course of studying a group of depressed women in New Haven, Connecticut, we noted in a number of them temporal relationships between their depressive symptoms and recent moves. These women often did not relate their illnesses to the moves but more often attributed them to other events in their lives, such as financial problems, increased loneliness, increased marital friction, problems with children, career frustrations, identity confusion. In most cases, however, these other events were the by-products of faulty adaptation to the stresses and changes created by moving. We suspected that these women did not associate their symptoms with moving since it is such an accepted part of American life that it is almost taken for granted. These women instead internalized the stresses and blamed themselves for their problems. The result was an emergence of depressive symptoms.

Most of the women were patients in a research clinic and were being treated for depressive episodes. They showed the usual symptoms of depression, including feelings of helplessness and futility, hopelessness about the future and persistent sadness, impaired capacity to perform their work and other usual activities, and a loss of interest in friends and family. We were led to examine their experience of moving in detail and we found that, in some cases, the move itself was the last straw in a series of stressful events and interpersonal difficulties. In other cases, moving represented an abortive effort to solve other problems, often financial or marital. However, in some cases, the move itself created new stresses and interpersonal difficulties which had not previously existed. This pattern of depression occurred even though the moves were voluntary and related to presumably desirable circumstances such as improved housing and financial status. This sharply contrasts with reports suggesting that moves produce detrimental effects only if they are involuntary or undesirable.*

Once a woman recognizes the effects of transiency, there may seem to her no answer to her dilemma. She is caught in the middle, for she must either sacrifice her own needs or ask her husband to sacrifice his career goals for some stability. In his recent book *Corporate Wives, Corporate Casualties?* Dr. Robert Seidenberg quotes a letter from a lonely transient wife:

Although I have the feeling that too much of the burden for trying to stay alive (mentally and emotionally) is on my sloping shoulders and that I'm on a treadmill that moves backward faster than I can make forward progress, I cringe at the prospect of more years ahead as an isolate—yet feel like collapsing at the thought of taking on another round of trying to break into another new community (for a few years only) and meanwhile trying to see to the needs of my family, domestic responsibilities and working. (p. 21)

Dr. Seidenberg believes, and women's liberationists would certainly agree with him, that much of the plight of the transient woman stems inevitably from the contradictory demands that the corporation and society place upon her. A woman is not supposed to work, or if she does, her job should be secondary to her husband's, and she should sacrifice her own career and drop everything to move when her husband must. She is supposed to be dependent on her husband for most things, and yet when high mobility exaggerates this dependence by removing her from a larger community, she is blamed for being what society made her—weak.

* Weiss, *Loneliness*, pp. 155, 156.

It is when the self is lost or communication with the self is severed that "the other" becomes so desperately important. Being alone then becomes a particularly fearful experience because there is literally no one at home. The house is empty because the person is. That is the tragic irony of the corporate wife's plight. She is scolded for being fearful and dependent; yet she is literally picked because she is dependent. Selflessness is deemed her most admirable attribute, but when she exhibits the inevitable effects of loss of self, she is called troublesome and lacking in emotional maturity.

The entire corporate life style encourages her to live solely through and by her husband; any personal aspiration or ambition is to be promptly extinguished. Any interest or pleasure with other people is prohibited. And she is not to be fearful or lonely when he is away? The mad rush to the suburbs has added to her miseries by cutting her off from the civic and cultural centers. (Seidenberg, p. 105)

A woman is thus damned to loneliness if she does not protest the transiency of modern life, and she is damned to contempt if she does.

Many women sink into apathy because of this almost impossible situation in which they find themselves. To recognize transiency as the enemy is a very risky business, for that would mean refusing to go along on the next move. When a woman does that she threatens her marriage, the very thing she depends on for whatever meager support she can get. Difficult as this is to do, there are increasing numbers of women who are refusing to pick themselves up and move at the beck and call of their husbands' companies. They are beginning to complain to their husbands and demand that something be done either about moving or about the problems in family life. To many men such complaints often come as a shock—a shock they resent.

Because the issues of loneliness differ for men and women, the transient male may not feel (or at least not recognize) loneliness as a resultant problem of mobility. Men do complain about the effects of transiency, but their complaints have more to do with their wives' inability to adjust, or with difficulties at work. Ms. Margolis says that the men she interviewed were concerned with the lack of impact they had on the jobs, but did not—consciously,

at least—connect this concern with their own high mobility.*
Similarly, the man worries about finding the right neighborhood
in which to live and the right home to buy. Once those problems
are solved, his worries, at least about his family, are over. Thus
when his wife begins to rail against moving and the stresses of
that life-style, her husband will often deal with such troubles by
ignoring them. When they become so overwhelming that she is
forced to seek some kind of therapeutic counseling, her husband
may allow her to go to the therapist but will resist accompanying
her. The couple's problems, he insists, are her problems. Once
she has solved their problems for him, everything will return to
normal. "If a counselor suggests," says Reverend Stewart Mac-
Coll, "that the husband come for counseling as well as the wife,
he may do so, but with some resistance. In a counseling situation
it is always, or almost always, the woman who seeks counseling,
and the man always, or almost always, reacts negatively to that
decision."

This resistance to a therapeutic solution to a couple's problems
is characteristic of the socially conditioned reluctance of men to
admit to feelings of weakness. To go to a therapist means that
something is wrong, that all is not under control. It further means
that whatever is wrong cannot be solved by individual effort
alone. It is all right if a woman needs help. But being a man includes doing things for oneself. It is difficult to overcome such
prejudices, particularly when they are intensified by business' traditional bias against psychiatry. What often results is that a man
will go into therapy in an attempt to placate his wife. He will re-

---

* This complaint of lack of impact is documented in many studies on
work in America today. The HEW study *Work in America* states that
workers feel they have no input or importance to their work and are thus
no different from a machine. And a study by the American Management
Association surveying its membership, conducted in 1972, revealed that
middle managers and personnel executives are deeply disturbed about the
lack of input and impact they have in their jobs. Entitled "Manager's
Unions?," the survey reported that one half of those questioned would favor
unions for managers, and one of the reasons for this choice was that managers felt they had little "opportunity for direct participation in the decision-
making process."

main in therapy for only a few sessions. Then he will refuse to continue. At that point it is again up to the woman to solve the problem. The wife resents this load, and the strain on the marriage can become unbearable.

This strain is especially hard to endure when the lateral supports of an outside community of family, friends, and neighbors are absent. And in transient groups "community" has been reduced to its bare minimum. Rather than indicating a group of people who share a place of residence, similar ideas, interests, religious beliefs, and traditions—the *Gemeinschaft* described by Ferdinand Tonnies in *Community and Society*—community today is reduced to what Tonnies calls *Geselschaft*. Community, according to this latter formulation, is where the house is rather than where one's historical and personal roots are. There is no personal closeness in such communities, because to get close to one's neighbors, to make deep friendships is antithetical to the nature of a society that says you must be free of any encumbrance so as to be able to move—up the corporate ladder—whenever the need arises. Friends, as Lloyd Warner says, are not assets but encumbrances. When you know you have to move, friends only mean additional pain at the time of departure. What was true in the fifties, when Whyte first wrote on the effects of transiency, is no less true today:

Above all they (transients) do not get too close. The transient's defense against rootlessness, as we have noted, is to get involved in meaningful activity; at the same time, however, like the seasoned traveler, the wisest transients don't get too involved. Keeping this delicate balance requires a very highly developed social skill, and also a good bit of experience. "It takes time," explains one transient, "I had to go through fraternity life, then the service and a stretch in Parkmere (a transient community) before I realized you just get into trouble if you get personally involved with neighbors."*

And indeed, it is very rare to find transients who cultivate

---

* *The Organization Man*, p. 403.

deep, lasting relationships. What transients may have instead, if they are not so depressed that they withdraw entirely from relationships, are pseudofriendships. Reverend MacColl notes that the most mobile residents of his town resist deep involvement with others. They get involved only superficially with people in community organizations. "For," he says, "they feel the less you give the less you lose."

Again, life is concerned with minimizing losses. To get close to people when friendships can only be short-lived entails the pain of saying good-bye. That good-bye, despite rumors to the contrary, is generally permanent. "People say they will keep in touch," comments Diana Margolis, "after they move. But an example of the infrequency of such contact is a woman who told me she wrote to her *best friend* six months ago. And that was her last communication with someone who was supposedly her closest friend."

To protect themselves against the pain of parting, people learn to limit contact with others. They set up subtle restrictions that indicate the point beyond which closeness can go no further. They also learn that any problems they may have with a friend or neighbor need never be confronted, because they can always escape that person and problem when they move again. As one army wife commented, "There are many advantages to moving. You don't have to be nice to your neighbors. Anybody doesn't like you or you don't like anybody, you just move."

The result of all this is that there is no one to turn to when an inevitable time of need comes.

It is difficult to maintain the vision of mobility as a great adventure when one recognizes the casualties of its excesses. Yet there are those who, despite all the contrary evidence, think moving all the time is a wonderful thing and the kind of relationships mobility fosters are the promise of our century. Alvin Toffler's apology in *Future Shock* for the friendships that result from high mobility is an excellent example of such mystification:

In a brilliant paper on "Friendships of the Future," psychologist Courtney Tall suggests that stability based on close relationships with a few people will be ineffective due to the high mobility, wide interest range, and varying capacity for adaptation and change found among the members of a highly automated society . . . individuals will develop the ability to form close buddy-type relationships on the basis of common interests or sub-group affiliations, and to easily leave these friendships, moving either to another location or to another interest group within the same location . . . Interests will change rapidly. . . .

This ability to form and then to drop, or lower to the level of acquaintanceship, close relationships quickly, coupled with increased mobility, will result in any given individual forming many more friendships than is possible for most in the present. . . . Friendship patterns of the majority in the future will provide many satisfactions while substituting many close relationships of shorter durability for the few long term friendships formed in the past. (pp. 107, 108)

Quantity again replaces quality, for the "close friendships" easily formed and easily dropped are, in the cases described, neither close nor friendly. Unfortunately Toffler fails to realize that the acquisition and loss of a friendship are not like the acquisition and loss of a new dress or book. People frequently attach part of themselves to those with whom they are close. And so loss of a relationship, in addition to loss of a friend, means that an individual has given up part of him- or herself. Uprooting oneself is more complex than leaving a house and garden. People invest places and people with their identities, and their identities are in turn confirmed and denied by the roots they establish or destroy. The process that John Bowlby describes in children who are torn away from their parents, in which they increasingly detach themselves from any human contact and feeling, is precisely that described by the lonely transient housewife. What happens is not, as Toffler posits, a different kind of attachment, but rather *detachment,* a loss, and the concomitant disconfirmation of the individual's identity.

In *The Lonely African* Colin Turnbull writes of the effects of the destruction of community and tribal life and the psychological results of that process on the native who leaves his or her village for the city. Our own dilemma appears in the following lines:

In the towns there is virtually no belief, only a way of life that the majority accept. There is no belief because in being forced to abandon traditional beliefs, in being taught skepticism, even shame, for tribal ways, the African has learned to be equally skeptical of Western beliefs and ways. He behaves as he does because of convenience or from expediency. . . . The rural African coming into this kind of society may feel shame, but not those who are born into it. And even the rural African, if he stays long enough, loses his sense of shame because he quickly learns that here he is no longer a member of a family, even of a tribe; that his neighbor is not bound by the same beliefs that bind him, and so cannot be relied on to behave as a reasonable man. The only sensible and safe thing to do is to mistrust one's neighbor, to think for oneself alone, to have no consideration for others. (p. 125)

Mobility, the disintegration of community, the erosion of communication because of unfulfilled expectations, the isolation of women—all cause intense loneliness in many people today. And all affect marriage in this society. Marriage is not simply a personal statement; it is a social statement as well. It functions not only to situate the couple in relation to each other but also in relation to a larger culture and community in which they, by virtue of their vows, take part. Without this communal participation, marriage and the family it creates lose their proper context. And when the society deserts its human responsibilities, the couple is left truly alone with each other, and with the world. What remains is the problem of adjusting to aloneness after togetherness—or pseudotogetherness—is dead.

Chapter Six

Jim Costello

They found him on a country road in Pennsylvania. The small car resting on its side in a ditch at the shoulder of the road looked like an insect desperately kicking its legs and trying to right itself. When the police came he was sitting about ten feet away from the wreck, rocking himself against the night. He took no notice of them or their questions, and they gentled their usual gruffness as they pulled him off the ground. It was a shock to see such a big man surrendering himself up to their care like a baby, repeating to himself over and over, "My wife's going to leave me, she has a lover, right in our house."

"Poor guy," one officer said, looking through the man's wallet for a license.

"Yeah—who do you think he is? Says here he comes from Cleveland. Sure is a weirdo."

"We'd better take him in."

They sat him down in a corner of the station house. No use locking him up. He was so quiet—docile almost. He noticed nothing—the officers walking by, the queer looks. After about fifteen minutes the phones began ringing more often, and the conversation, already dominated by the fact of a rare presence in the country precinct, grew more animated, more stares moving toward him.

"Say," one of the policemen shouted, putting down the phone, "what do you know about this! They think he's the guy that broke those windows at the high school."

"Hell—are you sure? He don't look like he could do nothing to no one."

"Well," the other responded, "he fits the description of the guy seen near there, and his car was seen near the place. Better ask him some questions."

Do you know so and so, where were you at such and such a time, why did you come here. . . . ?

He seemed to hear none of it. Finally they decided to put him in a cell, because he might, after all, be dangerous. They had telephoned his wife in Cleveland, who said she would leave for Pennsylvania immediately. And because of their description of his condition and the charges made against him, she said she would bring a friend with her, a psychiatrist. But it would take some time to get there.

It seemed for a moment, when she arrived, that he would recognize her. A tight-lipped, erect woman, whose carriage did not quite fit the loose, rather hippy-looking clothes she wore, she bent over him, repeating his name—"Jim, Jimmy, are you all right? Jimmy, what happened?" But his glance had closed in on itself. And so, after several hours and many consultations, it was decided that charges could be pressed later, after he had re-covered from whatever it was that was troubling him. In the car, his wife, Meg, again tried to talk to him, to explain, and finally to apologize. But he remained silent and shut off—as he was when they took him into the hospital, as they left him when they locked the door to his room, to the ward, and to the world.

He had been a happy, boisterous man. The most outgoing in his whole group. At meetings of the antiwar group he and his friends had built into a large and influential force he outlined strategies with good-natured, almost naïve belief in whatever it was that was happening in the Movement around the country. There was always a cheerful assurance that things would work because he and his friends were behind them. He was a leader not because he had original ideas, or because he wanted any kind of power over others, but because he wanted to share his enthusiasms, be there at the front lines to cheer when change occurred. After the Revolution, they would proclaim to one another, all would be well. And since he knew that that revolution would not be long in coming, all would work out quite soon indeed. It was the pioneer's faith he had, the heritage of a large Italian family that laughed and fought with warmth and great self-confidence.

He brought that same enthusiasm to all his dealings; at parties he leaped into the center of the room and danced with the simplicity of a peasant dancing by the sea, moving round and round after the others had fallen from fatigue. He chided his wife for her waspish humors, for the stiffness that she could not, despite all her efforts, completely overcome. But he had great faith in her potential. They had been married almost ten years, and she had already come a long way. Politics and the sense of support he got from the community of people he worked and played with daily gave him an endless hope. He had only occasional bad moods—depressions. But, his friends assured him, if he had manic-depressive tendencies, they were mostly on the manic side. Nothing to worry about in that.

He had started out in politics as a liberal in the early sixties. An activist in the civil rights movement, he went on marches, read books on black/white problems. As a social worker he tried to bring his insights into the homes of the clients he could never help enough. Then came the Vietnam war, and he joined a small, peaceful protest group. As the war escalated, and teach-ins and marches began, he was stirred by the motion around him. He had been waiting only for a catalyst of the right proportions.

Cleveland was a city that reminded one of the reality of racism and poverty. A city where integration was preached but prejudice was as pervasive as in any southern town. A city surrounded by black and blue-collar ghettos, there was something in the unremitting bleakness of Cleveland that made him recognize the maliciousness of American affluence, something that tied him to the city like a man trying to change the woman he has married.

He soon saw that that change would not come if he remained a liberal. There was something too passive in that stance, something too cautious, that would not match the breadth of his hopes. He became a radical, expounding his new vision to his wife each night when he came home from work until she was pulled along by the buoyancy of his monologues.

They set off in earnest—rallies, teach-ins, meetings. Political involvement had once taken up perhaps one evening a week. Now it took up almost every night and weekend. People were constantly at their house, some staying a couple of days, others a couple of months. These guests brought a flush of possibility to their marriage, which had, like most, settled into variations on a routine. Rarely having time for each other, they found themselves the center of a community they had never expected to find, where people began by sharing political ideas and ended sharing their entire lives.

At first their social gatherings were enormous—large parties, with great platters of chili, and salads, and breads, contributed and consumed collectively. Beer and wine in great abundance. Soon, though, the parties grew so large that there was not a house big enough to accommodate all the people. And then grass made people less garrulous. Head trips were more comfortable with eight or ten than with a hundred. The large group broke into small ones, and Jim and Meg met continually with about four other couples, all with the same political penchant—for there were of course divisions within the Movement: those who favored Cuba or China, those who were too intellectual, too eagerly critical of every country whose socialism was not quite correct enough.

They came to be called a collective, formed opinions together, tried acid together, ate together at least two or three times a week. There were many hugs and great warmth and understanding. They of course recognized mutual attractions, such as jokes at which one cannot repress laughter. In different houses, on weekends, or on camping trips, they made of these attractions group games. Sitting on the floor, a man and woman, not mates, would face each other, legs crossed, eyes closed, hands running across each other's face, until laughter would break the stimulation, and then they would switch partners for two other people. They shared their excitement with the group. For it was the collective that was important. To move in new couples from the living room to the bedroom would bring more harm than the thrill of a new sexual experience was worth. Besides, they had a task to accomplish—to change the country—that was more important than any personal desires.

He was taken with the adventure of it all. No tactic seemed too outrageous, no attack on the enemy too ambitious. Neither he nor any of the other members of his group had ever engaged in violence, but they admired the courage of revolutionaries in other countries where change meant a rejection of every comfort he had ever known. He would have been pleased, almost, if he could have traded the paved streets of his city for the mountains of Cuba or Vietnam. Thus he believed there was a place for everything—teach-ins, terrorism, demonstrations, arrests, jail, even death. Some argued that America was not ready for too much revolutionary vigor, that it would require more time, more patience, more consistent and less dramatic effort. But he was an advocate of shock therapy for the country. Missing the connection, he did not understand that since he was against the use of such techniques on sick individuals he should be against its use on a sick society as well. But he was impatient with the vision of great possibilities—the potential of himself, his friends, and that buried in the land.

Others would have to accept that things would from now on be in constant flux. After all, he had accepted the turning around of his entire life. From liberal to radical, from working with blacks to working with whites, from working with students to working within a community that included white-, even blue-collar workers. Endless changes—in everything he had ever known. Now there was women's liberation, of which Meg had become a leader, meeting almost daily with the women of their collective, who formed with her a consciousness-raising group. At night she and Jim talked about the reorganization of the society now that this dimension of women's rights had been added to the struggle. A reorganization that would have to begin right in their own marriage—with dishes and cleaning and sex roles. To all these innovations he brought unflagging approval, each new idea seeming a revolutionary advance on the past. They were exhausted, he and Meg. They had lost that exclusiveness and contact they had when they met and married. But they gained things they had never expected.

It was only after several years, near his thirtieth birthday, that depression set in. Not only his depression but Meg's and their friends' and that of the world around them. After all their work, day and night, little had changed. The troops were still in Vietnam, and President Nixon, despite protest after protest, had sent bombers into Cambodia, extending rather than ending the war. Things all over the world were moving to the right rather than to the left. Homosexuals arrested in Cuba; May, 1968, in France ended with Pompidou; there was subversion in Chile; dictatorships in Greece and Brazil. He did not want to stop fighting and was still as committed as ever. But he had grown tired—"burned out" was the expression. Both he and Meg wanted a rest. There were other people to carry on—younger people. It would not be an abandonment, just time to get back to themselves. The problem was, they discovered when the motors stopped, they no longer knew who they were.

The marriage had not been a particularly bad one. But what had brought them together had occurred so long ago, and times had changed so much since then. In their effort to keep track of all the external transformations, it seemed that they had lost whatever it was that had made them a unit when they were twenty. And then that unit had expanded so much over these past years, had included so many people moving into their lives, their home even, that its boundaries had cracked from the strain. The effort of learning to change the language of their relationship had been superseded by the need to relate honestly to their collective, their comrades and their friends. So many events had occupied their lives for so long that now they no longer knew how to occupy each other.

After things had slowed down in the Movement they decided that, to save themselves, they would move everyone from the house, withdraw from politics, and work on rebuilding their personal lives. No more discussions with their friends—they would talk only to each other. Sitting in the living room of the house that had served so long as a meeting place—a house they had never really spent time making their own, although it was theirs on all the proper papers—they dissected the problem. They had grown apart; he felt she was cold, and she that his moods, rapid swings to high and low, prevented any serious discussions of things that troubled her. Were they incompatible, should they just split up? No, that would be too extreme, they still had too much feeling for each other. They would work it out if they just kept at it. But they always seemed to cover the same ground without finding a solution or a new problem on which to concentrate their energies and frustrations. The circle just seemed empty without others in it.

The group was still there when they came out again. They had begun a new adventure, a new revolution. Smashing monogamy, it was called. It had begun rather innocently, with one couple that had gone east for a year. He had slept with someone else, then she had slept with someone else. They were still together, they had talked it out, and since it had done little harm, it was something to share with the collective. Like all of them, this couple had married young; and after spending almost ten years exclusively with each other they felt liberated by their new experiment. An imported idea, it was worth testing among all of them. None of the couples involved wanted to separate. But to be making a revolution and to continue in bourgeois marital relations was not possible, was, in fact, hypocritical. They should be able to continue loving their mates and love others as well. Sex was not something that should split up a solid relationship. Their parents would perhaps divorce if one partner had an affair, but they—they were a new world.

Meg began. She found another man, Paul, whom she met at work. He was easy to get along with, not as political as she, but willing to change. And this new relationship was not complicated by years of problems. She had not slept with anyone but Jim in years, having been too young and moral to sleep around in college, and too old and attached for the sexual revolution. It was her turn now. She did not hide it from Jim. Being honest was what it was all about. You could not clandestinely smash monogamy. Jim appeared only a little jealous, a little more moody. And then he found someone else, a woman named Donna. The experience was new to him also, as he had had only one or two sexual encounters before marriage and certainly none after. It would be good for him, he tried to convince himself, good for both of them, all of them.

But he did not want to lose Meg, to simply find one day that in all the commotion they had ceased to mean anything to each other. He depended on her being there, cared about her, even though she was often too cold or preoccupied to return that feeling. He had hoped that with work they could move on. Maybe she needed the affair, and then, when she tired of it. . . . He had taken up with Donna mainly to keep up appearances, to make Meg think he was not against this temporary experiment. Now, however, he could see that it was not to be so temporary. Her friend, lover, Paul, grew more and more attached, as did Donna. Each lover, or friend—there was no acceptable word in the vocabulary to describe those relationships—tried to edge out the husband or wife. He had not expected this, nor had Meg, but she was more willing to carry on and see where it took them. Their other friends also encouraged them to continue. They too were exchanging partners, trying out new forms.

Meg and Jim saw Donna and Paul more and more often. They laughed when they said "Good night, have a good time" as one or the other walked out the door, or as they called each other to the phone, or welcomed each other home in the morning or the next evening. Of course the situation was uncomfortable at times, but that was something that had to be dealt with and overcome. That would be the easiest thing to overcome. Less simple was Paul's desire to be with Meg more and more frequently, in fact, to live with her—a desire she reciprocated. It was just that she didn't want to leave Jim. There must be a way that she could be with them both—and they could find that way, the four of them, only together. They were all involved, after all.

The living room again became a meeting room, the four of them sitting together till late in the night, trying not to divide loyalties, to agree on all that would happen. So one night it was suggested, as if by all and yet by no one in particular, that they should live together, the four of them. The house was large enough. No one wanted to leave anyone, but all wanted to spend more time with their new friends. Meg wanted to be with Jim and Paul, and Jim wanted to be with Meg and Donna; Donna wanted to be with Jim and liked Paul, and Paul. . . . It seemed a valid idea, certainly one in keeping with their political beliefs. The decision was made. The foursome had absorbed their marriage.

They moved in together, cooked together, ate together. Said good-bye to one another as each new couple went out. Each person had his or her own room and was free to spend the night alone or with whomever he or she chose. It was always Meg who chose first—with Jim following, then Donna and Paul—Meg who directed those choices in subtle ways, like a player pushing a pin-ball machine ever so gently so as to get the best results. At night Jim could often hear Paul and Meg making love. He recognized her cries, and found it hard, when those cries were for him, to forget the times when he was only listening in. It grew harder and harder over those next two months to forget, harder and harder to be with her, to be with Donna, to be there in that house.

They all began to notice the change in him. He was more and more moody, laughed less. His best friend, a man uninvolved in this new sexual trend, tried to talk with him, bring him out. But the silence had moved from his eyes throughout his entire body. His walk was no longer an enthusiastic stride. Meg also tried to talk to him, as did Donna and Paul. And then one day he took the car, and for hours, despite their phone calls to everyone they knew, they had no word. Until the police called from another state.

He got out of the mental hospital after eight months. They had given him shock, tranquilizers, groups, therapy. He knew more about himself. It was not all Meg's fault; there was his past—insecurities, his parents, sibling rivalry. He had thought a lot in the hospital, where he was alone not only because of his illness but because of political convictions no one shared. His politics made him almost laughable to the doctors and nurses, an example of where such things get you. He held to them, but less militantly. He no longer wanted to be that jubilant, rebelliously accepting person he had been. He would have to continue to see a doctor when he got home, as it was on that condition that charges were dropped regarding the high school windows he could not remember breaking.

Meg had asked Paul to go, and Donna had of course left after Jim entered the hospital. So Jim returned to their house. He tried to get back his old job, but his radical reputation and psychiatric history did not make him a favorable choice. Too unstable. He worked wherever he could and Meg contributed to their support. Since he had become ill she had gotten a good job that she liked. She had not returned to politics, and was a bit warmer, trying hard to be sympathetic to his needs. But the house was too small for the two of them and the memories of all that had happened. After several months they decided to split up. It was something, they agreed, they should have done long before. They had discovered very painfully that they couldn't be together and independent at the same time. And then, Jim's lingering depression was difficult for Meg to cope with. He understood.

He found a small place of his own where he could have quiet. He could not stand too much pressure. He had come out all right, but certain springs were weak and could not be replaced.

His friends had all expected that he would smile again. That his breakdown would be like that of a car, requiring extended repair time, of course, a large mechanics bill, continued care before those around could enjoy full use of the vehicle. The seventies had brought not peace and love but bad times for all of them. Broken marriages, broken friendships. They understood what he was going through. But after a while, even though they loved him, had such fond memories, it became too trying to be with him. They could no longer slough it off as recovery time or a bad mood. He had changed and would not change back. So finally he was left alone.

Chapter Seven
Divorce

I was sitting in the airport the other night waiting to pick someone up. Suddenly I remembered a day thirty-three years ago when I was a student at college. I was nineteen years old. I had been doing well in my studies, especially my studies in French. I wanted to continue studying French, to go to the Sorbonne. My French teacher was very fond of me and encouraged me in that wish. My family felt it was too far away and opposed it, but they had never completely refused to let me go. So I felt that one day I would work things out, and that I had a lot to look forward to. And then this boy that I went out with in college, with whom I was involved the way you were involved in those days, when you had the constant fear of pregnancy, and all those awful condoms and such—well, he came to me and said he was going to go away. He wanted me to go with him.

Well, I remember that day so well. When I heard he was going to go away, I felt that awful hole in my stomach, and that void of what would I do when he was gone. And just because of that, that terrible fear of being alone, I decided that I wouldn't go on to finish college, that I wouldn't go to France. When I look back on it, the relationship only existed because we were both lonely. He wasn't all that important to me. Not important enough for me to have given everything up for him. I did it, gave up a career and married him, just because I was afraid of being lonely, so afraid of his not being there that I couldn't stand it.

Sitting in the airport I got very into that feeling of loneliness, and I had to stop thinking about it, because it's all past and I could really

*send myself into a terrible depression because of something I could
no longer do anything about.*

Helen Bixby is fifty-five now. Hers was not a happy marriage.
But it lingered on over the years despite her dissatisfaction with
her life, her husband's inability to communicate, and, finally, her
own alcoholism. That began because of loneliness, because, she
says, of that need tugging at her to unite with another person.
The person was, she admits, less important than the satisfaction
of the need. By the time her marriage ended, in divorce, her relationship with her husband had disintegrated into a series of
long drawn-out silences broken by sporadic hostile interchanges.
The need, the loneliness, had never disappeared.

Nor did it disappear after divorce—although Helen managed
to achieve a temporary numbness with enough alcohol. When
the effects of drink had worn off, there was still that void inside
her, as though her body had been drained of all its feelings. It
took Helen a long time to be able to face that void without a
drink in her hand. And a longer time to give up drinking entirely.

Being alone, she says, without a husband or a drink, left her
feeling vulnerable to myriad insecurities: "You think a lot when
you're alone. You think about things you don't really want to
think about. You feel that no one will ever love you. That you
aren't pretty anymore. That you have nothing to offer. That's
the worst part of loneliness."

Divorce is one of the loneliest of modern rituals. Before, during, and after the actual culmination of the legal process it is an
ordeal that rips people away from their roots, their important
relationships, and a part of themselves. There is really nothing
like it—except perhaps war. For unlike most rites, the modern
divorce does not bind a person to a community or tribe or family.
Tribal rites of passage reward the initiate with full participation
in the group. The divorced person, in going through a change
of status, is excluded from a former group and given nothing in
return. The victim of divorce consequently undergoes a test unlike any other. There is no assurance of welcome on the other

side of the unknown, no path to follow that leads to salvation. The modern divorce is a ritual marking separation and severance rather than initiation and acceptance.

This new ritual is now affecting more and more people. Between 1963 and 1969 there was a 25 percent increase in the number of divorces, so that one out of four marriages was ending in divorce (one out of three in California). In 1973 alone 13,000 people were divorced; in the state of California in that same year there were 170,173 marriages and 117,677 divorces.

Because divorce is a process rather than an event, the loneliness that often accompanies it passes through several transformations. Before the lawyers, the courts, and the adversarial proceedings come the disillusionment and unhappiness attendant upon the recognition that a marriage will not survive. Most divorced women and men point to this as a time of desperate loneliness. Their spouses—companions in their misery—are people with whom they can no longer communicate. They often feel more alone with their mates than they will feel when they are on their own, says divorced psychologist Cecile Goodman.

I've never been as alone in my life as when I was trapped in a lousy marriage. Because there was no one to talk to. I didn't come from the era that said you could cry on your friend's shoulder. I came from an era that said "Get involved, get busy, plan things to do." So that was my way of handling it. And I used to feel that there wasn't anywhere to turn, and I used to go to bed feeling very depressed. To me loneliness and depression were absolutely synonymous. I felt that I didn't care whether I lived or died.

Even with today's liberal attitudes toward divorce, many of those who suffer shattered marriages are unable to confide in their friends or their families. If their marriages have failed, they feel that they have failed, and they will not admit that failure until separation makes it impossible to hide the truth. They then have no alternative but to explain their situation. "I felt so ashamed," commented a thirty-year-old recently divorced woman, "that I couldn't even tell my best friends or my women's group what was happening between me and my husband. It made me feel like a hypocrite. But how could I tell these women that my husband would get physically violent?"

The energy that should be going into confiding in others and working out problems before the decision to divorce, goes instead into putting up a façade of happiness. That façade also serves to maintain a status quo that, no matter how painful, people are reluctant to trade against the unknown. If Jane tells Mary that the marriage everyone thought to be so perfect is in reality a nightmare, if she tells Mary that her husband may strike her when angry or that she gets no support from him, Mary might logically wonder what Jane is doing in that marriage. If Tom tells Ed that his wife constantly belittles him or is unfaithful, Ed, like Mary, might tell Tom he should consider doing something about it.

When the hostilities of marriage have built up to a certain point, however, doing something to rectify the situation may lead to divorce. "One of the biggest fears people have when contemplating divorce," says Dr. Laura Singer, a marriage and family counselor in Manhattan, "is that 'Oh, my God, I'm going to be alone. And alone means lonely.' So people will stay together out of fear."

Contrary to popular belief, the liberalization of divorce laws does not mean that people seek divorce without batting an eyelid. As Joseph Epstein, author of the recent book *Divorce in America*, says about his own divorce and others, it is always a most difficult decision. And to avoid that decision people will endure the shabbiest treatment from those who are supposed to love them.

Mr. and Mrs. Archer are a good example of the mutual acceptance of torture. They had been married for twenty-five years and were both in their early fifties when they divorced. Mr. Archer drank excessively, and Mrs. Archer often joined him. She did not, like him, hold her liquor well, and she would become angry and excited even though she knew their two daughters could hear the quarrels she would instigate. After several years of fighting, the couple lapsed into silence. When Mr. Archer entered a room his wife would leave, and vice versa. For five years the two hardly exchanged words. Mr. Archer paid the bills, because he did not want his wife to have any grounds, such as nonsupport, for divorce. But his wife had no intention of initiating such proceedings. She had made a rather disturbing peace with the situation. She went on her vacations and he on his. The only problem was the children. But the two girls were almost grown. Whatever worries their parents had concerning their welfare were dismissed on the grounds that they were old enough to take care of themselves.

They also used their Catholicism as an excuse to keep them from the divorce courts. Anything was better than saying "I've had enough" and losing the silent, hostile companionship to which they had grown accustomed. It was only after both daughters left home that Mr. Archer, having met another woman while at a convention, finally divorced his wife.

The Archers' pattern is typical. Not all couples, of course, maintain a five-year silence. But the reluctance to give up companionship until things become completely unbearable is common. "It was only after we had a baby and I saw how my husband treated the child that I asked for a divorce," one separated woman explained. "I had taken all sorts of things from him over the years. But I lived under some romantic illusion that things would work themselves out. But he would never even play with the baby. I just couldn't let myself risk what would happen to my child if I stayed with him."

Another typical element of the pattern described above is the reluctance to seek divorce until one spouse finds another relationship. The fear of loneliness often accounts for the fact that one partner—or both—will find a lover and then ask for a divorce. The partner may or may not marry that lover, but the new relationship does function to replace, in advance, the one they are going to lose. One divorced person, at least, will not be alone after separation.

Despite the surface security that such relationships appear to provide, the rebound syndrome can create more problems than it solves. A person jumping directly into one relationship before his or her old relationship is terminated may never have the time to figure out why the former relationship soured, why it was entered into in the first place, or what purpose it served in the psychological scheme of things. Falling in love again can conveniently erase such unpleasant considerations, because one is so involved in the new that the old is forgotten. But the old may not disappear, and the same mistakes may be repeated.

Ex-wives and the experts insist that divorced men have a greater tendency than divorced women to replace their former mates with either new lovers or new spouses. Opportunity is one reason for this. Men have traditionally had more freedom than women. A man may meet an attractive secretary or colleague at work, while the only male contacts the housewife has are the milkman and her husband.

The lack of tolerance for loneliness is a second factor that explains why men get attached to other women quickly after a separation. For a man the replacement of the woman in his life by another woman may be a necessity. If men traditionally depend on the women they love to be their only close friends and confidantes, the loss of those women leaves them completely friendless. Because men cannot easily confide weakness in other men, and because they need someone to talk to if they are having marital problems, it becomes essential to find other women who will play the role previously assigned to their wives. The new woman becomes the confidante, replacing the old. Men may feel resentment and bitterness because of divorce, but the loneliness of the adjustment to single life is an experience that their greater opportunity to find mates allows them to escape.

Not every man or woman is, however, willing or able to take the path of least resistance. And for the man or woman who divorces and then must live alone (and according to statistics, 1.3 million divorced men and women below thirty-five have not remarried)—either again, or perhaps for the first time in his or her life—the problems of loneliness are daily, depressing occurrences.

Two kids, two divorces—at thirty-four Linda has been through a lot of changes. She was only nineteen when she married for the first time. After one child and three years of marriage she and her husband divorced, she says, because they both grew up. Then came two years with her family, and she married for the second time. That ended because, after five years of marriage, her husband discovered that he preferred men to women. There was more astonishment than bitterness associated with their divorce. They are still friends.

Linda has been on her own, with her children, for close to a year. And it is only now, after six months of therapy, that she likes living alone.

It's only within the last four months or so that I've gotten to a place where I like being by myself. Therapy helped that a lot. At the beginning of the year I went through some pretty heavy emotional trips about loneliness. I was going through the standard routine which I've discovered since that a lot of people go through. You know, here I am at thirty-three, not particularly wanting to get married again, but also not wanting to face the possibility of being by myself for the rest of my life and knowing that my friends won't be around forever. And looking at some older women who are living alone and dealing with it in a way that I don't want to deal with it. Just going out and trying to find anybody to ease that loneliness. That frightens me. I don't want to be in the position of just grabbing anybody that passes by. And the whole point is that I wasn't comfortable with myself. Because I wasn't really sure who I was.

It took me a long time to realize that I was capable of handling the problems that come up. With myself it's been from one situation where there were people around to another. You know, high school and college, parents, to a husband, back to parents, to another husband, to a roommate. There's always been somebody there. There's never been a time in my life when I was entirely alone—with all my own decisions and actions—and that was what frightened me. Making wrong decisions and not having anybody to put it on but myself. There was always somebody there to help me. Or if there wasn't I would always make sure to get someone over or go somewhere fast. When I first lived on my own, I'd visit a lot, I used to watch a lot of television. Just because it filled up a space. I also used to drink a lot, and ate little. It's only now, after individual and group therapy that I can let myself be lonely and not try to escape it.

Jim's divorce was not particularly bitter either. After twenty years of marriage he and his wife had simply drifted away from each other. The last years were not torn by fights or recriminations but by boredom and a lack of interest. Each wanted to do different things, and so they finally decided to terminate their marriage. The fact that their separation was so amicable, however, did not make it any easier for Jim to go out and find an apartment and take care of himself after so many years. He rented a small apartment in Los Angeles and began to date a woman with whom he knew he could never get really serious but who had a large house where he could go on weekends to putter and cook meals and pretend, if only for a short time, that he had a sort of family—a place where his presence was still important.

He still saw his four children frequently. That period just after separation was confusing, especially to his youngest son, whose erratic off-and-on behavior toward Jim was perhaps the most unpleasant thing with which he had to deal.

You realize that the boy is having problems. He resents you for leaving, and he still wants to make sure you love him, all at once. He also resents the fact that you may be going out with women other than his mother. It's very hard to deal with while you're having problems yourself.

I found that even though I was no longer living with my family, I still wanted to play an important role in their lives. I would go to my old house and look around to see if things were as I left them. I wanted to make sure my presence was still noticeable.

And then there's living alone. After twenty years of marriage you don't know how to keep house for yourself. At first it's very exciting, fixing an apartment, getting furniture, having your very own place. But one day I went to Woolworth's to get silverware and a tea strainer. With my arms full of things I went to the check-out counter. And suddenly I found myself watching what I was doing—a forty-

four-year-old man starting over again. And I thought, What the hell am I doing in this position?

Jane had never been married. She lived with her boyfriend and had his child. Yet when the two split up, it was, Jane says, no different from divorce. No courts or lawyers, but just as wrenching. Jane took the boy and moved into a small apartment and got a job to support her schooling. She had not had much of a problem with loneliness before she left her "old man." Although she had a large family, she did not have many friends. A sickly child, she could not participate in many of the usual school activities. So she became a loner and was used to being by herself. It was only after her "divorce" that she began to feel lonely being alone.

I've always had a sense of aloneness. I always dealt with it really well until I left Michael's father. I was always independent enough, brave enough, to find people, so loneliness never bothered me. But after I left Michael's father it got to me. It was all the responsibility of having a child alone. So I would smoke a lot of dope or play with my plants and fish.

I'm really looking for a partner. There's got to be a man somewhere I could get along with. Someone to come home to at night. I like to cook. I like to put dinner on the table. I get pleasure out of it. But there has to be somebody there to eat it. It's a drag when you're alone with a small child. The child doesn't eat much and I don't care much about fixing food for myself.

For a while we got into the habit where the only things I'd buy were snacky things, things you could get by reaching into the refrigerator. And we'd eat all day. As long as it was wholesome food I didn't care how we put it together. But it's no fun that way. It was more fun to sit and eat at a table and share with people. It makes food a whole different trip. For over two years Michael and I didn't have a table, and so we ate at the coffee table or sitting on the bed watching TV. Our meals were just so weird. And I didn't enjoy it. You see, there were six kids in my family, and dinner time was when everybody got together around the table. And meals were sharing,

*supportive trips. You share the day with others. Mealtimes should be
a mellow, sharing time. But when you're alone, they're the worst time.*

Richard Davies had no idea there was anything wrong with
his marriage. He loved his wife and two children. He enjoyed his
work as an attorney. He was well suited, he liked to think, for
marriage and family life. Having a home and a wife and children to care about provided him with a purpose. Unlike his colleagues who complained of household noise, he even felt more
comfortable working at home in his study, hearing the sounds of
housework and play below. He had worried before his marriage
that his family background would hurt his chances of conjugal
success. His mother had died when he was small and his father
had been remarried to a woman with whom he was unable to
get along. Richard was sure that these circumstances had not
helped his emotional development, for there was little affection
in his youth. But that had not affected him, it seemed. His was
as nearly perfect a life as he could imagine.

When Richard's wife announced to him one day that their
marriage was not nearly as perfect for her as it was for him, it
came as an enormous shock. Suddenly, when she reached the age
of thirty, married life lost its charms. She had had so many ambitions for herself, and now, at thirty, when she was too old to
really do anything to change her life, all she had to look forward
to was housework and their children growing away from her.
On Richard's salary they couldn't afford the material things that
would compensate her for her losses. If he wanted to, she said,
he would have to do better. He would have to earn more money,
take her out more, and let her buy the things she wanted. True,
she had never asked him to get a job that would earn more
money, and she had said that he could practice the kind of law
that does not accumulate great profits, but she had changed her
mind.

Richard could not grasp what was happening. He liked his
work, and things had been all right until now. But they were to
be all right no longer. There seemed no way to make up to his
wife for what she thought she had lost, and no way to rectify

whatever errors he had made. When they decided to split up, his wife kept the house, and Richard moved into a small apartment on the top floor of a building in which the other apartments were vacant. With his dog, he began living alone after ten years. Without his two children, without all he had thought he had been building toward, he was left with the task of mulling over his life to see where exactly things had gone amiss.

Looking back, I could see that there were things I could have done. I used to work on weekends, write up cases, and articles for magazines. I was happy enough, but I can see that we didn't get out enough. I didn't make the effort. It always seemed so difficult to arrange. We would decide to go out and then we had to get the children ready. Our son would be ready to go, but our daughter would be asleep. Or one would have clothes on and the other wouldn't. It seemed too difficult to coordinate. So I'd get frustrated and decide it wasn't worth the trouble, and we wouldn't go. Then if my wife and I wanted to go out at night, we'd have to find a baby sitter, and that was expensive and a bother. I suppose I never made the effort because it wasn't that important to me to get out. I was out all day. But it was important to my wife. She felt that she was suffocating. She wanted to be an actress, to do something with her life. That threatened me. But even when I did encourage her, she said it was too late. She said she wanted to find someone who could give her more than I could.

I miss my children terribly. It's awful to think that my ex-wife will remarry and that my kids will have another father. I see them on weekends, but it's not the same as having them all the time.

Do I get lonely often? Every time I think of my family. It's worst at holidays. The first Christmas, when I had to visit my parents alone, was terrible. We had always gone there together, my wife and me and the kids. When I went alone, after my wife and I separated, it was like being a kid again, in mommy and daddy's house. There was no one to talk to, no one with whom I could share anything I was feeling.

Separation is almost always a frightening experience. There may be occasional feelings of elation at finally being out of a bad relationship. Recently separated persons may find it exciting to set up house without having to worry about another's wishes. They may find it exhilarating to have the freedom to deal with life without considering a husband or wife's needs. One young woman said that it was finally her loneliness with which she had to deal, rather than the loneliness created by the presence of another person with whom she no longer had anything in common. But whatever relief she felt at regaining her own life was only a temporary phenomenon, which would come between periods of acute depression.

Coming home to an empty house, eating alone, sleeping alone —divorce means adjustment to a new way of life. For many people the experience of living alone after separation is the first in their lives. Many people marry immediately after leaving their families or college. They have never known what it is like not to have people around them all the time. There is no experience of having made it alone to which they can refer for help in the future.

Things may be a bit less terrifying for the divorced person to whom living alone is not entirely new. But the adjustment to an unfamiliar way of life will always be difficult.

If people have friends or family, loneliness is somewhat mediated by their support. But marriage often means that the threads of life are woven into a very special pattern. Because of the reluctance of couples to have single friends, a divorced woman or man who used to be regarded as a welcome guest is, when he or she is no longer part of a couple, regarded as a potential enemy. And it is a typical and unfortunate pattern that a divorced man or woman—particularly a woman—finds that he or she is no longer included on the guest lists of their "good" couple friends.

Family may also be looked to for support by the person going through a divorce. But, depending on the particular family, parents may respond critically rather than supportively when they find out what is going on in a child's marriage. Divorce may be par for the course to the younger generation, but it is not taken lightly by the older one. Prying questions and subtle accusations that it was "your fault" that things went as poorly as they did are not appreciated by people trying to put their lives back together again. A recently separated person may prefer to back away from family obligations rather than face such problems. What newly divorced people often learn is that they have only themselves and a few of their closest friends—if they are lucky enough to have good friends—on whom to count.

The loneliness of divorce is combined with a sense of helplessness about life that differs somewhat according to the sex of the person involved. Men have a great deal of trouble setting up house for themselves. Most women keep the house, and so the man must make a home for himself after having had a woman to tend to his needs and create an atmosphere in which he would be comfortable. If a man works all day, he will be surrounded by people and things with which to keep himself occupied. But nighttime is the time he used to spend with his family, and coming home to an empty house, which is generally a rather thrown-together affair, increases his depression.

A man may also have problems finding friends if he loses those friends that he and his wife shared as a couple. Men often let their wives arrange their joint social lives. Even if a couple's friends are the husband's colleagues, the woman does the social planning. Women find other women for friends, and the men are drawn into the relationship. Divorced men can feel at a loss as to how to make friends or provide themselves with a social life outside of work. And so they will try to find a new woman to serve as social organizer.

Women who do not work are faced with the loneliness of staying home all day unrelieved by the prospect of having any communication with an adult in the evening. Or a woman whose only qualifications are those provided by the experience of being a wife and mother may suddenly find she must go out and find a job. She may then feel lost and alone both out in the world and in her own home.

And, of course, both sexes must face the dilemmas brought on by wanting to go out with members of the opposite sex after having been out of circulation for a number of years. Married and divorced people point to marriage as a haven from the discomfort of the rituals involved in forming an intimate relationship. But divorced people, if they want to find mates, must run through those rituals all over again. The divorced man or woman finds that he or she no longer knows how to approach a member of the opposite sex. They are pained at their own awkwardness and fear; all say that it is "like being in high school again." Yet a divorced person's loneliness pushes him or her out into this rather terrifying world that they thought they had left behind them.

If a woman living in the suburbs keeps the house and children, she will often find herself in a particular sort of trap. Divorced men who have lived with their families in the suburbs tend to move back into the city after a separation. Thus the divorced woman in the suburbs may find it very difficult to meet available men. She will be surrounded by a couple society, many of whose members shun her. The traditional solution to loneliness following divorce—the immediate absorption in another romantic relationship—is difficult for her to achieve. She will, furthermore, have difficulty maintaining the friendships she had when she was married, and she will find few available attached women with whom to have more than friendships in the afternoon hours when their husbands are at work.

The problems of loneliness are felt most acutely during the hours and days society says should be spent with a partner. Holidays, Saturday nights, mealtimes—those times when you are supposed to be near a loved one. Many recently divorced people find just coming home difficult, for the silence and emptiness of their houses mirror the emptiness of their lives. So many divorced people, like this young woman in California, avoid home for the first few weeks or months after they leave their spouses.

I didn't want to come home after my husband and I split up. The house reminded me too much of what had happened. It also reminded me of my mother's life. My father died when I was young and she lived alone the rest of her life, rattling around in her house. My worst fear was that I'd be like her. I also felt desperate and lonely because I felt I was overreacting to the split, and I couldn't tell anyone how I felt because they'd think I was crazy.

When I finally came home I played blues and rock music loud constantly during the night and day. I didn't want to hear the silence of the house, and I guess I felt dead inside and the music made me feel alive.

The adjustment of living on one's own is often complicated by the sense of failure that accompanies divorce. The intensity of the shame of failure to be a good wife or husband depends on who left whom in the divorce. If the divorce was mutually sought, both partners may share the guilt and pain equally. But if one partner sought divorce against the wishes of the other, or if an affair was involved, the unwanted partner may feel rejected. This spouse has failed to keep a husband or wife, and may also feel that he or she has lost the ability to attract and hold any member of the opposite sex. It then becomes important to find someone else who will love the rejected one and who will prove that he or she is still sexually attractive.

This need to regain lost self-esteem leads people into relationships for which they are not yet ready. The end of one complicated relationship is not the best time to attempt to start a fresh one. And like teenagers and singles, divorced people respond to the fear of loneliness and the societal prejudice against solitude by rushing into liaisons for which they are ill suited. It's no wonder that many of the quick remarriages of recently divorced people also end unhappily.

The opposite reaction—withdrawal from close relationships—is also common. Having been hurt once, Helen Bixby explains of herself and others, a divorced person may decide that never again will he or she get involved in a serious love relationship:

Having been hurt makes you very cautious about getting involved with anyone again. I'm fifty-five years old and sometimes I feel that I'd better grab onto something quick. I've already done that and I don't want to do it again. There was a man, but it was a bad relation-

ship. I was able to fill up his emptiness, but he wanted to possess me. And I was pulled in two directions at once. I had a hunch something was wrong. But I was so afraid to give up a relationship with a person and go back to being lonely that I didn't listen to my hunch. And he pulled me into his own loneliness. I couldn't handle that responsibility. And now I am very cautious about getting involved.

Many people operate on the maxim: Nothing ventured, nothing lost. This type of reaction to divorce is typical of many men. Harold Jackson, a businessman in New York and a frequent patron of singles bars, has been divorced for three years. He was in love with his wife, but things did not work out as planned. Rather than figure out what happened in his marriage so that he would not make the same mistakes with another woman, Jackson has discovered that the simplest way of dealing with women is to keep things light and end an affair whenever any signs of a more intense relationship develop. He has decided that once was enough. "I have had my relationship," Jackson insists.

The aftertaste of divorce has also made Eric James, a businessman in northern California, cautious about deep involvement with women. After a five-year marriage Eric was divorced four years ago. There was a great deal of bitterness at his divorce, he says. Bitterness because his wife did not understand that he wanted to get ahead in business, and complained because he worked for fifteen or sixteen hours a day to do a good job. Having never finished college makes a man ambitious to do as well as college-educated men. He had asked for his wife's help, and he wanted her to stay with him. But she left in spite of his desires. It would be insane, after such an experience, to get married again or even to become seriously involved with one woman. Why risk going through all that bitterness again?

His divorce has not soured Eric on women. He likes several quite a lot. With one of the women who keeps him company when he is lonely he shares only sexual attraction. They drink a lot and sleep together. She admires Eric's golf score, and, well . . . he admires things about her. Joann, a woman fourteen years younger than he, satisfies both his sexual and intellectual needs. He could, in fact, get quite attached to her if he were to let himself. But he's made sure that will never happen; he discovered even before he asked her out that she has another boyfriend. The boyfriend—Captain Africa, Eric calls him—has been in Africa for the past year.

I guess I got into the relationship because, you know, psychologically or subconsciously I felt that the guy was around. I don't know. But if he called up tomorrow and said to her that he was going to marry some dictator's daughter, I'd probably split. I made it clear from the beginning that I didn't want it to get too heavy. I met her at my office—she works for me. Then around Christmas I went over to her house with a box of wine and cheese, and she got out the candles and it was real nice. But I told her then that I didn't want it to get out of control and that I would just split if it did.

There were times when Eric wished that he and Joann could settle into a more permanent relationship. The time, for instance, he discovered Captain Africa would be back in a few weeks he got awfully depressed.

She found out two weeks ago that Captain Africa was coming back. And so we said adios. It was pretty heavy. I was pretty wiped out. But she didn't know it. If I feel more for her than I say, she just won't know it. I don't want it to get too heavy. I know if I feel bad for two or three weeks now I'll get over it. I'll play some golf, hang out, take some sauce and it'll be all over.

Work will keep Eric occupied. And he does have a couple of good friends, men he met before he quit college. They don't live in the same state as he, but they visit every once in a while. His best friend just came West for a stay. Eric and he played golf. Then his friend—a married man with a couple of kids—said he wanted some action. So Eric called his business manager, who told him of a great whorehouse where for $45 you could get a terrific lay. Eric and his friend went to the whorehouse together, and while Eric sat drinking, his friend went off with some broad. Sex is something Eric won't pay for.

Whorehouses, singles dances—these things, Eric thinks, are for emotional cripples or men whose minds are still in high school. His friend might need that—a little fling to get away from the wife. But Eric can find women by just being friendly and talking to people. The other day, for example, he was playing golf and some cute little girl came out and offered tea and sandwiches to the golfers. He refused her refreshments, and when she exhibited amazement at his refusal, he said he'd have a 7-Up and her address and phone number. Out she came with the cold drink, and under the glass she had slipped a card filled with the essential statistics. Just like that. That was easy enough—so why should he be lonely?

Fred Willis, a real estate speculator who divorced two wives he found dull, says he will marry again, but not a woman he loves. He has experienced the loneliness of feeling that something is missing in his life, the feeling that everyone else is out there having a good time. Fred does not intend to feel that again. He wants someone to be a companion, to fill his bed perhaps. But romantic love is foolish. When he finds another woman, the basis of their relationship will be either money or convenience.

We marry for insane reasons in America. For romantic love. But when romantic love is gone, then we find we don't even like the person we're living with. That's happened to me twice, and it won't happen again. If I marry again it will be for socioeconomic reasons. For money or position. That's an eminently sane way to do things. I have six uncles in France and all of them married for those reasons. They all have mistresses on the side. The only problem with that would be to find an American woman who would put up with it.

Men, it seems, have a lower tolerance of pain than women. And whereas many women will go into therapy after a divorce in order to try to understand their failed marriage as well as the rest of their lives, men tend to stay away from psychiatry and try to solve the problem of good relationships by not relating at all except on the most superficial levels.

No matter how they choose to deal with it, the loneliness of divorce is a problem for almost all of those who are separated. Some, however, have more freedom than others with which to deal with readjustment. If there are no children involved, things are often easier. But if there were children in the marriage, loneliness is increased. And in many cases divorces involve children: about 40 percent of those divorced have one or two children, while 20 percent have three or more children. In such cases both the husband and wife feel they have harmed their children by deciding to divorce. And whoever does not have custody of the children feels lonely for them, while whoever does have custody may have a more difficult time than the spouse left childless, because he or she must deal with personal feelings of loneliness plus the problems of raising children alone.

The single parent has a lonely struggle.* Child rearing is hard enough for two people, but to be both father and mother to a child in addition to coping with the dilemma of recent separation is often unnerving. Women in such a situation may feel anger, guilt, shame, and resentment at their predicament while they simultaneously love their children. They resent the fact that they do not have any help with child raising and that they must take on the full responsibility of a growing child. Pat, a twenty-six-year-old mother, explains that she is angry when she thinks of her husband's freedom to do as he pleases without having to consider a child's needs:

My ex-husband is always complaining because he has to see our daughter on weekends, and because he has to contribute something

* Mothers have traditionally had custody of their children. I will refer here mostly to the problems of single mothers. However, things are changing and some fathers do take their children. The problems discussed would be the same, therefore, for single fathers as those described for single mothers.

to child support. I used to feel guilty about asking him to help. But now I feel, what the hell, he can go out whenever he wants to, he doesn't have to worry about child care. And he can cop out on commitments to taking the child on weekends too. I've just had to finally say to myself that our daughter is my total responsibility and that I can't count on her father.

It's very hard to get yourself together after a divorce if you have the responsibility of caring for a child. You just don't have any freedom. And you feel a tremendous burden—that everything you do effects your child—and there is no one to help. If anything happens to your child it's all your fault.

Linda, the thirty-four-year-old divorcée whose husband left her to become an active homosexual, says that the responsibility of raising a twelve-year-old girl and six-year-old boy makes her feel alone:

I have a really hard time handling my daughter. There's a lot of really heavy competition going on, and it's worse because her father is not around. It really amazed me when I would see her reacting to men who come into the house, playing these little games and doing these little scripts to get attention. And I thought, My God, where did she get that from? And of course it was from me. It was like seeing a portrait of myself and not liking it at all. But not really knowing how to tell her that I don't dig it. Having kids increases my sense of loneliness because I'm aware of this overwhelming sense of responsibility. And I often want to escape from it and I resent my kids' presence. I just want to have responsibility for only me sometimes. So the resentment piles on top of the loneliness and intensifies it.

For those women whose husbands cannot afford or will not pay either alimony or child support (and in the majority of cases women do not get either), and who must go out and find work, life can seem pretty unfair. Nancy is a twenty-six-year-old single mother who decided to go to law school. Being a lawyer would allow her and her daughter to live more comfortably than they could if Nancy were doing more traditional "woman's work." She finds that the responsibility of both studying and taking care of her daughter keeps her from doing as well as she could in school. Looking at her fellow students whose parents pay for their tuition and who have no other commitments but study causes frustration and anger:

The professors don't make any adjustments for a woman with a small child. If I have to turn in a paper or take an exam and if my child is sick and I have to take care of her, I'm in a real bind. Of course my child comes first. But then I either do badly on the exam or turn the paper in late. So I get penalized in my grades.

Sometimes you feel that you're never going to get anywhere. And there's no point in trying. And then I hate my child and the responsibility I have. Since I really love my child, it makes me feel very guilty. I feel I have no one to turn to.

Many single mothers would like to have another relationship with a man and perhaps marry again. But it is not easy to find a man who wants to take on both mother and child. The care of a child, furthermore, does not allow them, single mothers say, to indulge in the kind of sexual experimentation made possible by more liberal attitudes toward sex. "One of the things that keeps me from getting involved with a man," says Pat, "is the guilt about how it will affect my child. I can't just experiment, and I have to really consider the effect of any relationship on my child. Sometimes the guilt of that is just devastating."

Susan, who has two children and has been divorced for five years, also feels the bonds of her responsibility. She is in love with a man who wants her and her children to come and live with him, but although she wants very much to do so, she is hesitant. "I lived with another man once for six months," she explains, "and it didn't work out. But even though we only lived together a short time, my kids still got attached to him. When we left, it was as though they had lost a daddy twice in a row. I can't risk that happening again, and having them go through that again."

The loneliness of a single mother is compounded by her worries about her children, her resentment at not having the freedom to do what other women without children seem to be doing, and by the child's problems with the adjustment to living without a father. Although a single mother may, some women say, use her concern for her children's welfare to protect her from involvement with another man who might again hurt her, most single mothers have problems that increase the loneliness of living without a man.

Coping with the loneliness of divorce also includes special problems for another group of women—women who are approaching either middle or old age. There is a typical syndrome in divorce that affects the older or middle-aged woman. Frequently a man who is approaching middle age will find another woman to replace his aging wife. The wife is a reminder to her husband of his coming old age—a reflection of an unwanted self. The man will find a woman ten or even twenty years younger than he who will make him feel more youthful. The blow to a woman's ego when her husband abandons her and a relationship that they have built over the years is often crippling.

In the advertising world a man is surrounded by beautiful women—models, secretaries, assistants, actresses. Jeanette's husband, a successful illustrator, could not, after fifteen years of marriage, resist the temptation presented to him every day at the office. His first affair was with an assistant, his second with a model. Jeanette knew of these little flings, but she tried to ignore them. Her pride, she felt, was less important than keeping her family—her husband, her thirteen-year-old son and herself—together. She and her husband had had a good marriage, at least for the first ten years. With the beginning of the second decade of their relationship, things began slowly to change. Not only were there affairs—with women who made Jeanette, a reasonably attractive housewife, feel totally inferior—but there was also her husband's unwillingness to communicate. He was tired or busy or irritated. With one excuse or another he warded off conversation and intimacy.

Then Jeanette had an operation which left a large scar across her abdomen. As people get older such things happen, and both husband and wife accustom themselves to the changes in their respective bodies. But Jeanette's husband could not, it seemed, accept such transformations, and after her operation he said he felt only disgust when he looked at her. Such disgust that he could no longer stand touching her.

For a year Jeanette and her husband shared the same house, communicating little. He continued his affairs and she continued her tennis lessons and her lunches with friends. The two hosted the large parties for which they had become famous in their circle of friends. Finally, however, keeping up the façade that had replaced their marriage became too arduous, and Jeanette asked her husband to leave.

He has been gone a year, and their divorce is almost final. Jeanette has the large house, the child, and alimony. Her husband has his posh apartment in town and the freedom to sleep with anyone he wants—a privilege he is not loath to use even when his son is there for the weekend. Jeanette envies that freedom. For her it is not easy to find a man. Although she is only forty-one, still slim and active, she rarely meets available men. At first she was shocked when her women friends dropped her, and their husbands came round to her house expecting that she would sleep with them. Then the loneliness and frustration of living alone began to get to her and she gradually abandoned her principles.

Now she finds the only men she meets are either married or police officers. She has never been particularly fond of policemen. One night, however, she heard a noise in her basement, and since her husband was no longer home to protect her, she called the police. Two officers came to her house and looked around. While one officer was searching the grounds the other noticed some liquor on a table. It looked good to him, he said. To which she responded with the offer of a drink. Oh, no, he answered, he couldn't drink on duty. But he would be off at midnight. Jeanette took the hint and suggested he stop by after work. By midnight, she knew, she would be needing company, and the officer wasn't bad-looking.

The officer came by every night for several weeks. Once he brought his partner, and the two men convinced Jeanette to sleep with both of them. Otherwise he came alone. After little conversation, he and Jeanette went to bed. All she knew about him was that he was married and had an arrangement with his wife, as well as with some other divorced women in the neighborhood he patrolled. The women, like Jeanette, were lonely, and he was obliging. After all, he said, a woman alone needs a man around the house. There was nothing wrong with such a thing, he and Jeanette agreed. It was to be nothing permanent. Just some fun. After a year alone Jeanette had learned to take any kind of companionship she could get.

When she was fifty, Rachel's husband informed her that he was leaving her for a woman thirteen years her junior. They had been married for twenty years and had four children. Shortly before her husband's announcement Rachel had found evidence of what she was sure was an affair between her husband and another woman. It was a typical scene of confrontation when she asked her husband if her doubts were well founded. Her husband admitted his "sins" but assured her that it was nothing serious. Finally, however, her husband's affair destroyed her marriage.

The pain of rejection was heightened by the fact that her husband's affair had begun while both Rachel's parents were dying and she had had to leave home to care for them. And in marrying a younger woman, Rachel felt, her husband had not only abandoned her at a difficult time in her life but had made her feel ugly and worthless. She was to be, from then on, the unwanted older woman who had nothing to offer. Several very lonely and desperate years after her divorce Rachel understood that her husband's actions were not meant to hurt her but were rather signs of his own weakness. "A younger woman would admire a man more, maybe. I wanted my husband to be a friend, I wanted him to talk to me and share things with me. But he didn't want any demands made on him. And I think that because he was getting old he wanted someone to assure him that he was still attractive. Someone to look up to him. I'd been with him twenty years and after that amount of time you know someone too well to stand in awe of them."

If a man is getting older, he can often find a younger woman to give him the assurances about his virility and worth that he may need. An older woman cannot find a man with whom to have an intimate relationship so easily. When a woman reaches forty she will look for a man her own age or older. But when a man reaches forty, he is interested in women who are younger than he. This means that a woman often discovers that the men she finds attractive are all out chasing after women in their twenties and early thirties. Simply because of her age, she is unwanted. A woman may have friends of the same sex with whom to share her problems, but that does not satisfy her needs for either emotional or sexual closeness with another person of the opposite sex.

At thirty-eight Anne finds herself alone with her four children. She is an attractive woman, very intelligent, very active. But working as a therapist at a mental health clinic does not provide the best opportunity for meeting men. And after several years of living alone, in which she has seen her husband marry again, Anne would like to have a permanent relationship with a compatible man. Despite much looking, she has not come across anyone who would interest her. She has tried singles bars and they have not worked, and she is too well acquainted with therapy to go to an encounter group that she would be qualified to lead.

Berkeley is a hard place to find a man. Everyone is a dropout or a freak. I have four children so I am not interested in someone like that. But I'm still looking. I've almost given up on San Francisco. In San Francisco you figure that there is so much to do that people you are interested in would be going to the opera or theater and wouldn't go to something like a singles dance. So you go to the suburbs to a singles dance because you figure that in the suburbs there is nothing to do. Maybe there will be some interesting people there. Anyway these are the delusions and myths a divorced person lives with. Probably all the people there will be terrible.

All this gets pretty tiring and you wish you could meet men other ways. But there are very few. With six or eight women to every man, every man is overloaded with dinner invitations from his friends who have female friends who are available.

Anne finds that the men she does come in contact with are often threatened by the fact that she is an independent woman with a life and ideas of her own, who wants to be treated as an equal.

Most of the women I know have just given up on men. What you have to do to find them is not worth the trouble, especially when you think you could be reading a good book or just having a nice night at home. Most men I have gone out with just talk about themselves and they don't pay much attention to who a woman is. They don't even have the sense to ask what I do, or who I am. And you can't challenge them about how they act because they just get upset if you get angry at them or talk about feelings.

Men have a much easier time finding women. They can get rid of their wives and go out and find a younger woman.

Men have been taught to value women who are younger and weaker than they. The middle-aged man shuns a woman his own age and looks for one younger than he. And because many younger women seem to be attracted to father figures, men are successful in gaining youthful mates. Women, however, have been made to feel that there is something undignified and slightly perverse about having a love affair with a younger man. The older divorced woman is often left alone, made to feel a failure because she has lost her man.

There are those who may, with the help of the textbooks, turn divorce into a creative experience. Ending a bad marriage may lead to a new and happier life, with new and healthier relationships. The ability to turn a destructive experience into one that is creative depends, to a great extent, on the ability to confront loneliness and to ride through inevitable periods of depression without seeking immediate relief in a relationship that will be only more of the same. Such a happy ending is also dependent on the age and sex of the divorced person. The younger a person is the easier it is to begin a new life and exchange old habits for new ones. The older a person is the more difficult it is to adjust to an unfamiliar way of life and find new companions. Remarriage may bring an end to the loneliness of the divorced, but remarriage is not something all divorced people can count on. The fear accompanying divorce is that what appears to be only a temporary period of loneliness will lead to a permanent condition. For many who have gone through a divorce there is the lingering prospect of a solitary, lonely old age.

Chapter Eight

Mrs. Emily Pierce

The grass has not been planted yet, and the garden (or whatever small patches of it there are by the sides of the building) is unfinished. When she asks the gardener what he is planting, his accent obscures his words. She doesn't understand, and he is too busy to repeat. "Crazy old lady," she imagines he says to himself in Spanish. There are only the hills to stare at—golden hills burned out by the California summer sun. There won't be any rain now for six months at least. Just fog rolling in at night, chilling her. The weather will sit with her, predictable and silent, like her companions and her days.

They no longer have anything to exchange, Emily Pierce and the world. Abruptly, about five years ago, when she was sixty-six, a heart attack—second main killer of Americans—divided them. The insurance firm in southern California, where she had worked for twenty years as a clerk, fired her. "It was a bitter pill to swallow," she says, "after twenty years of good work. But they didn't want to have someone around who'd been sick, even though I could still do the work." And so she became one of America's retired senior citizens whose promised golden years become an accounting of personal and economic loss.

For Emily Pierce the first loss was her health and the second her house. The gardening and cleaning had become too much for her. She had prided herself on keeping the house spotless and the garden well cared for—a concern she shared with her Japanese neighbors. They might be a different color, she realized after they moved in, but they shared her finickyness. But she was forced to leave her house and her neighbors for a smaller home in a retirement community. "Paradise," she says now, "the retirement community was paradise. Your own home, your own car, people around who weren't too much of a bother. When I got there, why I just went hog wild, taking classes. I took stitchery, painting and sewing. I was too busy even to clean house. It was such a new life."

She had her independence for a while. But soon the doctor began chipping away at it when he refused to let her drive. "He said it would be too dangerous, that he wouldn't want to be driving in front of me or in back of me. I told him maybe I wouldn't want to be driving near him either, but he wouldn't renew my license."

She had had the car for only a year, she had been in her new home only a year when she had a stroke. In the hospital the doctor told her she would have to stop smoking. Looking down at her in the bed, he seemed rather like a huge white statue, the kind that stands in front of old movie theaters. Could she stop smoking? "When you can't move, what else can you say but yes?" Now, three years later, another doctor says she must stop eating. She must lose twenty pounds or it will be bad for her heart. It seems such a lot to lose when you can't move half your body. One arm and one leg drag along beside her like parcels.

Her stroke and paralysis meant that she would have to leave the community, since the full-time help she required would be too expensive. And such places do not provide life care. Retirement "communities," as the ads say, are for independent living among mature adults. Once you become ill, you are no longer mature—you are old. And old people live in retirement homes and convalescent hospitals. After a year in a home in Los Angeles, which she considered more a prison than a place of rest, Mrs. Pierce moved again, to live near her daughter and to try a new retirement community, The Pines.

That was almost three years ago, in December—a December

that brought with it more rain than the area had seen in years. The rain mixed with the dirt of the newly constructed facility to form huge areas of mud—a rather dismal introduction to her new life. She brought with her some of the furnishings she had had in her previous homes. A table, a bed, a dresser were pretty much all she could shrink into her one-room "studio." And some other reminders of her former life—a wall of pictures of her daughter and her daughter's children, two paintings she had done while at the retirement community, a snowscape by one of her old friends, now dead. But no matter what she does to brighten up the place, her mind constantly returns to one thought: This is it, the end of the road, the place where the action ceases. "Old age isn't what you think it will be," she says. Her face, which can almost be pretty when she smiles, turns bitter with the preoccupation that shuts out everything else. "I thought that finally I would be able to do all the things that I had wanted to do. But I can't do anything I used to do. I guess things just don't ever turn out the way you think they will."

Life at The Pines is certainly not what she had in mind for her last years. Here retirement doesn't mean rest, it means withdrawal—a mutual pact with the world that it will ignore you and you will not protest. But, then, why should she protest? She could come and go as she pleased if she could only walk. She has a clean room, neighbors around her who are the same age and probably share her background and concerns. Outsiders would say that she should consider herself lucky to be here at all. It is just that to her all this freedom and luck seem illusory. The world outside is unattainable.

Community and friendship with her neighbors seem to her to be equally illusory. To her these older people are not friends, but rather reminders of the old age she would like to flee—of illness and death. She often recounts an experience she had when she first moved in.

There was an old lady who lived across the hall from her. She was a nice old lady, small and bent into herself. But a bit daffy. "One night when I was asleep," Emily says, "the old woman walked across the hall in her nightgown and got into bed with me. Well, it nearly scared me half to death. I called the night watchman and they took her back to her room. I used to keep my door unlocked, but after that I lock it every night. I never have been able to understand why the old lady did that. She died shortly after."

It was a frightening experience, and it made Emily afraid that she might become like that someday, that her mind would reach back to childhood and forget the years and years she had lived in control of herself. It would be better to forget that such things as senility exist. But seeing the faces around her, she can't forget. The women sitting by the front doors all day doing nothing, silent, looking ahead of them as if they expected someone to come and release them. One woman eventually falls asleep in the same chair every afternoon. Her head falls back and her mouth opens, and she lies there, sleeping in the middle of the day, for everyone coming and going to see.

Mrs. Pierce feels trapped among these tired, abandoned people —and what is worse, she is dependent on them too. She must eat with them and get what little amusement she can with them. Three times a day one of them must push her to the dining room and push her back to her room. But aside from such necessities, her contact with people is fairly limited. She is not interested in most of the activities provided at The Pines, such as slide shows and classes. She never was much of a reader and she has seen the travel slides many times. Besides, she will never be able to go to any of those places, and seeing them depresses her. The residents' council can also do without her participation, although she shares many of the complaints it brings to the management. As a former dietitian she knows how badly the meals are planned, and the food would be better if she had a say. But the management isn't very much interested in changing things. Whenever she asks for something, such as a reading light or getting a spot on her rug cleaned, the answer is always: "The budget doesn't provide for such things."

It infuriates her that she must always be dependent on other people and their whims, that she has become a recipient of charity—even the charity of her own children. Occasionally her son, who lives in another state, comes to visit and her daughter will come and take her out to a family dinner or for a ride. But those times are rare. After all, she tells people in that tone of resignation that is just several steps away from an explosion of anger and hurt, "My children have their own lives. My daughter is busy. She does come to pick up my laundry every week, and that way I get to see my grandchildren." But what is it that her daughter is so busy with, Emily thinks. Doing needlepoint, going out and buying antiques. Things that should hardly be enough to keep her away from her mother. If she could only get out, sit up and drive, she wouldn't need help. Or if she did, she could give something in return. Now she can give nothing. She cannot even get one of them a present without their help. If she could use her old kitchen, where she loved to cook and bake, she could have cookies for her granddaughters. She cannot keep back tears when she thinks of that—that she can give nothing that her granddaughters will remember her by. Just a tired, bitter old woman unable even to hug them properly.

When she thinks of that sour, depressed look sinking into the lines of her face, she reminds herself that she ought to change. But there just seems no reason to do anything. Her arm and her leg become a good excuse for her lack of interest. She no longer takes the paper, she says, because it is too hard for her to turn the pages. She no longer reads, because the book is too heavy. She is supposed to walk as much as possible, but the distance from her room to the porch, or sitting area—just a small distance really, no more than thirty steps—stretches out in front of her into a corridor length. She holds onto her steel walker with one hand, and her breath, going in and out, becomes a steady moan. One foot moving away from the other, tentatively, like a child afraid to move away from its mother. She could probably walk faster if she tried, if she didn't consider each slow step just another sign of failure. But instead of quickening, the pace slows with each tiny accident, each fear that the person holding her, helping her up a step or into a car, will somehow let go and stand there watching her fall, that the hands, gentle at times, will shift and become impatient, pushing where they used to support. Or worse, that they will cease helping altogether and abandon her because she will have become too much trouble.

Her doctor has assured her that if she does her exercises religiously she may regain partial use of her arm and her leg. And twice a week she goes to therapy sessions where he helps her do the exercises that should reawaken her muscles and teach them again to do their appointed tasks. With her good hand she must grasp the fingers of her bad hand, pulling them open and shut, open and shut. Lying down, she must pull her bad leg high, until it reaches her chest. But sometimes her anger at being ill and helpless is so great that when the doctor tells her to exercise more, resentment wells up, blocking the passage of the messages her brain sends through her body.

It is so difficult to adapt to all this. She thought old age would be utopia, a time of rest and relaxation. With one half of her body gone, the simplest things have become impossible. There is no rest when you cannot cut your own food, cook your meals, or get dressed. There is only constant humiliation; if she is in a restaurant and has to go to the bathroom, she cannot even lift herself from the toilet. She tried various things to keep her mind occupied. Like painting. But she gave that up. "I don't have much talent." There was also the constant frustration of her paralysis. "You cannot imagine how many paints I spilled. How much time I spent picking the brushes up off the floor. Just like my pills—you cannot imagine how many pills I've dropped into the toilet trying to get the cap off the bottle with just one hand. Such expensive medicine too," she laments. "I've thought about trying painting again, but there's only this one room and there's no place to work. And it would smell so."

The one thing she still enjoys is bridge, which she plays at least once a week. Emily is classed among the serious bridge players in the "community"—those who really play, as opposed to those who just play at playing. They are special to each other, these women. But their intimacy consists only of the game and chatter —about the food, which has not been good enough lately, or their ailments. Her bridge partners are her only friends. But she would never impose on them. Some have cars, but she would never think of asking for a ride, and they don't volunteer. "After all," she says, "they have their own lives. They don't want to give people rides because they don't want to be responsible if someone falls down or needs help." Nor do they want to be responsible for each other's personal problems. "I would never ask anyone to help me if I had a problem," she explains. "I want to be independent. Besides, you never know what their response will be. You never know what problems they might start to tell you about."

Remaining independent becomes almost an obsession for older people like Mrs. Pierce. For her it is especially difficult to get used to this new life precisely because she had lived such a hard and independent existence when she was young. Her mother died when she was only six months old, and from the time she was a child she worked—for her father and brother, for herself, and later for her husband and children. There was really no time she can remember when she was not active. In the boardinghouse in Iowa where she and her brother were raised by a "very Victorian, very proper Scottish woman" she cleaned. When her father bought his own store and the family moved above it, she kept house. The only time of real freedom she can remember came when she went to college to learn to be a dietician. In those days she was a mischievous, lively girl who disobeyed the rules, sneaking into the dormitory after curfew. She still corresponds with some friends from those days. But many have died. And the person that she was fifty years ago recedes hopelessly when she looks down at her bad hand tightly clutching nothing.

She married late, in her thirties, after almost ten years of independence, working as a dietitian in the East and Midwest. After her marriage she and her husband and only daughter moved to Nebraska, and she gave up work to keep house. That career lasted ten years and ended in divorce. Not an introspective woman, she says simply, "It was better to leave than to keep on bickering." So she came to southern California with her daughter. She has never seen or heard from her ex-husband since, as she has never seen or heard from her brother, although he lives quite near her. What hostility there was when they were children is swept up in her condemnation of him. "He thinks the world owes him a living," is all she will say. Unlike her brother, she doesn't believe the world has ever owed her anything, and it seems disinclined to give out any unsolicited rewards for all her toil. "Perhaps that's why I am so resentful at being sick," she says. "I worked so hard all my life. I sort of thought that when I got old I could let up a little."

As retirement homes go, The Pines is a model institution. The rooms are sunny and airy. And unlike some retirement homes that demand exorbitant entrance fees that are not refundable if the resident is dissatisfied, The Pines costs only $350 a month for a studio and three meals a day. The halls are carpeted and nicely decorated and the facility is owned by a church, presumably dedicated to Christian charity. It is the best of the institutions available to old people who can no longer live alone and whose children don't want to live with them.

The problem with The Pines, of course, is that it is an institution, in which the residents must mold their lives around institutional limits, and where people go because they have been abandoned, by either health or family. Because of this, what is called a "retirement community" becomes an old-folks' home, a place where the elderly wait to die. It is difficult to imagine residents feeling a sense of community when they would much rather be someplace else and when efficiency discourages community living.

Mealtimes at The Pines are an example of such discouragement. They are the only times when people are gathered in the same room, where they could chat leisurely and get to know one another. But there is no time for leisure or for chatting. In order to accommodate all 160 residents, there are two servings of each meal, each lasting forty-five minutes. The dining room staff has half an hour to clear away the dishes from one serving and set tables for the next. Understandably, they rush people through the meal, urging them not to stay and talk but to hurry and go back to their rooms, where they can turn on their televisions and return to their isolation.

Recreation is also arranged in the interests of efficiency. Although six people have volunteered to come to the community and teach painting, no offers have been accepted, because the facility is carpeted and paints would make a mess. The volunteers have suggested laying plastic on the floor, but the administration seems to think that would be too much trouble. The residents will just have to await the completion of a recreational building. That, however, may be a long wait for people with little time, as federal money and loans have been held up by the administration's anti-inflationary budget, and no one knows if and when building will begin.

The only needs that are immediately met are medical. Doctors' visits are a sure way to obtain transportation to the outside. And a volunteer is in charge of getting other people from the local community to offer to drive residents to their doctors. But even this may not last, as the State of California recently passed legislation that would allow a rider to sue the driver if the driver caused an accident and the rider was injured. In Sacramento all volunteer driving has ceased, and it may be difficult in the future to convince people to drive the residents. Despite this law, driving continues for the moment, and illness provides one benefit to people who are confined. It is not astonishing, therefore, that the members of the community are fixated on illness, as it seems to be one of the very few things that call attention to the fact that these old people are still functioning, human organisms.

Other outside contact is limited. About two years ago the recreation director organized several expeditions to local concerts. Five volunteers brought cars, but only six residents showed up. The director then decided that the program was a failure, and there have been no more outings. She did not, perhaps, realize that old people are slow to take charity when they feel they have nothing to give in return. Furthermore, the program could have continued with just those six residents.

There have been other attempts to cater to the residents' needs. A local charitable group comes in several times a week to operate a store where such things as soap and toiletries are sold. A beautician works on a part-time basis. And a local church member, Mrs. Rebecca Alan, has volunteered her services as program director.

Mrs. Alan is a good, charitable woman who enjoys the ego satisfaction of helping others. She has nothing else to do with her time, as her children are grown and her husband works all day. Charity is therefore her business, even though she has no background in geriatric work and admittedly finds it difficult to talk to many of the residents, whose indifference to her efforts often astounds her. But she has initiated some programs. Once a week an outside church or high school group comes to The Pines to give a presentation. Every third Wednesday night there is a birthday cake at each meal serving for all the residents who have had birthdays that month. Bingo meets regularly on Wednesday night, a book-discussion group meets on Monday, and an exercise class on Thursdays—the latter events run by volunteers.

Through Mrs. Alan's efforts a group of junior high school students came to the facility every week of the last school year to visit with residents and run errands for them. Although Mrs. Alan considers the program to have been quite successful, the students themselves were rather discouraged. "It got to be kind of a drag after a while," one girl explained, " 'cause you'd go around and ask people if you could do anything for them and they would say they were busy, that we should come back another time. Just a few people seemed really glad to see us. So we'd keep on visiting them, and then we'd feel guilty 'cause we weren't seeing other people." Without supervision or guidance in understanding the problems of the elderly, who are unexcited about being dependent on children, the students came less and less frequently. The recreational director chalked it up to end-of-school slack.

Despite such problems, Mrs. Alan is delighted with her achievements and would like to do more, even though she feels a different class or program every day would not be necessary. "There are lots of people here who lead their own independent lives," she explains, "and they wouldn't need that much activity." Unfortunately, the majority of the residents at The Pines don't get out much and for them time is unalterably slow to pass. In spite of carpets and nice accommodations, as one woman complained to a volunteer, she and many others feel miserable and bored. But Mrs. Alan is not a woman to rush into things. And when that same volunteer suggested that there should be more programs because people are indeed bored, Mrs. Alan's only response was, "What's wrong with being bored?"

Mrs. Alan says that her aim is to turn The Pines into "a place where I would want my own mother to live" (rather than a place where she wouldn't mind living herself). Her attitude contains a patronizing quality usually present in attempts to decide what is best for others. She has, for instance, created a residents' council, but she refers to its members as "my assistants" and "my spokesmen." The council has no power to enforce its decisions, and, as she says, serves mainly to approve her plans and occasionally present suggestions. She is proud of the council, just as a mother is proud of a child who finally learns to walk.

It is not surprising that, as the recipients of such patronizing charity, the residents have so little contact with one another and so little enthusiasm for "community living." To ask people who have been raised in a society that discourages dependence to suddenly lose everything and then adjust to both that loss and a whole new way of life is asking too much.

Such an adjustment would be more likely if psychiatric help were available to residents. But The Pines provides no such treatment, nor does the administration suggest that people with problems seek outside psychiatric care. In this the institution is typical of the retirement communities, which view the traumas and loneliness of old age as purely physical problems. According to San Francisco psychiatrist Dr. Elliot Feigenbaum, an expert on geriatric psychiatry:

The general idea in retirement communities is that if you have a psychiatric problem related to old age, it is based on organic change. Obviously, a psychiatrist is not going to be able to change most organic problems, so no one bothers to get the older person psychiatric care. In geriatric institutions most people look at the problems of older people as manifestations of senility. And to them there is no question about what you do about senility. You do nothing.

Even if people are more sophisticated, and don't think those problems are caused by senility, you run into another myth about old age and that is that old people are just not suited for psychiatric intervention. Freud once said that if you're over forty, you're not suited to be a psychoanalytic patient because your defenses are so firmly fixed that you're just so set and concretized that nothing is going to help. Now that's not really true. Even if the patient is not suitable for psychoanalysis that doesn't mean that they are not suitable for some kind of psychiatric treatment.

People like Mrs. Pierce desperately need help in adjusting to old age, illness, and life in a retirement home. The meager activities that are available are not enough. Without support, people live together but isolated from each other.

The spot on Mrs. Pierce's carpet is still there. Despite her complaints, no one has come to clean the rug. But, she says, "Those are the kind of people who run this place. When I ask, the manager says that he has spots on his carpets too. Imagine people like that! If he wants to live like that, that's all right, but I don't want to live that way."

She is considering taking a vacation, getting away for a while. She has a friend she could visit in Florida, but there are so many steps at her friend's home that it would be difficult, and the woman is also old and ailing and could not help her. It would be too hard to maneuver alone. There are also friends in southern California whom she hasn't seen since she left. Maybe next year she'll go for a week or two.

Chapter Nine

Old Age

Affluence and civilization have not advanced the position of the 21 million people over sixty-five in America. The elderly represent 10 percent of the population, and because of increased longevity that percentage is growing. Yet, in spite of the fact that we try to keep people alive until they reach a ripe old age, the everyday environment bombards older citizens with the fact that they are unwanted, helpless, ugly, and unpleasant. Forced retirement in a society that does not value idleness means an end to work even though one may be perfectly capable of working. Mobility means that family and friends have traveled widely and may be far away from an older relation in time of need. So old people are shunted off to retirement homes and adult communities—euphemisms for the old-folks' home. If they are too poor to afford such luxuries, they are left in old, decrepit neighborhoods or sent to state mental institutions.

The ethic of industrial capitalism eats away at respect for the aged. The old person is no longer the giver of knowledge and the laws, as was true in less advanced societies. The advancement of technology is not dependent on an oral tradition or on highly developed craftsmanship. Technology is constantly changing, and the skills and knowledge acquired over a lifetime are less important than what is new. As the elderly lose their status as purveyors of tradition, they lose their worth to the community. Unless they are accorded another and equally meaningful role.

The older person in contemporary society, robbed of any position in the present, often has no alternative but to seek refuge in his or her personal past. The ability to relive the past may serve as an escape from a rather unpleasant present. Psychiatrists point out that a person who has inner resources and the capacity to relive old memories will have an easier time adjusting to retirement and inactivity. But in choosing to find solace in the past, old people may find themselves in yet another double bind caused by societal prejudice. Those elderly persons who fondly recount old memories and cling to the past are regarded even more suspiciously than those who cling tenaciously to the present.

When older people react negatively to the way that they are treated, becoming irritable and contentious, they are to blame for the problem, says Alvin Toffler in his book *Future Shock* (p. 19). Because older people, manifest such unbecoming conduct, Toffler suggests the following solution to *their* problem:

Older people are even more likely to react strongly against any further acceleration of change. There is a solid mathematical basis for the observation that age often correlates with conservatism; time passes more swiftly for the old. . . .
Whatever the reasons, any acceleration of change that has the effect of crowding more situations into the experiential channel in a given interval is magnified in the perception of the older person. As the rate of change in society speeds up, more and more older people feel the difference keenly. They too become dropouts, withdrawing into a private environment, cutting off as many contacts as possible with the fast-moving outside world, and finally, vegetating until death. We may never solve the psychological problems of the aged until we find the means—through biochemistry or re-education—to alter their time sense, or to provide structured enclaves for them in which the pace of life is controlled, and even, perhaps, regulated according to a "sliding scale" calendar that reflects their own subjective perception of time. (pp. 39, 40)

The force behind this statement appears to be the much disputed (but nonetheless popular) belief that the sometimes erratic behavior of older people is totally a result of organic deteriora-

tion rather than unfavorable social conditions. The former opinion, says Dr. Julius Weissman, a psychologist and specialist on
the problems of the aged in Manhattan, has it that aging and the
decline of emotional and mental capacities is due to a natural
and, at present, unchangeable process:

*There are two theories in the field of aging. One is that there is a
natural process of disengagement as one gets older. Some people will
dispute this theory and say that it is not a natural process but that it
is rather an enforced, involuntary process. And even people who have
the means are not doing it on a voluntary basis, but at least those
well-to-do people who form colonies for older people in Florida have
some options.*

Although nature is involved, it seems hard to believe, given
what we know of societal attitudes, that the disengagement
spoken of above and the difficult behavior of the elderly are
always solely results of biological processes. Yet despite what we
know about how prejudice affects behavior, the older person is
often regarded with outright contempt or with the condescension
with which an adult approaches a rather annoying, naughty
child. The older person is alone, and when you're shunned not
because of *who* you are but *what* you are, you're truly lonely.
The process of aging is often one accompanied by a series of
uncompensated losses.*

For the men and women who have spent their lives working,
retirement may be the first such loss, and its consequences are
merely a preview of things to come. The compensation for forced
retirement is supposed to be the privilege of leisure after toiling
for many years. An older person, armed with pension, savings,
and social security, is finally allowed to take it easy and do
whatever he or she wants whenever he or she wants. Few people,
however, have the money to enjoy old age. Social security (which
averages $129 per month to retirees) certainly does not allow the
elderly much luxury, and meager pensions, if a retired person is

* These losses may account for the fact that of the 20,000 who commit
suicide each year in America one-third are elderly persons.

lucky enough to collect, are decreasing in value in a time of runaway inflation. Half of the elderly have an income of less than $75 a week. Furthermore, most people who have the money to relax practice the social ethic that one should be constantly doing things that have a definite monetary value. Because of this they cannot simply lie back and let life pass by.

Retired people often find that there is no place for them and that they have lost the respect they used to have when they were contributing members of society. Executives, for example, suffer acutely in retirement, says James Clovis of the consulting firm Handy Associates:

There used to be pre-retirement counseling for older executives about to retire. But most men didn't want any part of it. They all thought, Well, I'll get a part-time job, or I'll get my real estate license or sell insurance. And they found that after they retired and had two or three months of fun, they wanted to get back into the marketplace, and they weren't accepted. There was nothing for an older person to do.

Losing one's position in the world, and consequently the esteem of those who still work, brings a loss of self-esteem. When people begin to feel worthless, abandoned, and lonely for the world to which they had grown accustomed, they understandably begin to withdraw from social contacts. Retired men and women become cantankerous. Even were they to be accepted by those who are still working, they may no longer want to be around successful people, because they will then feel all the more like failures. Such feelings of worthlessness can often affect men more seriously than women, says Dr. Weissman, because men have been socialized to take their identity from work. Once that identity is lost, a man can become emotionally disturbed:

The issue of independence is much more severe in older men than in older women. When the men break down they become very dependent. And it is harder for them to regain a sense of independence. When women are in the hospital, they can be restored to functioning much more quickly because they can get back their skills more easily.

The difficulties in adjusting to retired life can affect the relationship between a husband and wife. The retired man is suddenly home all day with his wife. The wife, accustomed to being alone during the day, finds her husband constantly underfoot, and she is irritated by his presence. She wishes he would go out and do something and leave her in peace. Feeling this rejection and sensing that there is little to be done to remedy the situation, a man becomes morose. A rift develops between wife and husband, the man is not comfortable anywhere, and there is nowhere for him to turn.

Retired people, some suggest, could turn to other retired people for the support that would alleviate their loneliness and disaffection. And, indeed, retirement communities—where 500,000 people live, including those in lifetime-care facilities—comprised solely of the elderly, are often said to be the way out of the loneliness of old age.

The excuse for the segregation of the elderly is that they would prefer to live among other older people. Older people are said, for instance, to dislike children. Living in a neighborhood that is populated by young children, the myth continues, grates on the older person's nerves. So why not help the elderly by building communities where children are not allowed—where no one under forty-five, in fact, is allowed? This would immensely please the elderly, developers say. In all my talks with old people, however, I was unable to find one person who did not like to have young children and younger people around. One older woman living at a retirement community explained that other older people do not like children, although she likes children and, as it happens, so do her neighbors. The myth justifies segregation. We, the young, do not like the old, so we project our dislike onto them.

The adult community is created as a solution for people with whom we do not wish to deal. Rossmoor, for example, is one of the growing, nationwide chains of "adult living" communities. There are no children allowed and no one under forty-five may live there. If an older person can manage to put $2,000 down and pay monthly maintenance charges, he or she can buy a $22,000 unit in the typically suburban environment Rossmoor offers. No one walking on the streets, no one chatting in the gardens—a home for every elderly person and a lot of activities to keep their minds off things. Pools, crafts, cards, occasional concerts. "If you are lonely," one old woman commented, "with all this to keep you busy, then it's your own fault." The Rossmoor philosophy seems to suggest that if your exterior needs are met, your interior needs should fall into place; and the fact that you are segregated from society like a leper, even though the leper colony is rather comfortable, should not bother you.

But many people are bothered. "I don't know what's wrong with me. There are all sorts of things to do here," one resident said, "and I still feel bored and lonely." Some of those who cannot adjust to all they are offered in adult communities move back to the city and a more natural environment. While others languish in their loneliness. A swimming pool cannot make up for exile; and even though younger people may think all older people are alike, old people do not necessarily share the same interests and ambitions.

The loneliness that arises from the awareness of being an unwanted member of society increases as the older person loses those who were close. The morning paper often brings the news of a friend or acquaintance who has died. And little by little, those with whom life was shared disappear. The worst is the death of a spouse.

Five years after the death of his wife Howard Adams has still not been able to get over the persistent feeling that there is no one in the world who will ever care for him again. The couple was childless—although he and his wife had always wanted children—and the only person he was ever really close to was his wife. But she died of cancer. He had been retired for two years before that happened. And for two years the two had lived frugally on his social security. He had never, because of some bureaucratic mix-up that he has never been able to comprehend, collected the pension he feels was owed him. So there was not much money for him and his wife to help them enjoy their old age. Howard's health was not too good; having been a house painter had weakened his lungs. After his wife's illness and death his financial situation was disastrous.

During the following year Howard struggled to keep their small house. But taxes increased and he could no longer afford it. Reluctantly, he sold the house to pay off debts and moved into a small apartment in a not very cheerful section of San Francisco. Even that became too expensive, and he was forced to move to a room in one of the hotels in the city's Tenderloin area, a grim neighborhood frequented by bums and those old people, like himself, who had nowhere else to go.

He has a small room that's supposed to be cleaned daily but isn't, since most of the hotel's elderly residents are too depressed and apathetic to complain.

During the day Howard sleeps a lot or sits downstairs in the lobby watching people outside pass by. They stare in at him briefly and then quickly go on their way. It is common in this hotel to pass the time this way—looking outside watching life pass by. There are other old men and women in the hotel but they do not often converse, except to chat about their failing health or the weather.

Christmas and holidays are the worst times. The family that owns the hotel have a supper for themselves, but the residents aren't invited. "It's a shame," the hotel manager's wife says, "that these old people have to stay by themselves during the holidays. But I suppose if they're lonely it's because they want it that way." Neither this woman nor the family that owns the place has ever thought of preparing even a small get-together for the residents at holiday times.

There is a senior citizens center in the area, and every once in a while someone in the hotel goes there. But Howard has never gone. The walk is too difficult, and besides he has been away from people so long that he wouldn't know how to behave. At times he sees someone who seems to be a nice person walking by the hotel and wishes he would come in for a chat. But, then, he tells himself, that would be impossible. It's against hotel policy to let strangers come in, and the manager is right there in the lobby. They might, the owners say, upset the guests.

Mrs. de Angelo lives only ten miles away from her children. Her husband has been dead for five years. He and she had worked hard all their lives, and they had both looked forward to retirement as a time when they could finally relax. They had even planned to take a trip to their native Italy, where they had come from forty years before to make a new life in America. They had indeed done well. Her husband, at his death, left her a good income and a large house to live in for the rest of her days. But the money and the house could not compensate for her loss. The house was too big for her, yet she didn't want to sell it, as some of her friends had done after their husbands' deaths. That would mean moving into an apartment, and then, if she became ill, to her children's house. At least, she has the comfort of knowing that, unlike other children, hers would care for her if she were sick. They would not, she is sure, put her into one of those places for old people.

In the daytime Mrs. de Angelo travels by bus to a senior citizens center nearby. She plays cards and occasionally uses the crafts room to make a gift for one of her grandchildren. The days are not so bad. It's the nights that are hard to get through alone in that big house. If her children lived closer to her she could baby-sit once or twice a week. But they are too far to come and fetch her just for that. Sometimes the noises at night scare her. And there have been phone calls that have upset her. Twice she had to have her number changed because of those phone calls—a man saying obscene words to her. It would have been unheard of in Italy in the village where she grew up. Such things never happened. But, then, in the village where she grew up nothing ever changed. You grew old and died among family and friends. You may have been poor, but you were never friendless, even when you were old. Sitting at home alone at nights, Mrs. de Angelo thinks often of Italy. America, she says to herself, may be fine for the young. But for the old it is not so good.

The death of a loved one is always difficult to accept. When you are old, however, it is particularly difficult to adjust to living by yourself, as the five million old people who live alone must do. In the past the death of a spouse did not necessarily affect the relationships between the survivors and their large families and friendly communities. Today communities are no longer friendly, and families are scattered over wide areas. Children, when they are grown, have their own lives and often live far from parents. Thus if widows or widowers want to live near their children, they must either move to new locations (abandoning old and familiar places and people), where it will probably be difficult to meet people their own age, or they must forget about living near their offspring and content themselves with phone calls and infrequent visits. Whatever they choose, they may feel they have become burdens to their children.

Since women tend to marry older men and outlive them, it is most often women who lose their husbands, making widowhood a common fate for a woman growing old.* Many women have never in their lives lived by themselves. They have had family around them, and then husbands, and in most cases growing children to occupy their days. It is a terrible shock, says Mrs. Ann Parks, to have to face the fact that just when her children are grown and she feels she and her husband could have time together, he is dead:

I am very lonely for my husband. I have had a male companion for so long, since I left my family's house. I just can't get used to that— not having him. The period of acute loneliness, when I thought I'd crawl the walls, has passed. But I still miss that every-day intimacy, sharing the little things that happen every day. It's having intimacy that I miss. Someone with whom you can be completely yourself.

* One out of six women over twenty-one is a widow, thus constituting a population of 10 million widows in America.

Because intimacy, the freedom to be completely yourself, has traditionally been limited almost exclusively to male-female relationships, or to relationships within a nuclear family, recovery from the shock of the death of a husband may be dependent on the support of children. Like many other women, Mrs. Parks says she depended on her children after her husband died, but their help, as is so frequently the case, could be counted on only for brief periods because they live so far from their mother.

To the loss of a spouse and the absence of children is added a loss of self-esteem, because of society's view of the elderly. As Mrs. Parks says, "I don't even like to think about how old I am; it scares me." Similarly, the friendship of other widows and older people scares her, for typically, she does not like old people, even though she herself is old. "I have a lot of younger friends," says Mrs. Parks. "I have some older friends, but old people complain so much. They talk about their aches and pains, and I just don't want to hear that."

Disparaging remarks made by widows about older women are motivated not only by dislike of the aged but by women's traditional socialization. Women of that age have been taught not to value one another's company and to prefer the company of any man to that of the most remarkable woman. Too late to be much affected by women's liberation, many older women do not relate well to other women. "I am too old to change," one woman explained to me when I asked why she had never thought of sharing an apartment with another woman to ease the loneliness she felt since the death of her husband. A widow may be terribly lonely, but she will suffer rather than depend on another woman for the support and security she has been taught to seek in a man.

Still, another woman like herself may be her only possible source of stable companionship. Couples with whom she and her husband have been close may not accept her as a widow. She may think that because she is old, she is no longer a threat to the wife, but to the woman, she may be a rival still. Lynn Caine, a widow in her forties, whose book about her own experiences after the loss of her husband documents so many of the problems of widowhood, comments on the pain she felt at being excluded from get-togethers to which she was always invited when her husband was alive:

I was really stricken when I found out that a very dear friend had not invited me to her annual Sunday-after-Thanksgiving dinner. This had been a tradition among our little group for a good ten years. There were eight of us, four couples, who always got together for dinner that Sunday night. The year after Martin died, I wasn't invited. In my naïveté, in my self-centeredness, I thought at first that the dinner had been canceled because the hostess thought I would be too sad. But no, the dinner had been held. Instead of the Caines, another couple had been invited. Lynn Caine, widow, was no longer a desirable dinner guest.*

Even if friends do not abandon her, a widow experiences a certain awkwardness in having couple friends. A widow, for example, may feel that she should be financially independent. She will wish, therefore, to pay for herself if she goes out with a couple, or at times she may wish to treat the couple to an outing. But, chivalry has it, a woman alone should be paid for. A couple may not invite a woman out simply because they don't want to pay for her or because arguments and discomfort ensue about who is going to pay the bill if they offer to. Added to this is the problem of repaying couple friends for dinner invitations. Many women feel when they become widows that their role as social initiator is over and that without a man they have little to offer, and so they are reluctant to invite people to their homes. They then find themselves in the embarrassing position of being always on the receiving end of a friendship with nothing, they believe, to give in return.

Widowers do not seem to feel the same sense of inadequacy as widows. If a man is a widower and is aggressive enough, he can initiate social contacts with couples after the death of his wife. For example, Joseph Stein, a lawyer and widower in

* *Widow,* p. 179.

Boston, has dealt with his wife's death by keeping himself busy with friends almost every night and weekend.

After my wife died, and after the first month of friends coming over and relatives staying, there was a sudden silence of the telephone. No one called to invite me anywhere. And I felt abandoned by all my friends. But I began to call them and say, "Why haven't you called?" It was as though they avoided me because of death. But once I started calling I kept on. Now if people don't call me I call them and arrange to go out. That way I don't have to be home alone so much.

It is perhaps men like Mr. Stein, who are used to the role of aggressor in the hostile environment of the business world, who are best able to overcome the sense of rejection by friends that is experienced when a spouse dies.

A widow may look hopefully to the prospect of remarriage as a stable relationship to replace both the husband and social life she has lost. The fulfillment of that hope is, however, rather unlikely. Because many men die before women, there are fewer men of the same age to go around. And 70 percent of all men over sixty-five are married, compared with 30 percent of all women over sixty-five. The widower or older man may be besieged by widows who wish to remarry. With four or five women to every man, the chances for remarriage for a widow are slight. Older men, furthermore, have the freedom to marry younger women. Society may look askance at the sixty- or seventy-year-old man married to the forty- or fifty-year-old woman. But the man may still laugh in society's face and marry the younger woman. The reverse—the older woman marrying a man many years her junior—is almost unheard of.

The problems of sexual frustration increase the loneliness with which a widow or widower has to cope. The solution to this problem is especially difficult because of society's outmoded ideas about the sexuality of the elderly. Popular belief has it that once a person passes the age of fifty, he or she is no longer susceptible to sexual desire. If one is beyond sixty, the current notion seems to be, the suggestion is laughable. An older woman or man who does feel such stirrings is regarded as perverse and lecherous. The prohibitions against sexuality in the elderly make the man or woman who still recognizes these human feelings feel more alone, as Simone de Beauvoir writes in *The Coming of Age:*

The elderly person conforms to the conventional ideal that is offered for his acceptance. . . . He inwardly accepts the watchwords of propriety and continence imposed by the community. He is ashamed of his own desires and he denies having them; he refuses to be a lecherous old man in his own eyes, or a shameless old woman. He fights against his sexual drives to the point of thrusting them back into his unconscious mind. (p. 324)

Keeping sexual desire unconscious is, however, particularly difficult in today's world of liberalized sex.

If an older woman wants to regain her independence and make new friends after the death of her husband, and live on her own, she will find that many avenues through which young people gain self-confidence, respect, and companionship are closed to her. Discrimination on the basis of age is a policy in many businesses even though it's illegal. Women and men over forty or fifty have a hard time getting work. Furthermore, many women have never worked, or if they have, it was years before. They have been out of the marketplace for twenty or thirty years.*

Having a job and a place where a woman feels she is contributing can help immensely, Lynn Caine writes in her book *Widow:*

I can't stress enough how important my job was to me. It was not simply that it was interesting and paid a salary that enabled me to get along. More than that, it gave structure to my life. I had to get up in the morning, get dressed and get to work. Even at my lowest times, when I was torn by anxieties and fears, the very fact of having

---

* There are also strict provisions in the Social Security legislation preventing a person from earning over a certain sum of money. A person exceeding that amount must forfeit part or all of Social Security benefits, depending on earnings.

a job gave me emotional security. I belonged somewhere. No matter how alone I was in the world, I had a place where I belonged. Work to do. (pp. 156–157)

There is always volunteer work. But many women, educated in a society that believes work is work only if you get a paycheck, believe such activities to be worthless. Older people could make wonderful use of their time if our society placed a significant emphasis on contemplation and learning. But we value activity rather than thought and education.

One way to be free of the problems of old age is to pretend not to be old. Polly Bergen in her national ads suggests that her cosmetics will do a lot to cure the symptoms of age if used early enough. A few privileged women (and some men) have the money for plastic surgery. For from $2,000 up, lines are lifted, wrinkles smoothed, and according to noted Beverly Hills plastic surgeon Dr. Maury Parkes, the problems of aging may be lessened.

You get old and you get depressed. You are alone, people have died and you look in the mirror and you look awful. And you feel more depressed. So you don't want to go out and see people. And then you feel more depressed. But you still don't go out and see people. And then you look in the mirror and you feel still worse. So it becomes a vicious circle.

Plastic surgery is super. It makes people feel better. It can change their lives. Women find men they never thought they would find. We live in a society of youth, and it makes people look more attractive.

This solution, of course, requires constant touch-ups and cannot be accomplished in one visit to the doctor. It is available only to the rich and to those who are not too old. The risks of surgery and face lifts increase as the age of the patient increases. But what about those whose faces are revamped and who find companions because of their newly acquired ability to attract? How does one feel being loved for a false image rather than for the person one really is?

In America we do not suggest that the widow immolate herself on her husband's pyre, but the role we assign to the older woman whose husband is dead can be nearly as fatal. If society has decreed that they are useless without a man, women feel that they might as well be dead. Death is at least quicker, some women believe, than an extended old age with nothing to look forward to.

Perhaps the loneliest fate reserved for the elderly is the life in the many retirement homes and convalescent hospitals to which those who are too weak or friendless are sent. In the best of these retirement homes the old are treated as bothersome creatures who should do what they are told and be silent about the conditions in which they live. In the worst they are treated no better than animals, left to sit in their own excrement, tied to chairs so they will not wander off, referred to by number when they are lucky (or unlucky) enough to attract attention.

Recent investigations of the nationwide nursing home industry and New York State nursing homes reveal the extent of such conditions. When the New York State Health Department made spot checks of New York City's nursing homes in 1973 it found two-thirds of those institutions had "serious operating deficiencies." Provisional figures released in 1975 from an interim report by the U.S. Department of Health, Education and Welfare in their study of long-term-care facilities indicated that in the 23,000 nursing homes in the nation, lack of compliance with nursing-home safety codes "reflected serious concern and implications."

Although not all old people live in such institutions, experts estimate that 25 percent of the elderly will spend some time in a nursing home. Homes for the aged vary in purpose from the retirement homes, designed for people who are not disabled or only partially disabled, to the convalescent hospital, where full nursing and medical care is available. Most frequently older people do not choose to go to a retirement home. They are forced to do so. Their old neighborhoods decline and it is too dangerous for them to continue living there. They are ill and need a certain amount of nursing care, and their children cannot or will not provide them with that treatment. Their spouses die and they simply feel they no longer belong in society. One seventy-five-year-old woman who is currently on a waiting list for one of the better retirement homes in Illinois explained that she decided to apply for admission because she is getting on in years and, having no children, she wants to be in a place where she can have life care should she become suddenly ill.

Life care is a major concern for the elderly. Many nursing homes do not provide such care. If a person in a retirement home becomes too ill to stay in the home and must go to a hospital, that person's room may be given away. Should the ailing one recover, he or she must find a new place to live. Thus nursing homes that provide life care are at a premium. This concern for care in cases of serious illness is a manifestation of the difficult plight of old men and women who cannot count on anyone to care for them when they are ill.

The price of care in retirement homes varies. In some homes the residents pay not only entrance fees and monthly maintenance charges but they must also agree to leave much of their assets to the home. Should a resident decide to leave the home, he or she faces forfeiture of assets. Other homes ask only monthly fees. For those who can afford neither alternative, there is always the state mental institution.

Whatever the fee, however, the nursing home business provides a good opportunity for profit. Aside from high payment by residents for what is often poor, if not cruel, treatment, nursing homes receive funds from federal and state governments. Medicaid reimbursement formulas give nursing homes the cost of care plus a 10 percent profit based on those costs. In 1974 Medicaid payments to nursing homes in New York State alone came to $600 million. And investigations allege that many of these payments were not justified by actual treatment, and that the state and federal governments were billed for care to nonexistent patients.

The atmosphere in the very best retirement homes is not conducive to smooth adjustment and to the formation of new friendships. Very few people are acquainted with the residents in the home chosen for them. Their children move them close enough so that they can visit their aging parents when it is convenient, and far enough away so that their parents aren't a constant bother. Or whatever home is nearest and has a vacancy is selected. The shock of moving into the retirement-home environment is one from which an older man or woman accustomed to having his or her own home may not recover.

In her excellent paper "Hello in There," concerning her experience in a nursing home, Judith Klein, companion to an eighty-six-year-old woman, Mrs. Davis, writes about Mrs. Davis' introduction to her new life:

She [Mrs. Davis] had married late in life a widower with one daughter. . . . Her step-daughter lived in another state. Mrs. Davis later, and for many years, lived with a close friend and colleague. When the friend died, Mrs. Davis lived alone in an apartment building where some of her friends still live. More than a year ago, her closest friend noticed that Mrs. Davis seemed unusually confused, and in her concern she asked the director of a nursing home for advice. The director met Mrs. Davis on two occasions and based on these meetings, she recommended that Mrs. Davis come to live in the adult home. But Mrs. Davis was not eager to move in. She reluctantly signed the necessary admittance papers at the urging of her trust fund executor. Two weeks later a niece and nephew came, and that weekend Mrs. Davis' apartment was emptied and she was moved, with a few selected belongings, to the home. "She was stunned," one employee said. "She just stood in my office and watched them carry her things upstairs and arrange them in her room. She was very confused; it all happened so fast. I felt sorry for her." She was angry with her friend for a long time, and no relatives have visited since. (pp. 6, 7)

After such an experience Mrs. Davis, Ms. Klein recounts, became more and more confused. She believed things were taken away from her, as indeed they were by a staff that worried more about their own convenience than the residents' comfort. She was put on Thorazine (a heavy tranquilizer often used for the acutely

mentally ill), again to make caring for her easier.* Although
Ms. Klein was hired to take Mrs. Davis on outings, tranquiliza-
tion was still administered before Ms. Klein came for her daily
visits. Thus Mrs. Davis was practically asleep and behaving
strangely (due to side effects of Thorazine) when it came time to
go out for a walk or other excursion. The nursing home would
not, at Ms. Klein's request, stop tranquilizing Mrs. Davis, although they did occasionally reduce the amount of tranquilizers
before the old woman was to see her companion. Ms. Klein suggested that patients might be better off without sedation: "I
asked the director if the doctor had seen my report (recommend-
ing that patients not be so heavily tranquilized). The director
said she and the others had read it, but it was decided not to give
it to the doctor because prescribing medicine was his domain
and he would, most probably, have been offended by my recom-
mendations" (p. 31).

Because the staff and directors of many nursing homes want
the "inmates" to be as little trouble as possible and remain quiet
and docile, the fact that residents relate only superficially, if at
all, to one another is perfectly normal, and little is done to improve things. Even when a facility hires a social director—which
is infrequent—the mental state of the residents can preclude
improvements.

Older people have absorbed the image society has of them,
and they feel valueless. They are afraid, because of their low self-
esteem, to open up to others and thus show their weaknesses.
Many older people were also raised in an era when the social
ethic was one that said you should not confide weakness to
others. Weakness was looked down upon, and so one hid one's
feelings. As one resident of a nursing home commented, "I think

* A Senate subcommittee of the Senate Special Committee on Aging
studied the misuse of drugs in the nation's nursing homes and reported
that "There is ample evidence that patients are given tranquilizers to keep
them quiet and make them easier to handle." The committee called tranquilizers "chemical straightjackets." It also reported that many nursing home
operators receive kickbacks from pharmacists or pharmacies equivalent to
25 percent of the drugs used.

loneliness is sheer self-indulgence and selfishness." With the prospect of facing such a rebuke to the confession of one's emotions, many older people prefer to remain silent.

Directors of old people's homes share the feelings of the society in which they function. As Dr. Martin Berezin, a psychiatrist in Boston who specializes in the problems of the elderly, comments, "Unfortunately, the attitude of many nursing homes is that the best old people are dead old people." If their residents cannot be dead, in which case they would no longer bring a profit, they can at least be tranquilized until they act like ghosts, or treated as though they don't exist. The concern, again, of those who run such institutions is most often their own convenience, and the excuse of the patient's health is generally a rationalization to do what is easiest and least expensive. Thus when Ms. Klein quit her job as companion to Mrs. Davis she was told by the director of the home that the next companion chosen for the old woman would be instructed not to interfere in nursing home procedure as Ms. Klein had done.

Tomorrow is my last day.

Mrs. Davis and I went shopping today and she bought a lovely black and white straw hat with a wide brim.

There has been no mention of a companion to take my place, although I do know that several people have been interviewed. The job will be more specific now, and, as I understand it, close personal involvement with the residents will, somehow, be discouraged, because, as the director explained, close friendships make it painful for the residents when the companion has to leave. (p. 35)

Because life in a nursing home represents the final abandonment by the world and purported loved ones, death is a particularly frightening subject that is generally avoided. The experience of dying, when no one loves you and cares for you when you are alive, is the final experience of loneliness. It means oblivion. No one will remember you when you are gone and you might as well have never existed. Not only does the world shun those who are ill and dying but residents of nursing homes typically avoid contact with the ill and dying in their midst. There is a woman, Mrs. Willis, who comes to visit the patients in the hospital at Heritage Home in San Francisco because the residents there refuse to visit anyone who may be terminally ill.

The nursing home seems to crystallize what is going on in society at large—the denial of the humanity of the elderly. Old age is in such places a most excruciatingly lonely experience. Even if the retirement home is moderately comfortable and the care efficient, it is no more, to an old person, than a fancy prison. Some old people would even prefer a prison sentence, in which there is hope of early release for good behavior. The sentence to a retirement home, however, appears final. We seem, with our civilized methods, as Jules Henry argues in *Culture Against Man*, far worse than savages when it comes to the treatment of the old:

In many primitive societies the soul is imagined to leave the body at death or just prior to it; here, on the other hand, society drives out the remnants of the soul of the institutionalized old person while it struggles to keep his body alive. Routinization, inattention, careless-ness, and the deprivation of communication, the chance to talk, to respond, to read, to see the pictures on the wall, to be called by one's name rather than "you" or no name at all—are the ways in which millions of once useful but now obsolete human beings are detached from their selves long before they are lowered into the grave. (p. 393)

Considering the attitudes of our society toward the process of aging and the aged, the fear that one's old age will be spent alone and forgotten cannot be simply dismissed as an unfounded delu-sion. A lonely old age is indeed what many people have in store for them. Whether loneliness is aggravated by life in an "adult community," by retirement, or by widowhood and loss of friends, it is an inevitable outcome of the process of growth in a culture that teaches its citizens, from childhood onward, that old people are irritable, worthless, and crazy. It is no wonder that the young treat the old with such callousness and that the old regard the young with suspicion and anger. Nor is it astonishing that the old regard each other as senile, troublesome, and useless.

Part Three
The Loneliness
Business

The problem of loneliness is becoming more and more pervasive. Millions of people are searching for solutions that will put an end to the emptiness that threatens to engulf them. The traditional solution to loneliness has been the immersion in an intimate relationship with another person and membership in a larger, tightly knit community—or, in lieu of an intimate relationship, absorption in the community.

In the past, people either married and stayed married, or they never married and were spinsters and bachelors for a major portion of their adult lives. In either case they lived in social situations in which they were part of a definite community, linked together by family affiliation, work interest, place of residence, and common beliefs and rituals. Being part of a couple did not totally determine their status in a group.

In a tightly knit community, united not only by superficial social or financial interests but by blood ties, economic interdependency, traditional and religious custom, and place of residence, people's bonds with one another were dependent upon a whole array of factors. Being part of a couple was but one of the links among many others in a solidly welded social network. When one's status in a couple changed, because of death or a rare divorce, one's membership in the larger group might not be affected. Similarly, if one had never been part of a couple, but shared nevertheless in the community, that sharing might last as long as one chose. A relationship with one other special person might have been lacking, but this lack did not necessarily cause the forfeiture of other social relationships.

Life in large families, small towns, and urban neighborhoods, furthermore, provided a common ground that gave people the *permission* to form relationships. We have been taught not to speak to strangers. We need mechanisms through which to approach those unfamiliar to us. At dances, encounter groups, or meetings where strangers come to hear a common speaker or to engage in common activity, people will often remain silent until a leader comes into the room and by his or her presence gives permission for people to begin intercommunication. Following a leader is one of the mechanisms by which permission for inter-relating is given.

A second method by which people overcome strangeness and gain the confidence necessary to approach one another is through participation in a common social network—a large family, a group, a neighborhood or work-related community. Going to the same job, worshiping at the same church, living in the same close neighborhood, shopping at the same small stores—even repeatedly encountering people as they walk past your house or wait for a bus at your stop—can give you the sense that you belong somewhere. Such commonality gives you the permission to smile at the person walking down the street, to say hello to the person sitting next to you in church or at a town meeting, to talk to a person going to the same butcher or baker. The regularity and frequency of encounter leads to a nodding acquaintanceship that allows for the development of friendship.* Frequent contact also allows you to test the safeness of the potential relationship.

In the past, engaging in the occupations and interests necessary for physical and emotional survival, people met other people who would be important to them in their personal lives. And the more human scale of social, neighborhood, and work institutions was conducive to the forging of interpersonal relationships.

Today many community groupings that provided peripheral

---

* It is interesting that in an increasingly violent society we are asked to form relationships with people we do not know at all. Thus not only do we have to worry about possible emotional conflicts with a new acquaintance, we also have to worry about our physical safety.

relationships and the common ground necessary for the formation of new relationships have disappeared. And finding people with whom to relate, far from being an outgrowth of social and work activity, becomes a major occupation in and of itself. As soon as a man or woman leaves college or high school that person enters an unstructured world where most of the living and working conditions encountered foster not stable contact but anonymity and transiency. In such an environment the only possibility of a stable relationship remaining to many people is with one other person. If a couple relationship does not materialize or if it is only transient, the means for developing a stable social network are more limited and less apparent.

In trying to adopt the couple solution to loneliness in contemporary American society, the first problem is where to go and what to do in order to meet a potential mate. Most of us have experienced this dilemma either personally or through our friends. Where do you go in New York, Los Angeles, Detroit, or Des Moines to meet people? If you feel you have mastered all the recently advertised skills of human relating, where do you find the relationship to which those skills can be applied? Not at church, not at home, not at the movies. Even parties are no longer popular—as they were, for instance, in the sixties.

The conventional ways of forming relationships are no longer operative in contemporary urban society. To fill the void left by conventional methods of beginning and continuing relationships a new multibillion-dollar service industry has grown in America. Encounter groups, growth and awareness centers, singles apartment complexes, bars and clubs, pseudoreligious and mystical groups—all have flourished, either entirely or partially because of the need of Americans today to find relationships that will help them assuage their loneliness.

Thus: The loneliness business.

In the "best" American tradition, the solution to emotional and social problems is left to the world of business. And so the business world has obliged by creating a circuit of activities through which lonely people desperately pursue their search for companionship. The new pattern of initiation into the world of the lonely often goes like this. It begins with visits to the local singles bar, followed by participation in various other activities sponsored by the singles industry, such as dances, clubs, and hotel weekends. Although some people do manage to score in the singles scene, many are disenchanted. At this point the growth movement takes over. Lonely people are likely to enroll in a variety of encounter activities—weekends at growth centers, weekly encounter sessions. When openness and honesty fail to achieve their stated aim—a significant relationship—then comes a possible last step—absorption in one of the various spiritual pseudoreligions led by any number of gurus who roam the United States in search of followers.

Unfortunately, the last step in this journey through one of America's newest and fastest-growing industries may be total disillusionment as loneliness tends to persist. And the loneliness business becomes another example of how profit-oriented industries that promise to correct a problem function only to aggravate that problem.

The loneliness business is a negative solution to this mass social problem that assails so many in our culture. Its reason for existence isn't to solve the problem but rather to cash in on it. It fosters the illusion that feelings of emptiness and dissatisfaction can be overcome solely by individual effort, such as finding a mate or getting one's head together. It denies the fact that loneliness is a social as well as a personal problem and that the solution to loneliness lies in social and political action as well as purely personal action. Finally, the loneliness business depends on loneliness for its continued well-being. You can't cure a disease upon which your very life depends. So, insidiously, the loneliness business actually exacerbates the problems of American life while insisting that its only aim is relief and happiness.

Chapter Ten

Dorothy Ames

Lively, loving teacher in
her forties, residing in South Bay, seeks
an intelligent, vital, and liberal man
to create and share life's adventures.

There. That seems to say it all. Only twenty-four words, but each of them leads to a whole chain of images and associations. Like pictures in a dream, if someone reads them and follows them, a whole lifetime of possibilities appears. Just those two words, "share," "create," mean so much. To think that in her original version of the ad she had not used those words. She had almost made a terrible mistake, and the first ad—"Lively, attractive college teacher in her forties seeks intelligent, vital, and liberal man, preferably South Bay"—would never have worked. Fortunately the leader of an Esalen singles workshop was quick to see the trouble. "You can't write that, Dorothy," he had insisted. "Why, that's sad, that makes me want to cry." Dorothy Ames realized that the man she was looking for would never respond to such a picture. The second ad was zippier, more intriguing. After a letter and a phone call she would finally have a chance to prove herself.

The likelihood of someone's seeing her ad was good. It was such a fine opportunity, the first time this singles press printed ads. There are so many ads in most papers that a man could get tired of reading after the first column. But not in this paper. The minute she heard they were printing ads she rushed hers in. She would have to wait a bit for replies; the letters would be sent to the paper and then forwarded to her. But after waiting almost ten years for a man to share her life again, a few weeks is so little time.

But even short waits pass slowly. When she walks to the mailbox each morning she can feel the excitement, and then, too quickly, comes the anxiety surrounding her hopes. In these past ten years, in almost all her forty-eight years, for that matter, there have been so many bad endings and so few new beginnings. Two divorces in less than ten years. And in the following ten so many disappointments as she went through dozens of singles parties, clubs, dances, and encounter groups. And still there are whole weekends when the phone never rings and she is all alone in her house, the only noises those her cat makes when he enters or exits through his trapdoor.

"Living alone bugs me," she says, "and it sort of annoys me a little bit when I hear people say, 'Well, everybody's lonely.' I know that's true, everybody's lonely, and you can also be lonely with people. I know you can. But I don't think that people who don't live alone realize what it's like. One weekend I was at an encounter group. And before it started some women were chitchatting. One woman said how she fasts every third day, and another was saying that she plans to have one day of silence a week. And there was something in me that got very angry. When I think of the enforced days of silence I have, weekends sometimes when I never speak to a soul." Her voice rises as she speaks, abandoning the meekness that is its general tone. It is as though she sees something outside herself, an enemy perhaps, or a force that treats her with a different justice from the rest. And as quickly as her anger flared, she grows resigned again. "Oh, I know, I just don't go out enough. I don't have enough good friends. I can't blame it on anyone else."

Dorothy has some friends. But the town in which she lives, San Jose, California, is not the best place to be single. A large

community, it is sixty miles south of San Francisco, but farther
in spirit. Most of her friends are married. They are nice to her
and invite her to dinner or come to her occasional parties. But
she doesn't like to bother them too often. A call to ask whether
they'd like to go to the movies or to dinner on the spur of the
moment would be an imposition.

When she first came to teach science at one of the city's educational institutions ten years ago, she had more friends—people
who were single and with whom she could get together spontaneously. She remembers those years as a wonderful time.

"I really felt I had found my niche when I went up to San
Jose," she recalls. "It was lots of fun. There was a large group of
us, and then there were four of us who were really close. We
were all single and it was really great. I felt as if I had finally
found the vital, stimulating people I had been looking for. We
stayed up all night, we would eat together two nights a week,
go to the movies, hop in the car and drive to San Francisco.
They were free people and I did things I had never done before.
But then I found out that one of the men was a homosexual, and
the other woman in the group pushed me out because she was
interested in the other man. Sex got into this foursome and
ruined it."

Since then she has been careful not to let sex interfere with
her friendships. "I bend over backward," she explains, "not to be
a threat to any couple I am friends with. And I must be sending
out messages, because I've never had a married man friend make
a pass at me. I'm just sending out messages all the time saying
that I want to be a friend to both the man and the woman and
that I don't want any of that other stuff."

Her messages have worked, but then she worries that she may
be sending out similar messages to men she really does want to
attract. Or perhaps she is unsuccessful with men because she
tries too hard, because they feel she is desperate.

But, no, that may have been true in the past, but not today.

Today she has learned so many things that have loosened her.
Just recently, for example, she finished being Rolfed. For ten ses-

sions, at $30 a session, she lay on a mat and was molded and pushed and pulled. As though the masseur's hands were lifting away lines of age and stress, Rolfing manipulated her body, releasing tensions deep in her muscles, tensions she had not even realized were there. When she had finished, her whole body was realigned, restructured. True, she was a bit disappointed when she looked at herself afterward. It did not seem from her reflection that she had changed as much as she would have wished. Her thinness still seemed more sparse than attractive. The lips were still too tightly compressed. And her brown hair continued to lack luster, refusing somehow to fall becomingly around her face. Her masseur assured her there was no reason to worry. These things take time to really work, he explained. If she waited, the changes would slowly make themselves apparent.

So now, with Rolfing, and so many other things she is discovering, she is sure she will find someone. "I'm in a tremendous process of change," she says enthusiastically. "I wish I could find a man who was going along the same road. But I really have a hope and a confidence too that when I get myself straightened out there is going to be someone there." Her face softens when she thinks of the image of her life when she will no longer be alone. She has formed a plan of what it is she wants, and when she is overcome with loneliness, she imagines the somewhat vague outlines of the presence with whom she will soon, she is sure, dress her home and her life.

"I want somebody intelligent, liberal, and vital"—so she describes him—"someone who is fun to be with. Someone I can really talk to. Intelligence is very important to me. People say I'm too fussy. But if it's not someone I can talk to, I don't care about bed. Sex just isn't that important to me. Maybe that's one of my problems. But there are a whole lot more hours to the day, and I want the communication to be around ideas and interests. I'm not looking for another marriage. But I'd like a steady relationship. Even someone in San Francisco wouldn't be bad. I could go there for a weekend, and he could come here another weekend, and spend his vacations with me. I think I would like that kind of arrangement better at this point than having some-one around all the time. I've gotten used to doing my own thing. And besides, my house is small and isn't set up for two people. So right now I'd like something where—unless something really important came up—we could spend every weekend to-gether. I mean, it wouldn't have to be every single weekend, but it would be something I could pretty much count on." Her dreams, and her ad, received, among others, the following reply:

Dear Lady of Personals,

I'm one of two hundred million people in the U.S. The odds against us meeting inside of an envelope are beyond the scope of love and imagination. Love being out of the realm of understanding and defini-tion.

The earth has moved in its spacial orbit forty-six revolutions around the sun since my release from the internal world of my mother's womb. During these revolutions my body and life have been in the experience of excitement, love, marriage, divorce, tragedy, beauty, poverty, wealth, ignorance, wisdom, self-pity, self-realization, sickness, health, and freedom. My height measures 5'11", and I weigh 140 pounds. Born October 28, 1927.

Animals are my brothers and sisters. . . . Therefore I humble my-self to all forms of life from the germ to the largest whale. . . . I am a vegetarian, not by choice but by the dictates of my physiological structure, evolved and determined over millions of years by the Laws of Life.

Exercising dominates my movements. Outdoors is my house and my home; the stars are my lights; the wind is my clothes; the sun is the door to my happiness. Sex evolves in my life as my emotions merge into the life of a living Queen. I am monogamous.

From all of myself as seen in the above, if you discover our rela-tionship, then we'll meet again inside of your letter.

And until then, the best of health, happiness and love.

                                                              True

Her search for this relationship has been long and full of dis-appointments. When she first heard of the idea of singles clubs and computer dating, she thought it would be the solution to her problem. She sent ads to magazines and went to clubs, encounter groups, and dances and entered her name with computer dating agencies. She did not, however, find her ideal mate.

"In my age bracket," she explains, sighing with pity and disbelief, "the men who go in for computer dating are the saddest, most defeated, gone-to-flab people. And the computer dating doesn't do what it might to help. I specified college-educated and I'd get truck drivers. All the men I met just seemed like jerks, like people who weren't alive. So I decided that computer dating has a built-in factor against my finding the sort of man I want, because the sort of man I want wouldn't have to even think of resorting to computer dating. He would be so interested in what he was doing, jobwise or whatever, and he would have enough of his own initiative to meet women. I think the women who use computer dating are better than the men, because women have fewer opportunities to meet men. So I hope you can't say that all the women who use computer dating are losers, because I don't consider myself that."

After computer dating she sent her first ad to the *New York Review of Books*. "I got some funny replies to that ad," she comments. "I did have a nice thing going for some time, by letter, with some fellow who taught at San Diego State University. I learned a lesson from that. I pushed—I wanted to meet him because I was sick of letters. But he had just gotten a divorce, and I think he was using me as an outlet for this great emotional turmoil he was going through about his divorce. When it came time for Christmas vacation I wrote and said I really thought we ought to get together, and I even offered to go down to San Diego. But he wasn't ready to meet me, and he let me know that he wanted our correspondence to end. I knocked myself for not being more patient on that one."

Her patience has increased since that experience, and she is no longer as shy as she was. Now when she goes to a singles dance she'll go over to an attractive man and ask him to dance. She can also do without some of the disguises she used in the past when going to singles activities. "I used to wear a blond wig when I went to dances," she recounts, "because this was enough to change me. Psychologically, it helped me with the idea of walking alone into a dance. It wasn't me at the dance, it was a disguise. But I decided that now I think I would want to be myself and I would want the man to want not a blonde but me. Especially if I went to a square dance, it would be awful if the wig slipped off."

Hoping to meet someone, Dorothy has gone on a number of singles trips. She took a raft trip down the coast of Mexico and another down the Colorado River with the Sierra Club. She has gone to England and South America. "I try to do things that are interesting and that I like to do, and then see if these are places where a more vital man might be. I suppose I should take up scuba diving. I met a woman at a singles workshop who does free-fall and is now learning to fly a plane and says that's the way to meet a man. But I'm not that athletic."

Next summer she is going to Japan, and recently she was in Hawaii on a singles tour, which was not, however, what she had hoped it would be. "It was a sham and a delusion," she says. "I went with a woman friend and so I wasn't disappointed. But had I been alone I would have been very unhappy. They said it was for singles. But when we got to Hawaii they just stuck us with a hundred and fifty other people—mostly couples—and we had to fend for ourselves. There were no singles activities arranged and they didn't help people meet each other. I've been thinking about writing a letter—you know, just to suggest that the next time they at least have a cocktail party for people just so they can meet each other."

Disheartened, she adds, "The thing that kind of bugs me is that I haven't even had a crack at making something work. I'm really getting very discouraged. But then I think that it must be the place that I'm in. And when I get to a better place, I can find the kind of guy I really want." The bleakness of her life has stiffened her, but it has not shaken her faith. She has only to set her mind on what is possible and it's as though she can see the light surrounding the coming of a miracle. In fact, she has just been part of what is the closest thing to a miracle she has ever known. It has changed her life dramatically, made her realize things that years of Gestalt groups, Esalen, and singles clubs were unable to make her see.

est: Erhard Seminars Training.

She'd heard about it from an Esalen group leader. The woman said it was just the best thing around, something that, as est itself says in all its advertisements, would open her life, allow her to really experience things, not by doing anything to change things but just by living. She called immediately and was lucky enough to be able to enroll for the next two weekend training sessions. And during those four days she sat with two hundred other people, who had paid $200 each, in a large hotel in San Francisco, listening to Werner Erhard, the originator of the trainings, explain and demonstrate. She cannot really describe what happened. It's something you don't understand, you experience. Something that flows out of Werner's lips and into your body. You can't reproduce that energy in words. Only Werner can really convey the ideas.

Werner is the closest thing to genius she has ever seen. Some people think he's too slick, a bit like a snake-oil salesman. But to hear him talk. . . . Suddenly she realized the truth of what he was saying—about all the "right-wrong games" she and others play. The way she is always trying to blame others, never to take the responsibility for her actions. After those two weekends she saw that if she is lonely, it's simply because she wants to be lonely. The world hadn't done it to her—she had done it. Something in her wants it, and she had chosen it. Two hundred dollars is certainly not too much to pay for that kind of knowledge.

Hello!

You are a very special person: sensitive to things that are quite above most people . . . to say the least! Some call it soul, some would say you are 'high'; anyway, I hear you loudly. . . . You probably love Gibran, Hesse, Watts, etc. You seem to be very high-minded, and will probably get the very best that life can offer you. Good luck!

If age means anything, I'm thirty-seven; a Licensed Psychiatric Technician by trade . . . by calling, not choice . . . Oh, I love the healing game, but I plan to get away from it soon. Twenty years is enough! In order to have my own business someday, and also to give my nature a creative outlet, I am going to start Beauty School next month. I like the feminine arts because I like women! Why not? I have been styling the patients' hair anyway; I like to do it!

Well, soul-sister, I hope I interpreted you correctly, but it takes one to know one, and I'm seldom wrong on this subject! Let's get together and share some adventures?

Est has now become one of the most meaningful parts of Dorothy's life. She has already attended the two post-training series, given once a week in San Francisco. The first was called "Be Here Now," and the second, in which she is currently enrolled, is "The Best of Sex and Money." It's astonishing how really ridiculous her hangups are, she has learned. "The first night," she says, "we were told to just spend the whole evening thinking about sex. Well, you can imagine how boring thinking about sex can get. Then for the money part, we spent three whole hours just looking at dollar bills, throwing them up in the air, touching them—to see that they are only pieces of paper. You begin to see how silly it is to make a big thing out of money.

"Est helps so much more than other things I've tried," she says, "because other things don't give you so many practical ways to handle things. At est they have various things they call processes—really examining things and getting in touch with things. They give you a whole procedure. There is one called the Truth Process. You do this with physical things or upsets. First you find the bodily sensation and describe it exactly. Then you begin asking questions. What emotion does this bodily sensation arouse, what states of mind, of attitudes, what posture? And then there are a whole bunch of head trips: what considerations, what have people told you about this, what do you think caused this, what have you thought about it, what have you read about it? You go through a whole intellectual thing. And then comes the most magical thing. Bring in a picture from the past that is associated with this bodily thing or upset. The theory is that if you can go further and further back to what caused anything, you'll blow it off."

The magic of the first two est weekend trainings was so great that much of the est philosophy was lost to Dorothy, and she is thinking of doing the training over again. She has also spent several weekends as a volunteer subject for people who are learning to be est trainers. "I signed up to be a volunteer for one Saturday, and I went down to San Francisco," she says. "It was fascinating. It was so much fun that I went back on Sunday also. Werner was there. He stressed that trainers shouldn't allow est to become a belief system. There are some people you know," she confides, "who are est freaks, who think that est is everything.

"I'm also going to an est party soon. They've rented the Civic Center, which can hold six thousand people. They're going to serve champagne and hot dogs. To tell the truth, I think that will be a good place to meet people. It won't be as contrived as a singles dance or encounter group. And I'm certainly not going to meet people staying home. And est people are so friendly. It's just a wonderful thing. Why, at Christmas they had a dinner for all the people in est who weren't having Christmas with someone. I was having dinner with friends or I would have gone. And they have some kind of class going on in San Francisco almost every night. It can become your whole life," she says, musing on the joy of that possibility, and then, remembering Werner's warning about belief systems, she adds quickly, "Of course that would be a bad thing. The idea behind est is that you should eventually stand on your own two feet."

Since Dorothy has found that living her own life is not worth while without someone to share things with, she has decided that any man with whom she becomes serious should also go to est. "I think it would be so much better to have a relationship with an est person. We would have a much better start. He wouldn't have bad ideas, be into things like right-wrong games and such. He would be interested in the right things, like sharing

and creating. I used those words in my ad in the singles paper.
Those are est words."

Dorothy has taken several of the men who have answered her
ad to est, where they have attended free introductory lectures.
None of them enrolled. There was one fellow who was a real
jerk. Trying to make it easier for him to meet her, she said that
she would be in San Francisco on a certain night when she had
an est meeting. She suggested that they have dinner before and
get acquainted. After they had eaten he asked where she was
going, and when she described est, he seemed interested and
asked if he might attend a lecture as a guest. Perhaps he had
been angry because his class had gotten out earlier than hers
and he had to wait an hour for her. But, no—there was really no
excuse for his behavior. She had come out of est feeling fine—
great. And then he began to put est down. Playing all the right-
wrong games est people were fighting against. He was a real jerk
and no one she would ever want to see again. But more than that,
he had really upset her.

Returning home in her car, she began to use the Truth Process
she had learned in training.

It was an upset. The man had put her in a bad mood. She had
come out of est feeling good, and after she had left that fellow
she was feeling bad. Now, what were the physical feelings associated with this upset? She felt tight, angry. She could feel the
anger twisting through her stomach. Was it also disappointment
she felt? Yes, a little. He had sounded nice on the phone. Perhaps the upset came from a break in understanding. Or perhaps
it was a break in communication, or maybe a break in affinity?
No, it was none of these; it was definitely a break in expectation.
That comes under the category of agreement. Now that she
could name it, she would have to think of something in the past,
some memory.

The gas station and store lights along the freeway seemed
almost to put her into a trance. Not enough so that she would
lose control of her car, but just enough to let her remember. A
break in expectation. . . .

She had had breaks in expectation before. It was two days

after she and her first husband had come back from their year's trip to India. He had gone there to teach a course in law. It was to be the journey of a lifetime. Not wanting to ruin their stay, they had buried all their problems. On their way home they traveled for three months through the Middle East. There had been tensions, but they never argued or discussed them. And when they finally came home, she hoped they could just go on. Things weren't that bad, and with time everything would be fine.

But the day after their arrival her husband went to keep an appointment with his psychoanalyst. They had both been in analysis with the same man before they had left. On the following day she had her appointment. She had those same feelings that day. Anger, hurt, disappointment. The analyst told her that her husband no longer loved her and wanted a divorce. She begged him to help her, to talk to her husband. But of course that would have been impossible. No one can make someone love someone else.

She fought the divorce. She even tried to commit suicide. But in the end it had come. After that he married another woman and had the children she was never able to give him.

Anger. She felt anger even thinking about it now. It could have worked. But the times were against her. The times and all those books telling women what to do and what not to do. Before they married she had been a teacher and had enjoyed her work. But back then, in the fifties, everyone said a woman should not work. A woman who had a career would become a psychological mess. So she set out to be the ideal woman the books spoke of. She adopted her husband's work as her own, which wasn't difficult as she found the law interesting. She gave up her job and never tried to find another. Even after her baby died she did not try to teach again. It would have been foolish to sign a contract, only to quit when she got pregnant. But she did not get pregnant again. In the end her husband accused her of being dull, uninteresting. And then came the final break in all her hopes—the divorce.

Amazing the things you think of when you work out the Truth

Process. From an upset at est tonight all the way back to something that had happened over fifteen years ago.

She can feel her intestines unwinding a bit, just from trying to understand the problem. But there are still things to figure out. What caused this break in expectation? Was it enforced, was it inhibited, or was it desired? Werner says a break in expectation can be desired. But that's hard to imagine. Why would anyone desire not to have her expectations fulfilled? Her divorce certainly wasn't desired. It was the times that brought it on. If they were married today she knows it could work. No, the times were against the marriage, just as they worked against the second marriage. If the times had been more permissive, she would never have married her second husband. She would have preferred simply to live with him. But back in the sixties a teacher really couldn't live with a man without marriage. And he was an egotistical, disturbed man—an only child. Her first husband had also been an only child, and she is an only child as well. Perhaps that was it. Only children shouldn't marry only children. It made for too many difficulties. And David Ames was certainly a difficult man, always trying to undermine her. And indecisive, confused. First he was an engineer. Then he decided he would write, and while he searched for words she was supposed to support them. Now, after their divorce, he'd become an artist. They were married for only two years, and she doesn't know why she kept on seeing him so long after their divorce. He was someone to fall back on. Maybe it was loneliness that drove her.

Now those times are over, thanks to est. Now she no longer has to feel such a failure for being lonely. She can accept it, along with the other parts of her life. The things that do work for her. Her house and her job.

Getting out of the car, she admires the small, one-bedroom cottage set back behind pine trees so that it is hardly visible from the road. It is a tiny, compact house, and she has managed to contain all her interests in its closets and bookshelves. What looks like a wall opens up, and there is her sewing machine and its paraphernalia. Her desk drawers double as file cabinets, and the shelves are filled with books from García Lorca to *How to Pick Up Men*. Out back is a small swimming pool, and in front a small garden. The wood and shingles, the soil all fit around her in a quietly nostalgic security. Everyone is impressed with her house.

Her job is another thing she can't complain about. The pay is very good for a single person, so that she has money to go on trips, to do pretty much what she wants within reason. The hours are short, with lots of vacation time. There is almost too much free time. During the winter she plans carefully the trips and excursions she will take on her three-month summer recess. Without those projects she would perhaps spend too many of her days envying those women whose lives are occupied worrying about families and husbands.

Definitely, the job and house are her two joys. If only there was someone, then everything would be perfect.

Some men have answered her ad. It keeps the phone ringing and the mailbox full. There is someone coming in the next couple of days. He sounded older on the phone, in his fifties. She didn't ask. Better to just keep age out of it. If she had asked his age, he might have asked hers. She feels hopeful, his letter sounded interesting and vital.

Hi there, "Lively,"

Your ad in the "Single Life" interested, especially since we live near one another. Maybe that's a good start.

I'm a "young forty," alert, alive, intelligent, blond, blue-eyed, 6'1", a trim and not-so-bad-looking guy. I enjoy books, conversation, classical music (mostly), parties, camping, theater, dining, making love, swimming, tennis, people, and ideas.

Why don't we meet some evening, or you write or give me a call sometime soon? Let's communicate. Okay?

Chapter Eleven
The Singles Business

The amount of "room" to move a person feels that he has is related both to the room that he gives himself and the room he is given by others.

This is dramatically illustrated by the report of a policeman who watched a little boy running around a block of flats. After the boy had run past him on his way round the block for the twentieth time, the policeman finally asked him what he was doing. The boy said he was running away from home, but his father wouldn't let him cross the road! The boy's "free space" was curtailed by his "internalization" of this paternal injunction.

R. D. LAING, *The Self and Others*

Every single or divorced person in New York City has heard of Maxwell's Plum. Even those who are only passing through Manhattan may have gone out of their way to look through the floor-to-ceiling windows that dominate the northwest corner of 64th Street and First Avenue. Equipped with a huge English-style pub bar in the center of the room, a glassed-in table area wrapping around the street corner, and a large dining room where couples can watch the action at the bar and men can invite a woman they have just picked up to an expensive and impressive meal following drinks, Maxwell's is the hottest and most elegant of the singles bars among Manhattan's East Side strip of singles gathering spots. And being jostled around the bar or waiting in line on the street outside of Maxwell's is part of being single or on the make in New York City.

It is only at night that Maxwell's becomes what it truly is—
a body shop where men and women come to look one another
over with the hope of meeting a mate. During the day the restaurant is filled with gray-haired ladies and businessmen lunch-
ing on large hamburgers. Then at cocktail hour the men and
women coming home from work stop in for a drink. Until seven-
thirty or eight Maxwell's would seem to the uninitiated to be a
rather elegant East Side bar, with nothing particularly special
about it other than its expensive décor.

After eight, however, people start arriving in cabs, on foot, or
by bus. The women come in groups of two or three and the men
come either alone or with a friend. Women rarely come alone to
Maxwell's. Although other women can be competition, the
traditional notion is that a woman alone is fair game for all un-
serious contenders. This discourages the lone woman from making an appearance in a singles bar. Many women today might
want sex and sex only, but they don't want to appear obvious.
That's not cool. So they come to Maxwell's with their women
friends and the understanding that once they find a man it's
every woman for herself.

Before nine or nine-thirty, when Maxwell's is packed, things do
not move quite as one would expect them to move in a "body
shop" or "meat market." There are no fast approaches, no men
coming up to women or women coming up to men with the
legendary "Wanna fuck?" People stick to themselves. Eyeing each
other rather casually, the men may smile at women, but while
the bar is only lightly populated most people talk to their friends
or stare into their drinks.

Once the crowd begins to grow the atmosphere changes. Being packed together around the bar along with hundreds of other
people tends to loosen you up. It's easy to talk to the man or
woman against whom you have been pushed by the crowd. And
at Maxwell's, as at other singles bars, the action has to do with
how many people are in the room. With a few drinks and a few
hundred people, conversations begin.

Swingers are interested in the here and now, and so what is

important is not what you do or where you come from but whether you are available for this or any other evening. One does not begin a conversation at Maxwell's with "What do you do?" or "Where do you come from?" The most important thing is to make a quick impression, be different from the hundreds of other people going in and out of the bar, so that you can get the name and number of the man or woman in whom you are interested before the crowd pushes you away or before that person leaves for the evening.

The only way to be different may be to be totally outrageous. There is, for instance, the man who asks to whisper in a woman's ear. When she asks why, he says he must tell her a secret. When she puts her ear up next to his lips he gives it a kiss. Sometimes it works and sometimes it doesn't. But there is always the chance that it will. Or the young salesman who wanders around the room approaching woman after woman with an offer of dinner at any restaurant of her choice, followed by the Broadway show of her choice, followed, if one should agree to the former, by bed and breakfast. There is always the one girl out of ten who will accept.

Most of the men and women at Maxwell's are not aggressive types. They will spend the evening standing in place, shifting with the weight of the crowd, and waiting for someone to make a move toward them. You see them at Maxwell's every night. The two women standing in a corner, expectantly glancing at each other every once in a while, then turning away to face the room. The man by the end of the bar nursing a drink, spending three or four hours watching various women on the other side of the bar. And you wonder why such people come to Maxwell's at all.

Then, when they leave alone or with the friends they came with, as do most of the men and women who come to Maxwell's hoping to connect with someone either for the evening or a lifetime, you understand by the look of defeat they wear as they go out the door why they came to Maxwell's this evening—and why they will come again yet another evening. It is because, like most people in America today, these people think there will be more comfort in being lonely together than in being lonely alone.

CONVERSATION I

HE (stopping woman as she moves around the bar at Maxwell's Plum): Why don't you stop and talk?

SHE: Okay.

HE: You know, you have bad breath. Here, open your mouth. (He pulls out a small can of some spray.)

SHE: Hey, what's that?

HE: Just open your mouth, it's nothing bad.

SHE: No, thanks.

HE: Okay—why don't we step over here? (They move toward an open spot.)

SHE: What do you do?

HE: Oh, I've been a detective, a bouncer in Vegas. Now I work for a frozen-food company.

SHE: Oh, that sounds interesting.

HE: Hey, listen, why don't you come home with me—I'll show you a good time.

SHE: No, I don't think so, thank you.

HE: Listen, if you don't like it you can leave.

SHE: No, thanks.

HE: Listen, you look pretty nervous, do you want a pill?

SHE: What kind of pill?

HE: You know, to calm you down.

SHE: No, thanks.

HE: Look, come on home with me.

SHE: No, thank you, I don't think so.

HE (angrily): Then why did you come here?

SHE: Just curiosity.

HE: Well, hell, that's a pretty bad reason. (He walks off and approaches another woman.)

With millions of lonely people searching for companionship in a social environment that is hardly conducive to the creation of viable personal relationships, the business world has been quick to recognize the commercial possibilities present in the loneliness experienced by many Americans today. In our cities and suburbs there are almost 49 million single, divorced, or widowed people for whom finding a companion for the evening is almost as challenging and difficult as finding someone with whom to share the rest of their lives. So, in the past ten years, providing a place where single people (who have an estimated purchasing power of $40 billion per year) can mate has furnished new uses for the bar, the hotel, the apartment house, and the computer, netting millions of dollars in profits for enterprising business men and women. In this process the business world has turned companionship into a commodity—like automobiles or deodorant—to be sold in a "free" market, where, as with most things today, the conditions favor the seller rather than the buyer.

The singles business began in Los Angeles and New York with several bars and apartment houses that offered either events for singles or singles living accommodations. Friday's, a bar in New York City, for example, advertised "Thank God It's Friday" night parties, to which people interested in meeting available members of the opposite sex were invited. With little publicity to advertise such get-togethers, Friday's was jammed on weekend nights. Similarly, when the South Bay Clubs in Los Angeles advertised singles apartment living, the idea was well received. And hotels in New York's Catskill Mountains offered singles weekends, which soon became popular and filled empty rooms. Entrepreneurs were soon aware that the singles population represented a lucrative and untapped market.

Before this market could be fully exploited, however, the would-be singles industry had to overcome a major obstacle to its future success—the antipathy of single people both to publicly identifying themselves as single and lonely for companionship and to congregating socially with other single people. Single people traditionally hid in their rooms on weekend evenings rather than venture into a bar or dance alone, thus admitting that they couldn't get dates. Being single past the age of twenty-two connotes failure. To admit to being single would thus be to admit to having committed a cardinal sin in our culture—that of being unable to attract or hold a mate. Thus the first and most important task of the singles industry was to make being single both an acceptable and even preferable state, so that single people would come out of hiding and choose to spend their free time with other single people. To do this the singles business has had to take the loneliness out of being single, or at the very least to convince people to repress their feelings of loneliness and failure behind a façade of cheerfulness.

Thus the myth of the swinging single.

The swinging single—an outgrowth of the sexual revolution and the new morality—is the creature upon whom the singles industry depends for its existence. The myth of the swinger began as a male image publicized by *Playboy* and TV. Unattached, cool, handsome, well-to-do, the swinger was the man who was surrounded by dozens of beautiful women with whom he engaged in endless sexual encounters. Equally comfortable at a bar or at home, equally successful in bed or at work, the swinger never, ever succumbed to feelings of loneliness. The successful swinger was judged only by the number of his sexual relationships. The superficial quality of those relationships was a deliberate choice—the door to bliss rather than loneliness.

While holding down a high-powered job, the swinger, according to Playboy Philosophy, could fuck 'em and forget 'em and go on to the next one, never considering for a moment the possibility of entering into a stable, much less a marital, relationship. Liberation was thus defined solely in sexual terms, and the problems of our society, said *Playboy,* had much less to do with social and political concerns than with the fact that men and women were sexually inhibited. Free was the man who could sleep with as many different women as possible in as many different places and positions as possible.

Television was equally important in creating the image of the unattached sexual swinger. With few exceptions the heroes of television series are and have been unmarried, and engage in only the most superficial romantic involvements that last for one episode in the series. Romance on television has been associated with attraction to shifting sexual objects. The hero may fall in love with a guest star one week, but that guest star must either disappear or be killed off so that the hero may fall in love with another guest star another week. In the "action series" (action, one wonders, in what sense?) there is no such thing as stable attachment to a member of the opposite sex. The message, over the past several decades, has been abundantly clear: the only way to lead an exciting and adventurous life is to be single and to have as many transitory sexual attachments as possible. If you don't believe it, turn the dial and watch the situation comedies in which the heroes and heroines are married. Their relationships are singularly unromantic and asexual. Can you imagine Bob Newhart and Suzanne Pleshette in bed, or to go back a few years, Robert Young and Jane Wyatt? Clearly not.

Following the lead of business, and in fact furnishing what business needed most after the war, television and *Playboy* created the mobile relationship to suit the mobile employee. Corporate policies of shifting people among various branches, which in effect made personnel interchangeable cogs in a well-oiled machine, was paralleled and reinforced by the message of the media that the swinger should engage in sexual relations only with interchangeable sex objects, with whom the sex act was to have only the most superficial meaning. Thus, in December 1963, the *Playboy* coloring book shows a picture of a man—the playboy—surrounded by three buxom women—the playmates—with the caption:

Every playboy should have several [playmates] to spare. That is because variety is the spice of life. The playboy likes his life spicy. Make one of the girls a blonde. Make one of the girls a brunette. Make one of the girls a redhead. It does not matter which is which. The girls' hair colors are interchangeable. So are the girls.

To demystify the puritan ethic decreeing that sex had to be sanctioned by the bonds of matrimony, and was even then acceptable only when its aim was procreation, *Playboy* turned the sexual act into a game. And as with all games, half the fun was in competition. The winner was the high scorer—the man who could get the most and best women into his bed. Hefner thus extended the competitive ethic of capitalism to sexual relations, pitting, as we see in these lines (again from the 1963 *Playboy* coloring book), the playboy against himself as well as against others:

This is the playboy's little black book. No playboy should be without one. Color it black. Do you have a little black book? Good. Write the names, addresses, and telephone numbers. Write down the playmates' vital statistics. Also write down your own vital statistics about your last date with this playmate. Did you get to first base, did you get to second base, did you get to third? Did you score? Isn't this fun. It's just like baseball, only better.

Sexual liberation, as *Playboy* defined it, was the only kind of liberation. Freedom meant not only scoring as many times as possible with as many different women as possible but never letting the sexual adventure become so all-consuming that it threatened to endanger the playboy's work life. The playboy was the man who could maintain the delicate balance described in Hefner's Playboy Philosophy in which the swinger uses sex to promote efficiency in business:

The upbeat can enjoy kicking up his heels, participating in the same set of fun and frivolity for which the Twenties are famous, but they are equally capable of knuckling down to a particular job and getting it done. . . . And because activity actually begets activity the man who works hard and plays hard too, will soon find that he is accomplishing more of both than if he tried to concentrate all or more of his effort in only one direction.

In the excitement of the moment no one seemed to notice that Hefner was merely extending the puritan ethic to include working hard at play and sex, nor did they notice that, as in the above, Hefner was putting sex at the service of work. To be sexually free would allow the playboy to be even more efficient at the office than he already was. Similarly, no one seemed to notice the contradiction in Hefner's philosophy of variety. On the one hand, he encourages the playboy to sleep with as many women as possible, because variety is the spice of life. On the other hand, his concept of *interchangeable* sex objects makes each woman the same as the next.

Of course, neither *Playboy* nor other segments of the media created the sexual revolution. Technological advances and their consequences did that. Newer methods of birth control, the breakup of the family and the disenchantment with matrimony, increased mobility and the need to make relationships which were better suited to the mobile life-style, the disintegration of the community—these are only some of the factors that actually spawned the sexual revolution. What the media did, with their philosophy of casual, unattached sex with interchangeable sexual partners, was to popularize the sexual revolution that broke down America's puritan heritage, making sex without love and marriage not only acceptable but desirable. The Playboy Philosophy of swinging liberation was quickly adopted by people who were no longer bound by family and community restrictions, and by an increasing population of divorced people whose painful experiences in bad marriages made the model of an unattached swinger seem particularly attractive.*

Business men and women latched onto the swinging philosophy of the new morality and used that philosophy to transform singlehood from a sad, shameful affair to an "in" status, with the singles bar, apartment, or dance as the vehicle for the swinger's success.

But one problem still remained unsolved: how to attract women to singles activities. The sexual swinger in the early sixties was, after all, a male image. In order for the loneliness business to succeed, not only men but women would have to voluntarily identify themselves as single and on the make. To be a bachelor, even before the sexual revolution, had never been considered as pitiable a fate as spinsterhood. Men have conventionally had the freedom to clandestinely satisfy sexual appetites

---

* And in the late 1960s and early 1970s the original Playboy Philosophy would undergo a slight change, for the playboy, disillusioned with work, would concentrate increasingly on play.

outside or before marriage. Nor had they ever had any reluctance to go to bars or social functions alone. Women have been traditionally loath, however, to admit to being unmarried, to engage in premarital sex, or to go to bars or to other social events by themselves.

Thus the singles business had to court women. Offering reduced rates for drinks at bars, reduced entrance fees to computer-dating services, letting women in free at bars or clubs were some of the ways which women were tempted. The success in attracting women was also dependent on the development of the birth control pill and found expression in Helen Gurley Brown's *Cosmopolitan* extension of the *Playboy* image to women. As an article in *Cosmopolitan* explains, being single is "it":

The single woman of the seventies—the divorcee included—has more sensational options at her fingertips than women have ever had before. The trick is in daring to use them! Many of the old, rigid rules have broken down, thank goodness, and the woman alone is no longer hemmed in by a handful of no-no's. She can have lovers galore and still be a lady, be envied rather than pitied if she comes unescorted to a party, buy her own summer home or travel alone to Europe. She doesn't need a husband—or even a steady beau—to entertain graciously, collect interesting friends or see unusual corners of the world. In short, an unmarried woman can . . . if she chooses . . . be a complete person *without* becoming attached to a man.*

Because of such changes in attitudes, among other factors, since 1960 one-third more women remain single into their twenties. The singles business encourages these women to become exact replicas of its idea of the liberated man—well-to-do, up on the latest sexual technique, and practicing on a variety of shifting sexual objects.

Not everyone, of course, is attracted to the image of the uninvolved sexual swinger. Many people wish that they could find lasting relationships with members of the opposite sex, but their

---

* In the seventies the *Cosmopolitan* creed was "refined" through such magazines as *Playgirl* and *Viva* and such TV shows as "Police Woman."

wishes may dissolve in the panic brought on by loneliness. When people are desperate for companionship they will do things they would not ordinarily do, go places where they would not ordinarily go, and listen to promises that they would otherwise find ridiculous. And despite the desire to have a "meaningful" relationship, making contact, no matter how superficial that contact may be, replaces or substitutes for the desire to find the "one."

Sex is one way to make contact. For the duration of the sexual act two people are physically close to each other. Such physical closeness is tempting because it can so easily be mistaken for emotional intimacy. And people can easily delude themselves into believing that a purely sexual encounter will eventually lead to a deeper relationship.

The singles business flourishes on such delusions. By fostering and then capitalizing on the confusion between sex and companionship, and intercourse and liberation, the singles business provides a camouflage behind which people can hide their loneliness. Ironically, despite its self-promotion as a new life-style, the singles business actually relies on traditional beliefs that finding a "mate" will cure loneliness—although this time the cure may be found in a series of sexual relationships rather than one intimate relationship.

Hardly anyone likes to go to singles bars. Virgins and veterans of the trade agree that an evening in a singles bar is almost always an alienating experience. The bars are too expensive and crowded. The kind of conversation one overhears and engages in is superficial. The people, excluding oneself of course, are interested only in surfaces—how pretty or handsome one is, how much money one has, what kind of car one drives, what address one boasts. Almost everyone agrees—and this includes the secretary and the accountant, the lawyer and the nurse, the journalist and the insurance salesman—that the rules of conventional etiquette are frequently flaunted. In their place, a style of relating has developed based on the premise that illusion and mystification are more interesting than reality and honesty.

Many of the lonely people whom I interviewed had had at least one if not many experiences in singles bars. These people were all looking for some sort of long-term relationship with which to end the painful emptiness they experienced. Categorically, the people I interviewed felt that the singles-bar experience was alienating and disappointing. It was something people went through because they had nowhere else to go and because they were desperate for company. Thus while many people who go to singles bars are interested in finding companions for more than just one evening, the atmosphere of most singles bars favors only very superficial contact. People who go to singles bars often have no more in common than the fact that they are looking for a mate—either for the evening or for a lifetime.

Most bars are located in one area of town, such as New York's East Side or Los Angeles' Marina (where 70 percent of the 7,000 population are single). Men and women come to these hunting grounds from all over the city. The choice of which singles bar to go to is not determined by its "cuisine" or clientele; there are no singles bars known to be visited by writers for instance, or especially tailored to a clientele of lawyers or doctors. A singles bar may cater to a younger or older crowd, and the age of its customers may be the only thing that distinguishes it. The choice of which singles bar to stop at is made on the basis of the bar's reputation. And the reputation of a bar is made . . . well, that is more difficult to determine.

Walking down New York's East Side strip on Friday night one sees certain singles bars that are so packed that people line up outside to wait to get in, while others are empty. The bars look alike, the bartenders seem to act alike, and the men and women going in and out seem to dress alike. When I asked customers of singles bars in San Francisco which bar provided the best action, I was told the name of a certain bar. When I went to that bar, and didn't find much action, I asked the same question of customers of that bar, who told me the name of another bar, to which I went, only to find that the place to be was not that bar but yet another bar. It would seem that the quality that makes one bar click and another fail is as intangible as the quality that makes one woman or man go home with someone for an evening and another go home alone.

The action at many singles bars seems to have less to do with the exercise of free will than with certain extraneous conditions —the day of the week and the time of the evening. The most popular evenings for going to a bar are Wednesday and Friday. Singles never go to a bar on Saturday night, as Saturday is date night. To be out alone on Saturday, an admission that one hasn't been able to get a date, is definitely against the code. When a bar is not crowded, people seem shy and passive. Once the bar gets crowded, however, people approach one another because of the flow of the crowd. The crowd, Jim Parker, a former waiter at Maxwell's Plum explains, does the work for you. "Because Maxwell's is so loud and chaotic," Parker says, "people are able to talk to people they wouldn't normally talk to. The people who go to Maxwell's wouldn't want to go to a quiet bar."

The person with whom one converses may be chosen arbitrarily, but the conversational patterns are dictated by a highly stylized set of do's and don'ts. Since the object of the conversation is to make the maximum impression in the minimum amount of time, one behaves differently in the bar than outside it; one becomes a player. But within the singles bar crowd, unconventional behavior—conversational and otherwise—takes on a conformity of its own. There are, for example, certain conversational topics that are avoided by common consent. One of the most stringent prohibitions is that against admitting to frequent use of the bar as a means of introduction to others. The swinger is the man or woman to whom sex comes without effort. Going to a swingers bar means that one has to go out of one's way to get sex. Even though this may be necessary in our anonymous world, it is still not considered to be cool. So swingers elaborately refrain from confessing to their history on the singles scene. According to Parker:

People tell people that this is the first time they have been to a bar—

because they don't want people to know that they come to bars every night. You never want anybody to know that, because you want people to think you have things to do, and that you're busy and worldly, and the last thing you want them to think is that you're in a bar every night. It's bad for the image.

Because a quick impression is of prime importance, and because the impressive person in our culture is the one with the highest income and the most impressive job status, the aim of many conversations in singles bars is simply to discover salary and position. But one mustn't be too direct, so, as Parker explains, one asks indirect questions that will produce the information:

The waiters at Maxwell's think of the bar as a zoo. I used to stand around the bar and watch people, and the sense of values there is so incredible I used to just stand in awe, because I didn't believe people were actually like that. You'll hear a regular income rap, "Where did you go on your last vacation, what kind of car do you drive?"—stuff you hear in commercials, or in movies. Nobody actually cares who someone is, but what they have and where they came from. I've actually heard conversations, like a one-to-one thing, who's got what, who's got things better than the other.

It is also important to discover a person's marital status, and thus his or her potential availability. But again, discretion of a certain kind is the key. Since sex is "in" in the seventies, you aren't supposed to be *too* concerned about the marital status of your sexual partner. Anything goes with anyone—in spite of the fact that most customers of singles bars are interested in some sort of long-term relationship. Given the rules of conduct at singles bars, it is thus very difficult to find out with whom you are dealing.

In the competitive world of singles, where many people—all looking for some kind of connection—are gathered in the same bar, certain guidelines determine who is a desirable partner for future contact. One criterion of desirability is the bankbook, another is place of residence. In New York, for example, a woman who lives in Manhattan will have better luck finding a man than would a woman who lives in another of the city's boroughs or in the suburbs. "You meet a lot of women in bars," one young man commented, "but it isn't easy to find quality women. You find a lot of BBQ's"—women from the Bronx, Brooklyn, or Queens. Because of where she lives, a "BBQ" is assumed to be substandard, while a woman living in Manhattan has that special something. "Men won't go out with a girl from the Bronx, Brooklyn, or Queens," says Mary, a nurse in Manhattan. "The first thing a guy asks you is, 'Where do you live?' If you don't live in Manhattan you're automatically GU—geographically undesirable. It doesn't matter how much a guy likes you, he won't go out with you, because he has to travel to take you out. And there are so many women in Manhattan, why bother with a BBQ?"

The unwillingness of men to take out women who are "geographically undesirable" is not motivated solely by callousness, but also, as Ernie, a young salesman in New York, explains, by financial considerations:

A guy doesn't want to take out a girl from the Bronx, Brooklyn, or Queens. It's like this. You have to figure that a guy comes into these places a lot. He doesn't have that much money, and he spends a lot on drinks and clothes so he can look good. If he meets a girl from BBQ, he has to go out to get her by subway. That takes a lot of time. Then, since mostly they go back to Manhattan, he has to take a cab, because it wouldn't look good to go by subway. So back by cab. So he just can't do it, because all that cab riding is too expensive. And you just can't ask a girl to take the subway. That wouldn't go.

Despite the fact that ours is supposedly an era of openness and honesty, the client of a singles bar is concerned with appearances. It is not chic to admit that you can't afford to take a cab, and although many women would rather go by subway than not go at all, men are nonetheless reluctant to confess to the weakness of their wallets. In the contest for a mate the BBQ is often disqualified from competition.

The heightened competition of the singles scene makes people who are already lonely feel still more so and increases the desperate need for companionship. Yet in the alienating environment of the singles bar, in which the size of the crowd and the nature of the rules make everyone look and act the same, how do you distinguish yourself from everyone else and convince someone that you are worthy of attention? What most often happens, because of this dilemma, is that men and women act more and more outrageously in order to distinguish themselves from the mass. Men will come up to women and pinch them, or simply introduce themselves with a "Wanna fuck?," or women will come up to men and, without even saying hello, ask them home for the evening. What is surprising, says Jim Parker, is that the use of such outrageous tactics sometimes works:

There won't be any airs or premeditation. I mean, I have seen guys at Maxwell's approach several girls with the same line. This guy would walk up to a girl and he'd pinch her ass. The first girl he did it to was very bummed out about it, and he said "Oh, it's very European." He wasn't a bad-looking guy and he was dressed well. He struck out with that girl. Then he went up to another girl, and they started rapping, and I assume they got together.

Most people are shocked, however, rather than turned on by the outrageous approach. Rather than take up an offer of a quick one-night stand, they are put off by such aggressive behavior.

The highly competitive action at singles bars is generally discouraging to the majority of people who go to such places. And the need to act quickly upon meeting a person intimidates people to such an extent that many can't act at all. Yet if one does not quickly indicate to a possible mate an interest in further contact, one runs the risk of losing a rare opportunity. Because singles bars are not neighborhood institutions where one may encounter a person again and again and thus have a chance to observe how that person acts over a period of time, snap decisions are necessary. "I can't imagine meeting people in a singles bar. I've heard stories," says Mr. Stein, a recently divorced man, "that you have to decide to ask a girl out right away without even seeing her again. I could never do that." Many people, like Mr. Stein, find the prospect of making such a decision based on so little contact too frightening. Many of them, says Jim Parker, leave singles bars alone, or if they are courageous enough to ask for a name and phone number, once they have left the highly charged atmosphere of the bar they may never use the information:

You don't find as many sexual contacts made as you think could be. Most people come in there to jerk each other off and in turn they jerk themselves off. Most people go home alone. Maybe because they haven't met anybody that meets up to their fantasies, they just meet the same kind of people over and over. So it becomes a futile thing, but they keep doing it because they have nothing else to do. They could sit home with friends, but I don't think a lot of these people have friends. They hang with a group, but I don't think they're friends to each other, because they can sit in a group with five or six, and four out of the six aren't even looking at the person they're talking to. The loneliness causes great desperation, and people feel they have to rush into things because they'll lose their chance. A lot of guys will approach a girl and take down her phone number and I bet half of them never call the girl because what would they say to her when they're alone? Maybe they do call, but I keep seeing them come in alone over and over again.

Most people who go to singles bars hardly live up to the media's image of "the swinger."

Despite all the hoopla to the contrary, singles bars must defeat their customers' expectations in order to survive. Profits would diminish radically in an atmosphere where customers could form solid, viable relationships.* The atmosphere of most singles bars

* A *Newsweek* article on single life in America (July 16, 1973) estimated that one singles bar owner, Michael O'Keefe, grossed over $1 million a year from his two New York City bars. One has only to multiply that figure by the number of successful bars in a large city or suburb to gauge how lucrative such businesses can be. Many bars, furthermore, charge not only for drinks but demand a three- or four-dollar cover charge just to get in.

is one that encourages precisely the opposite results. On a popular night at a singles bar there are so many people on display that it's impossible to selectively distinguish one person from another, to be selectively available—to turn on someone to whom you may be attracted while turning off someone you may find unattractive.

Walking into the typical singles bar on a Wednesday or Friday night is like walking into an overstocked dress department for an after-Christmas sale. All the lovely wares on display give you a rush of excitement. But after the first flash of anticipation you become discouraged and dismayed. How will you ever find what you are looking for in this mess of merchandise? There is so much, everything begins to look the same. You leave the store without any merchandise, blaming yourself rather than the shop owner. It was all there for the taking and you couldn't take. With this sense of failure as your only acquisition you leave the bar for the evening, with the idea that you will come back another day.

The whole task of meeting people at singles bars can be overshadowed by the expectation of defeat. It is common, for instance, to hear women who go to singles bars explain that they do not expect to meet a man in whom they would be interested. Ruth, a member of a large New York publishing house, often goes to singles bars in search of a man. Yet she does not believe that the kind of man she wants would be there: "You know that you'll never meet any man that you'd really like, because the kind of man you'd really like wouldn't be in a singles bar, he'd be interested in things and have an active social life. But you get lonely and you go anyway."

Similarly, Dorothy Ames (pp. 199–212), and Anne (pp. 159–160) insist that the kind of men they want would not have to go to a singles bar in order to meet women. Because women believe, not without reason, that men have more freedom in their jobs and personal lives than do women, they feel that an attractive man would meet people at work, at a museum or opera, rather than at a bar. Women, they feel, have to go to a singles bar because they lack other opportunities to meet people. Their presence at a bar does not indicate that they are losers. Yet they consider men who go to singles bars to be losers. Hoping that they will meet the one exception to this rule, women continue to come to bars, and indeed, because of their negative expectations and the nature of the singles bar, they are often disappointed. Men feel the same way.

"I would go to a singles bar," one young man confided, "but I don't think I would like any of the women I met there." And for people of both sexes, having to go out and actively look for company in a rather alienating environment makes them lose respect for themselves as well as for others. This sense of defeat further increases loneliness and helps to push people into relationships that, again, serve only to increase loneliness.

Thus many people who score at a singles bar feel after a one-night or two-week affair that they have been used. On this subject it is worth recalling a comment quoted at the beginning of this book by a divorced lawyer, John Atkisson, in San Francisco, who spoke of the results of many of the sexual relationships begun at singles bars:

For the most part the eminently respectable sons-of-bitches walking around the financial district of S.F. know how to get laid. The question is, is that what they want to accomplish, and the answer is "no." But that's what they'll settle for. They want, however, more than that. They want to accomplish "it" of course—the ultimate, mind-blowing experience, ultimate emotional experience.. What it boils down to is falling in love.

By this analysis, the cynicism of many so-called swingers is a result of disappointed expectations. A man or woman goes to a singles bar in the hope of encountering the person who will fulfill his or her image of a mate. Neither is looking for a person with whom to develop a relationship over a long period of time but rather for an instant relationship with a man or woman who will "blow my mind"—the modern equivalent of "love at first sight." Given the atmosphere of the average singles bar, it is difficult to imagine how this might take place. Since the chief effect of the singles bar is the reduction of the clientele to a common level of frustration and despair, the swinger's ideal described below by Atkisson is impossible to achieve.

What do people on the action circuit want? No matter how a person insists that they are only in the action circuit for the fun of it, they definitely want commitment; only they want to be driven to it because their minds have been blown. But the reason we're cynical is that while we realize that that's what we want, we realize that it's quite impossible. It doesn't exist. Not that the "one" doesn't exist, but that it isn't a lasting one, because human beings aren't built that way. It's humanly impossible to maintain that kind of fervor for long; a human being can't live that way.

This skepticism, in fact, underlies much swinging behavior. After experiencing or witnessing a painful divorce or separation, the possibility of another permanent love relationship is denied. The skeptical view is maintained to protect a romanticized and impossible view of love characterized by a desire for total immersion in the love relationship. The conflict between skepticism and romance sets up an ambivalence about lovers and possible lovers which is constantly hovering between ecstasy and disappointment. It permits both parties, after the deflation of an affair, to feel used and ill treated. And it propels the cycle of false expectations onward.

For those who, as a result of this constant disillusionment, don't drop out of the singles scene, the bars can become the arena for a cynical exploitation of the opposite sex in an attempt to gain as much—either financially or sexually—as possible while giving as little as possible in return. This cynicism is not characteristic of men only but, as John Atkisson argues, of both the men and women who are habitués of the singles scene:

More and more there is developing a breed of cat who knows that scene through and through. I know men who are great candidates for women's lib, they are not MCP's, but they find themselves lashing into a language that refers to women in very shoddy terms, very sexual terms, and all they are is on a different level of cynicism. At the same time there is also developing more rapidly a group of women who feel the same way—hard, crusty, severe, cynical—and who will frankly and openly and shockingly suggest that they want to fuck your brains out or who will recount their exploits.

Most women feel that they have been exploited by men, but it's like a narcotics habit, you know—they can't live with men, can't live without 'em. They just feel terribly guilty and remorseful every time they are with one—which is about three or four times a week.

CONVERSATION II

(*Man and woman in singles bar where they've just had a first date.*)
HE: I have to go now. I really don't feel good. I hope you don't mind. I'm really beat.
SHE: No, go ahead.
HE: Well, I'll call you.
SHE: Okay.
HE: I'm going to take the bus. Look, can you get a cab home?
SHE: Sure.
HE (*hesitantly*): Here's five dollars for the cab. Is that enough?
SHE: It won't be that much.
HE: Well, take five, and you can always buy me lunch with the change.
SHE (*skeptically*): Sure.
HE: Well, good night.
SHE: Good night. I hope you feel better. (*He leaves and she turns to another woman.*)
SHE: Well, at least I got cab fare out of him.

This attitude, says Jim Parker, is typical of the "hard-core" swinger:

Well, Maxwell's is really brutal. For instance, of the girls that go in there, 50 percent of them that go in there for a drink are looking to get dinner, to get the tab paid for, and 50 percent go in there to socialize like they would to every other bar. But it's very heavy, be-

cause everybody actively tries to be chic, and the way they try comes off as being very gauche—in their dress, their mannerisms, and their behavior.

You get a lot of women who are diamond diggers, gold diggers, women between the ages of twenty-three and twenty-eight, who are married and divorced, who might have children, or who haven't been married, and they are really looking to latch onto something. And then there are some women who are there just to goof on people, to get away with free dinners, a full night of drinking.

Like, say a girl goes in there and all she wants is to be able to drink, to be seen and to have dinner. She'll leave herself open to almost anybody, and I've seen it happen that the girls will just float around until some guy will offer them dinner. Here's a typical scene, for instance. A guy from Texas, in his forties, who comes to New York on a convention, he's staying at the Americana, he's married, and he comes up here and he thinks he's going to knock the world dead. He'll offer the girl the world, and she won't fuck in the end; at least if she got the guy off in the end, then he'd get what he wanted. The guy thinks he's gonna come to New York and it's gonna be easy, but it's not that easy, because these girls look at these guys as the jerks of the world, as real saps. So you've got this conniving bitch and this pathetic sap, and all they do is just split after the evening.

Women come in there to screw just as much as men. Before 1965 or so a woman would never admit that she had come to a bar to find a guy to ball him, but now women do.

In all this new freedom people learn to take advantage of one another's weakness and loneliness. Peter, a divorced executive well versed in the Chicago singles world, explains that if a woman comes to a singles bar because she is lonely and has nowhere else to go, she will find men who will use her vulnerability to get sex:

If you are a secretary in Chicago and you want to meet people, where else is there to go but to a singles bar? You come to the bar because you want to meet people and you're lonely. And you put up with a lot because that's what you have to do. Women may come here because they want to meet someone to have a relationship with. But

men come here only for one thing—sex. Naturally they will take ad-
vantage of anything—of a woman's loneliness—to get what they want.
Of course I'd do that—I'd take advantage of anything to get sex.

It is interesting that Peter expressed sympathy rather than dis-
respect for the woman's plight. And one wonders how men or
women feel knowing that they have scored by exploiting the
vulnerability of people weakened by loneliness and alienation.
Achieving sex in such a case is like stealing candy from a baby.
It demeans the thief more the victim.

The brand of male-female equality suggested by such cynicism
presents an interesting version of both sexual and female liberation. Men, for instance, rarely buy drinks for women in singles
bars. "A man won't buy a drink for a woman anymore," says
Rebecca, a secretary. "Things have gotten very cold and impersonal. A man may invite you to go to a bar with him, and then
you have to pay for your own drink." The refusal to buy a
woman a drink is not motivated by the belief that men and
women should be equal, but rather by the notion that male
sexual contact is in such demand that you no longer have to pay
for it with amenities such as a drink and dinner. "Why should I
buy a girl a drink?" asked Louis, a well-to-do swinger. "Why
shouldn't she buy her own damn drink? One time I was in a bar
and I picked up a girl I liked. She asked me to buy her a drink
and I said, 'Buy your own damn drink.' And she did and she came
home with me." Equality seems to be defined as equal brutality
for all and by all.

The effects of such a cynical attitude do tend, after a time,
to boomerang. John Atkisson insists that habitual swingers end
up hurting their health, emotional well-being and careers.

There are literally thousands of men who no longer remember what
it is like to be healthy and awake and unhungover. A guy stays out
every night until one or two in the morning. He may end up closing a
bar with his buddies, and not going home with anybody. If he gets a
girl to go home with him he's lucky, because then he gets some kind

of release. But he's killing himself every night. Mostly he destroys his health and his career. He comes into work late and he's always hungover. He may be able to survive that way, but he isn't going to advance.

Women, Mr. Atkisson believes, do not get as carried away with swinging as do many men, mainly because they can't afford to do so. "A woman paces herself more. They don't get as drunk. Also, they have more menial jobs and so they can't get too drunk because they don't have the privilege of coming in late to work in the morning."

Besides singles bars, the past decade has seen the growth and popularization of another branch of the singles industry—the apartment complex especially constructed for singles living. In 1974 alone 100,000 singles apartment units were built across the country. The singles apartment complex began in Los Angeles with the South Bay Clubs, and since the appearance of the first such facility in 1964 many such units have been constructed in southern and northern California, in Arizona, the Washington, D.C., area, Illinois, and other such large urban or suburban areas. Because of complaints that such a limitation made the units discriminatory, the singles complex is no longer advertised as solely offering singles living. They are now referred to as "country clubs" or places for "adult living." A typical complex has a scattering of married couples. No children are allowed in such "communities."

Studio, one-, and two-bedroom apartments are available at singles complexes, generally in the $250–$350 price range. Because of the rather high prices, many singles share their apartments with a roommate, and lack of sufficient funds to meet the rent each month is one of the reasons for the high transience in singles communities. As one resident of a singles complex in Los Angeles commented, "Hardly a day goes by when you don't see someone moving out and someone moving in."

In most singles complexes the apartments are furnished in what residents refer to as "Howard Johnson's" or "motel modern," and there is little difference between one unit and the next. The management discourages personal furniture by making the difference between the cost of a furnished and unfurnished unit minimal. The complexes are generally quite large, with a population somewhere between 600 and 2,000. Most have large recreational facilities such as swimming pools, tennis courts, indoor golf, and crafts and game rooms.

The singles apartment complex promises to do what the singles bar has not done—provide an atmosphere in which people can belong to a clearly defined community of people, with clearly defined activities in which to engage, in a clearly defined environment. Kitty Lawler, social director of Oakwood Gardens, formerly South Bay Clubs, Marina complex, explains that living at Oakwood provides people with friends and a social life and makes the need to leave Oakwood unnecessary. "Why leave," Mrs. Lawler asks, "when at Oakwood the name of the game is fun?"

Subscribing to the traditional belief that loneliness can be alleviated if people keep themselves so busy that they forget their predicament, the singles apartment complex engages a social director to think up social activities, supervise their execution, and convince people to participate. The social director is most often an elderly woman, reminiscent of the camp social director or fraternity mother.

The degree of participation in the activities of a complex varies from place to place. At the International Village in the suburbs of Chicago the management is said to put a great deal of pressure on residents to participate in scheduled activities. These activities include sports competitions between the various buildings in the complex. Other facilities schedule outings, Saturday-night dances, Sunday brunches, and barbecues, among other activities.

The amount of swinging or sexual exchange varies between complexes. At Oakwood's Marina complex, the population is younger, more transient, and more sexually fluid; while at the same company's San Fernando Valley complex residents are older, somewhat less transient, and the atmosphere is calmer.

Where there is a considerable amount of sexual activity, what to do when you have slept with many people in the complex becomes a problem. Some people feel they must move out if their sexual exploits are too well advertised.

Whatever the crowd and the amount of sexual activity, the thing that seems to attract people to singles apartment complexes are their suburban locations, the activities and recreational facilities they offer, and the possibility of community.

With his career and the opportunities he has of meeting exciting people, one wouldn't nominate David as a likely candidate for Oakwood Gardens. A well known stage actor must meet so many interesting people, and many beautiful women among them. And yet David stays at Oakwood whenever he is shooting a film for the movies or television in Los Angeles. His choice of Oakwood as opposed to any other apartment complex, he says, was primarily motivated by its location in the San Fernando Valley. Near the freeway and several film studios, Oakwood seemed a logical choice. The complex is also near his ex-wife and children, so that it is not difficult for him to see his kids when he wants to. The restrictions in the complex against children's use of facilities are a problem, especially for his youngest child, but still he finds Oakwood appealing.

There are a variety of activities with which he can occupy spare time. But mostly the atmosphere at Oakwood is not as anonymous as that of most other urban and suburban apartments. David does not go to many of the activities, but there are people to be met if he should want to meet them, and the silence of his apartment when he feels the need of privacy. There is something, David says, in knowing that you can say hello to a neighbor when you are walking down the corridor and that you will be greeted with a smile rather than a suspicious look, that makes Oakwood attractive despite its troubling plastic environment.

The tennis courts are the main reason Sue likes living here. A native New Yorker who only recently arrived in Los Angeles, she is delighted to be able to play tennis almost all year round for as many hours a day as she chooses. The friendly atmosphere at Oakwood is also part of the appeal the complex has for her. Moving to Los Angeles wasn't easy for a forty-five-year-old divorcée. She had one friend in the entire city, and living, as she did when she first arrived, in an anonymous high-rise did not make her feel welcome or secure. She was somewhat hesitant about moving into a place with a reputation for swinging singles, but she was relieved to find that if there was a lot of sexual activity at Oakwood, she wasn't aware of it. Oakwood may lack sophisticated good taste, she says, but at least there are opportunities for meeting people, people with whom one can have friendships as well as romantic involvements. And after having made a life for herself after a long and unpleasant marriage, Sue is in no hurry to remarry.

Playing tennis has given Sue the best opportunities of meeting people. She does not often go to social functions at Oakwood. She feels that the themes of many Saturday-evening activities— a Las Vegas gambling casino, dances, wine tastings—appeal only to the loser. She does go to Sunday brunches and Saturday-evening barbecues, where people can bring a plate and get a fairly good meal for two dollars. A group of her new acquaintances chat during dinner, and thus without appearing foolish by going to Saturday-night events, Sue meets the kind of people she finds interesting.

My theory is that the groovier, more sophisticated people are never going to show up at the mass functions—the losers are the ones who will go, more so for women. In singles groups generally the women will surpass the man, because the really good guys don't have to go to that shit. They have women hounding them, crawling all over them.

For the time being, Sue is content living at Oakwood. She has been there almost a year, and will probably live there at least another year, although she does not plan to remain on a permanent basis. She finds, however, that for a woman alone, whose children are grown, and who is new to the area, Oakwood living gives her the opportunity of having companionship when she feels lonely.

There are times when I just want some human contact. I have many casual acquaintances here, which is a great crutch for me. I am a people person. I just sometimes want some contact, just human contact. It may not be what I'd choose to have for a whole evening, so that this is a great crutch for me for now. Maybe when I feel more secure I won't be afraid to move somewhere else where I would be more isolated.

I could never make it in a singles bar. To me they are meat racks, you go in there and show off your wares. I could never do that.

Randy, twenty-nine, works for an advertising company while trying to break into acting in his spare time. He's never been married. He chose Oakwood at the Marina in Los Angeles because of its reputation as a comfortable place to live in a location where women were readily available. He has found after five months that Oakwood lives up to its reputation as a swinger's paradise. On weekends and weekdays, bronzed bodies, both male and female, line the sides of the pool. And when he tires of the women at Oakwood itself, there are 5,000 other single people living in the various apartments at the Marina. Randy has not had to make a date—that is, call a woman a week or so in advance—since he arrived in Los Angeles a year ago. There may be a lot of sexual transiency at Oakwood, but Randy finds that it is a mobility from which he can only benefit. There is a lack of seriousness about life in the Marina: it is hard to get people to talk seriously not only about their sex lives but about what they do, where they come from, and who they are. In this environment it's easy to get what you want and not have to worry about hurting yourself or anybody else.

Most singles complexes provide a good stopping-off point after a man or woman has separated from a spouse. Month-to-month rental agreements mean that it is easy to come and go without worrying about forfeiting money should one tire of the singles-living experiment. Furnished apartments appeal to the divorced man whose wife kept the house and furniture. And the kind of friendly, if not forced, atmosphere of the facilities gives the divorced person some sort of social life. The problem is that only divorced people without children have the privilege of using the singles complex to facilitate adjustment after separation. And for this reason most of the divorced people at singles complexes are men, as most divorced women have the house and the children, and children are prohibited at singles apartments.

Once divorced people make the adjustment to singles life they often leave the complex for traditional residential environments. George, a forty-five-year-old who lived at Oakwood in the Valley for a year after his divorce, was rather disillusioned by singles living. "It's easy to find someone to sleep with at Oakwood," he commented, "but it isn't easy to find a friend. Sex is in great supply in the Western world but friendship is not."

Thus some people find that they are able to develop a sexual community at the singles-living complex but that any other sort of community is illusory.

As a solution to loneliness the singles apartment complex is disappointing. It does offer a friendlier atmosphere, but the kind of "community" provided by such facilities is a false one. It excludes children, and their caretakers, the elderly, and the married. The complexes are generally quite expensive, with high rents and various extra charges for parties and other social events. Thus only the affluent or semiaffluent can partake of the benefits of singles living.

High rents encourage the kind of transiency about which residents in singles apartments complain. The transiency prevalent in so many singles complexes is also a result of the marital status of the residents for which they are constructed. Despite the *Playboy* and *Cosmopolitan* philosophy of the swinger, being single is, traditionally, considered a transient state. Although they may change, the majority of those who enjoy being single don't relish the idea of remaining so forever. Although singles complexes are open to married couples or men and women living together, they are not quite what one has in mind when one is beginning to create a home. Because of the transiency of the singles population, the effort, if it is indeed a serious one, to create an alternative community for Americans is undercut by the same mobility that causes disintegration of any other American community. The singles apartment may provide temporary solace, but it is not a serious solution to loneliness. Like the singles bar, it profits mainly contractors and managers rather than the lonely single man or woman.

If you are searching for a better social life . . . it is within easy reach! The Single American program based on experience, understanding and supported by the newest scientific technology now accomplishes for you in moments what you have been seeking through years of casual dating and ordinary exposure.

There is a right person for you and Single American can tell you who it is, accurately, dependably, scientifically and with deep regard for human dignity.

The future belongs to those who dare to reach out for it. Take your first step in to a happier, richer life now. Complete the attached answer sheet and blank referral form and return it today.

Perhaps the most impersonal and alienating method that the singles industry offers as a mating device is the date arranged by the computer or solicited by personal ads in a variety of newspapers aimed at the singles audience.

The rationale behind the computer-dating organizations that have grown in most large cities is that if you can't do it yourself, technology will do it for you. In fact, technology will do it better than you could do it yourself. For various prices, ranging from $15 to $100 a year, computer-dating companies promise to provide the customer with a number of matches selected each month by the most modern computer techniques. Each customer fills out a form requesting vital statistics concerning age, appearance, education, and religious beliefs, and including a series of questions concerning one's choice of a mate. The computer digests all this information and presumably finds a series of matches, each of whom conforms with the respective mate's requirements. Some companies even promise that the potential matches will be astrologically compatible. Both male and female subscribers are given the names of their respective matches, and the man is told to call the woman and arrange a date.

The personal contact involved in computer-dating services is generally limited to a single interview, conducted by an organizational salesman whose job it is to convince prospective customers that the computer is the best, if not the only, way to ensure compatible matching. Some dating services try to woo customers by promising that mates will be matched by the computer in combination with professional psychologists. The fee of Date-a-Mate in San Francisco, for example, includes not only computer readouts but interviews with professional psychologists or other social scientists. Computer matching promises that questionnaires will be read by professional psychologists who will then use their skill, plus that of the computer, to match mates. This combination of the computer and the social scientists, an advertising pamphlet assures, guarantees successful matching:

Today, a new form of compatibility matching has evolved using the best techniques of the computer—*and* the skills of trained experts in the field of human relations.

The leader in this field is Matchmakers who evaluates the individual as a person, determines his real needs, desires and personality to add the absolutely necessary "human element" which no computer by itself can provide. Then this information is correlated with the data on file in an IBM computer.

Can the dangerous down-curve in successful relationships be reversed?

Yes. The combination of computer and human selection developed by Matchmakers is proving that matching of individuals seriously interested in meeting those with whom they are compatible can definitely be achieved.

Many of those who have subscribed to computer-dating services in a last-ditch effort to find companions complain that the computer promises a lot and delivers little. Even should the computer service deliver a mate with all the superficial characteristics required, a computer, even combined with a psychologist, can hardly distinguish the subtle qualities that determine the attraction between two people. And one can surmise that if a successful relationship results from a computer match, that success is probably due to chance rather than the intuition of an IBM machine.

Singles bars, apartment complexes, and computer-dating services are the most popular branches of the singles industry. They are, however, only three of many services offered for a fee to those who are looking for mates. The singles press constitutes a growing specialty market in the newsprint industry. Dances sponsored by singles organizations and aimed at segregated age groups, singles cruises, escort services, ski clubs, and singles weekends featured by such hotels as Grossinger's and the Concord, in the Catskills in New York, are among the many other activities and events aimed at the single, divorced, or widowed population. In Los Angeles, for instance, in 1974, a young teacher named Barbara Samuels organized a Single-Life Celebration, which was held over a long weekend in a Los Angeles hotel. The celebration featured singles activities from sensitivity training to dances. And Saki's, one singles club in New York, alone has been able to attract 15,000 members and a mailing list of 45,000. Even New York City's rather stuffy Schrafft's restaurants now rent out rooms for singles dances.

In New York a group of businessmen recently bought a large estate that they have transformed into a singles-only country club. Chateau d'Vie, located outside of New York City, offers the usual country club facilities in summer, and indoor sports and social events in winter. The yearly fee of $500 permits the middle-class single man or woman membership. And, indeed, in its first year of existence Chateau d'Vie was flooded with applications. Aside from the obvious attraction of its recreational facilities, the club presents an atmosphere that is more congenial than that characteristic of the singles bar. "I came here almost every weekend last summer," a young salesman says. "It's a much more pleasant way to meet a girl than at singles bars. You can see her on weekends and you get an idea of what she's like. You don't have to make any snap decisions."

Chateau d'Vie, in the interests of its single members, excludes nonsingles from membership. Before a member can be accepted a thorough security check is made to determine marital status. This is aimed at discouraging married people who want to have affairs. According to one woman member, however, the club's security precautions are not all they are said to be. "I went out with a member who had just split up with his wife. I guess he was allowed in because he was separated. But he went back to his wife after a few months and I was left alone. I don't think he should have been allowed to be a member of the club. He was too recently separated."

Members in Chateau d'Vie say they enjoy the social events offered by the club, and they add that such activities allow them to make friends as well as to meet potential mates. Because Chateau d'Vie is limited to singles, however, any social circle of friends tends to be transitory. As much of the club's advertising relies on the implicit assumption that the club will be a place where people can find a mate, people may join the club with that expectation. If one's dream is fulfilled and a relationship results in marriage, membership in the club ends. All friendships with other members may end as well, or those friendships must be centered around social activities outside the club.

The singles industry as a whole creates a false and unstable community. And in the process it exacerbates the problems that have led to the disintegration of community life in America and the loneliness that many Americans feel. It is wholly dependent on the myth that love and intimacy can be realized only with a member of the opposite sex, and that freedom is something that begins in bed. It denies the fact that loneliness in contemporary America is the result of very complicated social problems, and fosters age segregation by limiting membership in social activities to strictly limited age groups; thus there are singles clubs for people between twenty-five and thirty, or thirty-five and forty. Finally, the industry forces people to search for love and companionship in a circuslike atmosphere where personal uniqueness dissolves into the chaos and frenzy of the crowd.

The singles industry was born of the disintegration of community in America, and it is dependent for its continued profits on the maintenance of the status quo. The industry is a business, and businesses are concerned with financial rather than personal growth.

As industry depends upon the planned obsolescence of goods, the singles industry depends on the obsolescence of personal relationships. And, indeed, lonely people who use the singles industry as a solution to their loneliness often feel even more lonely and isolated. What occurs at a bar or hotel or dance is merely a microcosm of what is going on in society at large. And the singles industry is a restatement of the problem rather than a model for the solution.

Chapter Twelve
The Encounter Business

You have approximately four minutes. The impression you make in this "tiny segment of time" says Dr. Leonard Zunin, psychiatrist and popular encounter group leader, will determine what happens next. Four minutes: the contact barrier, Dr. Zunin calls it. Breaking that barrier, he insists, brings an end to the Number One disease of our time—loneliness. And how do you break that barrier? Read Zunin's book, *Contact: The First Four Minutes*, or, better still, read the book and enroll in one of his encounter-style Contact Workshops.

To begin: buy the book. Answer the contactability questionnaire. If you agree with these statements, your contactability is okay:

I can talk easily to others, strangers as well. In new contacts I make an effort to have people trust me by being aware of what I say and how I act.

When I'm talking to a stranger, I try to convey the feeling that he or she has some special qualities. (p. 266)

But if you agree with these next statements, you're going to need a little help:

After initial contact with a stranger, I know I have many prejudices that influence the encounter.

I find it difficult to become interested in unfamiliar subjects other people talk about.

More than half the things I assume about strangers are usually misleading. (p. 267)

For those whose contactability needs revamping, Dr. Zunin's encounter groups for contact, such as the one he held at the Single-Life Celebration in Los Angeles last year, and others he holds for businesses as well as growth centers, give clear exercises that can help one achieve the Four C's of Contactability: Confidence, Creativity, Caring, and Consideration. For example, there is the Hello Exercise, in which partners stand in front of each other and practice saying "hello" in various tones with various facial expressions. Or the Goodbye Exercise, or the Handshake Exercise, or the exercise in which you practice telling your partner the assumptions you have made concerning him and his conduct.

After you have mastered the skills taught in Dr. Zunin's book and in his Contact Workshops, you need never be lonely again. Despite our impersonal culture, there is no reason, says Dr. Zunin, except lack of skill, for people to be lonely:

Too many people endure the pain of loneliness rather than taking steps to overcome it. Even in these fast-paced times, there is no valid reason to be lonely. The opportunities to meet people, know and really get involved with other individuals are greater now than any time since Adam and Eve had only God and the serpent for conversational partners. This is so for two reasons: 1) there are simply more people on earth than ever in the history of man, and 2) technological advances provide you with virtually unlimited mobility and means of communication. (p. 8)

Dr. Zunin's Contact Workshops and book are part of the increasingly popular Human Potential Movement (HPM), which attracts millions of Americans each year into its various groups, lectures, weekends, and weeks of "intensive" training in interpersonal skills. The leaders of the Human Potential Movement believe that the skills they teach are the answer to the loneliness and impersonality of an increasingly dehumanizing culture.

The Human Potential Movement has disparate roots and

equally diffuse methods.* Influenced by the thinking of such people, among many others, as Kurt Lewin, Abraham Maslow, Frederick Perls, Wilhelm Reich, Carl Rogers, William Schutz, the movement began in the late forties with interest in training social scientists in the skills of human relations. The first encounter group is said to have taken place at a National Training Laboratory in which a group whose task was helping leaders develop human-relations skills shifted its focus to the relationships within the group. Since the fifties, "unstructured groups which focus on their own dynamics"—as Carl Rogers defines the encounter group in *On Encounter Groups*—have sprung up all over the country.

The aim of the HPM is the expansion of awareness—the releasing of the locked-up potential in human beings. Such self-awareness is the key to health, and thus the motto of the HPM is "Be in touch with your feelings." If human beings are aware of their physical and emotional states, they can experience themselves and others fully. This experience of the self will lead to fulfillment, the peak experiences of which Abraham Maslow speaks in *Toward a Psychology of Being*, or joy, as William Schultz describes it in this passage from his book *Joy*:

The underlying philosophy behind the human potential thrust is that of openness and honesty. A man must be willing to let himself be known to himself and to others. He must express and explore his feelings and open up areas long dormant and possibly painful, with the faith that in the long run the pain will give way to a release of vast potential for creativity and joy. This is an exhilarating and frightening prospect, one which is often accompanied by agony, but which usually leads to ecstasy. (p. 14)

To be in touch with your body and your feelings is the first step on the road to joy. But to achieve full joy one must also be able

---

* The HPM is so vast that it is difficult to categorize its thinkers. For simplicity and so as to be able to talk about it at all, I will consider ideas and thinkers that represent tendencies in the movement. I will refer to these as "the leaders of the HPM"—although I am aware that many within the movement do not share their ideas.

to relate well to others, for, as Schutz says, "Ours is a communal culture, this means functioning in such a way that human interaction is rewarding to all concerned." Thus in the HPM the self is reflected in the eyes of the other.

The arena of this process of achieving self-awareness through interaction with others is the encounter group. The encounter group teaches the skills that will bring an end to loneliness, building bridges between the self and others and between the self and its hidden corners. Encounter groups appear in many different guises: under the label, for instance, of T-group (task-oriented group), sensitivity training, contact workshop, singles workshop, Synanon, Gestalt, or TA (for transactional analysis) workshop, and in industry organizational development. Yet, despite variations, the typical encounter group is recognizable through certain basic characteristics. The groups are generally small, normally with eight to fifteen members—although encounter techniques are currently used in groups that may include up to a hundred or more people. There is generally a leader, although the function of that leader is to facilitate group interaction rather than to direct, in traditional leadership fashion, all communication through him- or herself. The job of the leader or "facilitator" is to encourage the "open encounter," or the focusing of attention on "the process and dynamics of the immediate personal interaction," as Carl Rogers explains in *On Encounter Groups*. The facilitator is also a participant in the group and may be subjectively involved in the group process.

Although the typical encounter group may meet for only a short time—anywhere from a few hours to several weeks—the individual can learn much about him- or herself, Carl Rogers says, because of the intensity of the experience:

In an intensive group, with much freedom and little structure, the individual will gradually feel safe enough to drop some of his defenses and façades, he will relate more directly on a feeling basis (come into a basic encounter) with other members of the group; he will come to understand himself and his relationship to others more accurately; he will change in his personal attitudes and behavior; and he will subsequently relate more effectively to others in his everyday life situation.*

Teaching effective relating is perhaps the main application of the encounter technique, and it is this instruction that the HPM considers its most useful tool against the loneliness of our age. Because of the context of our society, the traditional methods of meeting and mating are no longer feasible, and so we need to develop, via the encounter group, new methods of getting to know people. "People need to develop skills to get along with one another because we no longer have instant communality of former times, where communities were homogeneous and there- fore people shared the same interests and values," says Dr. Wil- bert R. Sikes, a Manhattan psychiatrist. "So we need to develop techniques for discovering people's values and for listening to people." One of the aims of the encounter group is thus to shorten the getting-to-know-you period of a relationship.

There are a number of fairly standard techniques that the HPM uses in order to teach its followers to discard the masks that separate people from one another. First of all, we must learn to live in the here and now (an idea that derives from the work of Frederick Perls) rather than living either in the past or look- ing solely toward the future. To begin concentrating on the here and now, Perls suggests that people make statements using the words "here and now" about their feelings about themselves and their environment—emotions that they feel at a particular mo- ment. Interactions in encounter groups should concentrate on the here and now and what is going on when people meet. These statements include not only awareness of verbal communication but also awareness of what is communicated through the body— body language. Awareness of the self and the other is facilitated by exercises that encourage people to *really* see each other, such as those Emily Coleman, the popular encounter group leader, uses in the groups she leads all around the country.

* Carl Rogers, in Siroka *et al, Sensitivity Training,* p. 12.

Well, I have many techniques. First I make people look at each other and be aware of what they see. And then to be aware that each one of us has a whole system of wishes and prejudices when we meet someone, and when we are aware of that we can expand our repertoire of ways of reaching out. And then touching. I try to help people become aware of what they are communicating and learning from a touch. Learning to touch and also to push away a touch. Then another one is talking and listening. To teach people to really listen and also to help people say what they have to say. And that is a long, long, difficult process.

Another way the encounter movement teaches people to live in the here and now is by discouraging people from asking too many questions during their meetings with another person. Make statements and don't question, encounter leaders urge. Too many questions indicate that you are trying to hide from another person.

To be open and honest you must confront what you feel. This is one of the main tenets of the HPM. In encounter groups people are often asked to sit face-to-face, two people silently looking at each other for several minutes, during which time both partners are supposed to be aware of everything they feel. They are then asked to tell their partners what they thought. This encourages the open encounter. The expression of feelings also encompasses the knowledge and expression of expectations and desires, as well as the immediate feelings one has about the person with whom one is in contact. Jack Crickmore, director of Transition Institute in Berkeley, California—an organization that runs encounter weekends for divorced or widowed people—believes that learning to say "I want" is one way to neutralize loneliness:

The way we deal with loneliness is to identify what kind of "I want" isn't being fulfilled—if it's the "I want" of requited love, if it's the "I want" of company, if you have no one around you and there's an "I want" of caring, or sharing, then maybe there is a communication problem we have to deal with. The first thing to do is to say that's okay, to say "I'm lonely." To say "I want." Merely by saying "I want," identifying it, it owns the person less. There's less pressure on them. You have to stay with the loneliness, really taste it, and share it with other people, and once you do that, it no longer obsesses you and gets in your way.

Once you make your expectations known, another person can provide you with what you lack. Expressing needs and expectations, says George Bach, founder of the "pairing" technique of the HPM, prevents the mix-ups inherent in the old style of relating, in which people dealt with masks covering up the real aims and desires of the two people involved.

Another method suggested by Bach and other encounter leaders is to confront issues of attraction and repulsion immediately. Exercises in encounter groups may then concentrate on having partners say what they think of each other. If you find something special about a person, Bach says, tell him or her. If something disturbs you, say it. If you have assumptions about another person, Dr. Zunin says, reveal those assumptions. Not only should you express good feelings but also negative feelings. Dr. Bach's pairing procedure thus asks people to express anger as well as joy. By doing this, people will learn to be flexible and to discard assumptions and stick to reality.

Of course, being open and honest involves taking risks. In recognition of this the HPM believes that its exercises and processes will teach people to take risks outside the group as well as during group time. To be free enough to take risks with others one must, however, learn skills in how to trust others. One of the first exercises in many encounter groups, such as the drop-in encounters that take place every Friday night at the Topanga Growth Center in Los Angeles, is an exercise in developing trust. The group divides into smaller circles of people. One person stands in the middle of a circle formed by other members of the group. The person in the middle falls backward or sideways into the arms of another participant. That person must catch the falling person and hold him or her up. Members take turns in the middle and on the outside.

A similar exercise is the blind walk, or trust walk, in which one closes his or her eyes and allows oneself to be led around by another person. The presumption is that the "blind" partner will regress to a childlike or infantile state in which there was dependence on others for guidance. In experiencing that regression a person will learn what he or she did not learn in childhood—to trust others.

To fully express emotions, encounter groups discourage intellectualizing. Being abstract or theoretical about feelings is to leave the here and now and hide behind a mask of words. Perls has called intellectualizing "elephant shit," and many encounter leaders follow suit. An encounter leader at the Topanga Growth Center explained that the trouble with the world was that "people think too much and don't feel enough. If President Nixon didn't think so much and was closer to his feelings, Watergate would not have happened." Personal as well as political Watergates are discouraged by asking people to be as concrete as possible, get into their feelings, and experience rather than think about life.

These techniques (which are only a few among many) increase flexibility, encounter leaders say. Rather than game-playing or role-playing when you meet someone, the encounter group teaches you to be direct. Although this state of openness is called different things by different groups, almost all leaders insist that it permits people to get what they want out of life.

Bach believes that the skills taught in his "pairing" classes will make people what he calls "intimate people," who will have the "intimate eye and questing heart," and Jack Crickmore says that the skills taught at Transition Institute will make people "meetable":

Once you demystify, or detoxify loneliness, you can get on with the business of living, and then, my sense is that the loneliness pretty well takes care of itself.

Once you begin to satisfy the business of living and the "I wants," then "I want someone to fuck" is just another small step.

The loneliness gets solved not by trying to solve it but by getting on with one's life after putting the loneliness in a safe place. Before long my sense is that people are no longer lonely.

There are four billion people walking around the earth and half of them are male and half of them are female and there's a natural attraction between them. So it's almost impossible not to meet people, you have to be a recluse not to meet people, so that brings us to the getting-on-with-life part. And Transition Institute's part in helping people get on with single life is to help people become what we call more *meetable. Rather than putting people in a situation where they can meet people, we say the situation is having people have this glow.* What will bring you in contact with the person you want to meet is being meetable. If you're meetable you can strike up conversations with people on street corners waiting for buses, in restaurants, waiting rooms, the elevator—there's no end to the millions of people you can meet if you're meetable. [*emphasis mine*]

Once you become "meetable," "intimate," or skillful in the techniques of relating, such encounter leaders believe that you can take your pick of relationships. As Dr. Bach says in *Pairing:*

So anyone who can be open and genuine can approach anyone else with a probability of success. This probability frees people to explore the potentials of any number of relationships. For in a philosophic as well as a psychological sense, all human beings live in the same village and can greet each other as neighbors. (Bach *et al,* p. 137)

Not only can you begin relationships with these skills but you can also avoid the pain of ending relationships. Learning to say what you want means that you can end an affair when you no longer want it. And ending an affair at an appropriate time, Allen and Martin's book *Intimacy* says, avoids much of the pain of parting.

The end of an affair can be an unhappy time, but it is usually less so if the lovers have been emotionally as well as physically intimate. Then there has been enough honesty that they have always faced realistically the possibility that the relationship might not last. And there is enough empathy that they can take leave of each other without inflicting unnecessary injury. More important, both retain the personal growth that a creative alliance fosters. And this allows them to proceed to other relationships with self-confidence and realistic expectations. (p. 142)

The skills acquired through participation in the groups spawned by the HPM enable a person to make and break relationships quickly and easily. And speed is of the essence in our increasingly changing world. As Leonard Zunin says in *Contact*: ". . . it is necessary to speed up the processes by which friendships are established—and possibly consummated."

The founders of the encounter movement see the facilitation of adaptation to change as one of their most important services. Carl Rogers writes in *On Encounter Groups*:

Conceivably one of the most important implications of the encounter group is that it helps the individual in adapting to change. Very few people seem to realize that one of the most basic questions for present-day and future man is the question of how rapidly the human organism can adapt to the almost unbelievable speed of the changes brought about by technology. . . . Thus, our technology is forcing upon mankind a rapidity of change for which the human organism is poorly prepared. Certainly the encounter group with its various offshoots and related groups is an enormous help in enabling individuals to become aware of their feelings about change, and to make of change a constructive possibility. (pp. 177–78)

In the belief that awareness of one's feelings is *the* way to deal with social problems, Rogers argues that recognizing and expressing one's feelings about change combats the instability of our world. In a time of accelerating change the HPM promises that its methods will lead to "instant intimacy," as Bach calls it, both inside and outside the encounter group. This instant intimacy will alleviate the loneliness caused by high mobility. People will recognize each other's uniqueness, and this appreciation leads to a caring and accepting atmosphere. The person leaving the encounter group has gained a feeling of community.

And that sense of community alleviates alienation. As Rogers says in *On Encounter Groups:*

. . The more the movement spreads—the more individuals experience themselves as unique and choosing persons, deeply cared for by other unique persons—the more ways they will find to humanize our currently dehumanizing forces. The individual will no longer simply be an IBM card or a series of facts stored on a memory tape for a computer. He will be a person, and will assert himself as such. This is certain to have very far-reaching effects.

Similarly, the encounter group can be an attempt to meet and overcome the isolation and alienation of the individual in contemporary life. The person who has entered into the basic encounter with another is no longer completely isolated. It will not necessarily dissolve his loneliness, but at least it proves to him that such loneliness is not an inevitable element in his life. He can come in meaningful touch with another being. Since alienation is one of the most disturbing aspects of modern life, this is an important implication. (p. 176)

The HPM promises to wrap its clients in a womb of caring and community. And the skills that created this warm atmosphere can be applied outside the encounter group, thus reproducing the encounter climate in the outside world.

The problem with this exemplary goal is, of course, how to bridge the gap between the internal world of the encounter group and an external world beset by social, political, and economic chaos. The leaders of the encounter movement solve this problem in a variety of ways that are dependent upon their analyses of the origins of social problems and the way such problems can be ameliorated. Although the HPM is vast and its leaders hold many different opinions, for the sake of simplicity I will divide what I consider some representative arguments into two groups—the left and the right wing of the encounter movement.

Almost all of the leaders of the HPM insist that loneliness is a disease peculiar to our time. Those on the right believe this loneliness stems not from an increasingly dehumanizing environment created by a specific political system, but rather from the fact that people don't know how to benefit from what is offered them. They share a fundamental faith in the potential of our society. To them America is an affluent society in which the possibilities for self-fulfillment are limitless. America is a vast shopping center in which every possible kind of relationship is available. Anyone can find what is necessary for the satisfaction of a particular need. The problem is that people either lack the proper directions to get to the shopping center, or that, once there, they don't know the appropriate language to get what they want. Loneliness is not a psychological, sociological, or political problem; it is a communications management problem.

The dissatisfactions people express stem from either the failure to know what they want or the inability to express their wants and needs. Jack Crickmore of Transition Institute offers a very simple prescription for correcting this failure: just get up and do something about it.

I don't think there are social issues. If you're a woman teacher and you're working mainly with women teachers and children, and you want to meet a man, then get another job. If you don't like working with women and children, then what the hell are you doing teaching? Think of something. Go teach mathematics in a junior college, there's a way to meet a man. What about teaching investment principles in some extension department? I don't think there's a social problem there. What are you doing in that bad situation? I really have to say that I don't believe that there are physical barriers out there stopping people from meeting each other.

The left of the encounter movement believes that there is something fundamentally wrong with the structure of our society. Loneliness is a result of a dehumanizing culture whose profit motive is destructive to human development. When it comes to the question of rehumanizing America, however, the left begins to sound like the right. Again change becomes a question of attitudes. No political organization is necessary; the Revolution will be a revolution of consciousness. Influenced by the ideas of

Wilhelm Reich, the left believes that if everyone asserts what he or she wants, if everyone has the right attitude and openly expresses his or her emotions, then all will be well. If encounter group techniques are used in industry and government, in schools and colleges, a whole new society will appear—what Carl Rogers calls a "person-oriented society":

We will, I believe, see a more formless spread of the encounter group *spirit*, and *climate*. . . . There is no organized encounter group. There is simply freedom of expression—of feelings and thoughts—on any personally relevant issue. It takes somewhat more imagination to envision what an industry or college might be if permeated by this climate. And when one thinks of a bureaucracy such as the Bureau of Indian Affairs, or the State Department, it takes a vivid imagination indeed! Yet, it is not necessarily impossible. Will a person-centered organization always be a contradiction in terms? I believe not.*

Despite the fact that the different branches of the encounter movement spend a lot of energy distinguishing themselves from each other, their basic ideas converge around the dynamics of social change. The distinctions between the ideas of the right and left wings are only terminological. The latter calls change Revolution, and the former calls it change of consciousness. The right views loneliness as a purely personal problem, dissociated from the social conditions in which people live. Seen as a private affair, loneliness is amenable only to a private solution. The spillover from the private solution, as Emily Coleman points out, will eliminate any problems in the public domain: "We are pioneers. We have to make people realize that this is a whole new stage of life. And there are lots and lots of goodies out there for people. I think that if you help them realize that they can get what they want and need, I think then they won't be as belligerent and violence will decrease."

The left wing sees loneliness as both a more complex private

* *On Encounter Groups*, p. 175.

and public concern. But, again, the solution is to be effected
through private means. The encounter group is still the vehicle
for social change, and the proper application of the ideas of the
Human Potential Movement will create a harmonious world. The
desire for dominance over others will disappear; personal needs
will be shared with others; and if conflict appears, the very
awareness of it will somehow lead to a resolution. Both the left
and right judge the social environment only as an extension of
the attitudes of individuals.

In the past decade the ideas put forth by the HPM have
gained enormous popularity. Every major city in America has a
local growth center. A version of the encounter group called the
"singles encounter drop-in" not only helps its clients gain awareness but also functions as an introduction service for lonely people. Industries are using a version of the encounter group called
Organizational Development to promote good internal relations.
Churches use encounter groups, and so do high schools and universities. And the sexual liberation movement uses encounter
techniques to free people from sexual inhibitions. In Los Angeles
Emily Coleman is developing a million-dollar growth community
where people will be able to incorporate encounter techniques
into a residential community (in which, as in singles apartments,
no children will be allowed). And, of course, such established
growth centers as Esalen and Kairos are more popular than ever
before.

Millions of lonely Americans, many of whom see the HPM as
an alternative to the alienating atmosphere of the singles scene,
believe that the skills taught in the encounter group will help
them end their loneliness. The instant awareness and intimacy
offered by encounter groups are appealing to people who crave
companionship. Such quick results seem an advance on the previous psychotherapeutic techniques through which awareness
and intimacy were presumably to be facilitated. Before the encounter group became popular the place to go to get your head
together was the psychiatrist's office. Psychiatry, however, es-

pecially psychoanalysis, is a long, involved process that not only requires a significant time commitment but a significant financial commitment as well. Moreover, the outcome of analysis is not guaranteed. People who are desperately lonely feel they cannot wait even a month to get results, much less a year or two.

The encounter group, on the other hand, often promises to do in forty-eight hours or two weeks what therapy may not even do after five or six years. Encounter groups, furthermore, view awareness in terms of one's immediate relationships with others. You find yourself while relating to others. Not only can the effort at self-awareness pay off, but in the time it takes for you to gain insight into your emotions you may also meet someone right there in the encounter group. Or you may meet someone to relate with outside the group. You may get two for the price of one: a deeper self-awareness and a partner. Imagine how much more attractive this possibility must look to the lonely person than the prospect of sitting in a room with a psychiatrist who must be left at the end of the hour. The assertions of various encounter leaders, such as this statement by George Bach in *Pairing,* therefore draw more and more people into encounter groups and away from therapy:

Our philosophy and understanding of intimate relationships may be expressed by the formula: one plus one equals three. The three elements are: the man, the woman, and their relationship.

To us, the crucial element is the fire between the logs, the dynamic between the pair. While our students might take years to understand themselves, they can be taught to see and understand their relationships very quickly.

And when they are mobilized toward good relationships, the buried fears and angers within the individual tend to be resolved. Psychoanalysis proves to be unnecessary for most of those who can achieve intimate love by pairing. And most can. (Bach *et al,* p. 26.)

The encounter group can thus often function as an introduction service. Lonely people know that it is possible to meet an available partner at an encounter group meeting. Even the group leader may be involved in this quest for companionship and may form a sexual relationship with a member of the group. Meeting people in an encounter group, furthermore, does not carry the stigma attached to meetings in a psychiatrist's office. People are still somewhat reluctant to admit that they are in psychotherapy. But the encounter group is seen as an acceptable vehicle for personal growth. To say that one is trying to expand one's growth potential is very acceptable in a society based on the growth ethic.

Many people who use the HPM as a vehicle for both personal change and meeting people will swear that its methods are effective. They insist that they have changed, that their relationships with others are better, and that an evening or weekend in the encounter environment makes them feel less lonely. People gain insight into the way they function in social situations, and they feel more confident about their social skills. They share their feelings with others, and are relieved by "getting things off their chests." Many people with whom I spoke about their experiences in encounter groups felt that realizing that other people also had problems was a major encounter group contribution. As one young man said, "I really felt better after I left an encounter group, because hearing all those people talk about their lives made me realize how much better off I was than they were. It really felt good to know that compared to others I wasn't in such bad shape."*

Finally, the encounter group can provide a temporary sense of community, in which the glow of shared feelings creates bonds that will last for the duration of the group experience. At Esalen,

---

* An analogous solution to loneliness, in which people forget their problems by being in contact with others whose problems are more serious, is the "help others solution." People are told to find needy cases and absorb themselves in charitable undertakings. The worse the situation of the person being helped, the better. In that way the helper can feel that his or her own problems are insignificant in comparison. This solution, of course, posits a patronizing dependency on those one is helping, for without the victim, the helper is again assailed by loneliness.

for instance, people come from all over the country to enjoy the beautiful coast at Big Sur and experience feelings of intimacy with people who had been strangers before the group started. Fred, a real estate entrepreneur who goes occasionally to Esalen, found the experience very rewarding. "For a weekend we really got into feeling. There were about eighteen people there and we really got close. Also I met a nice girl from Florida and took her home for a day and that was really nice."

The encounter group is particularly effective if its clients are affluent and thus more able to act upon whatever insights they have gained inside the group. A thirty-seven-year-old professional from the East explained that his experiences at Esalen made him realize that he no longer wanted to pursue his successful career or live in the East. He really wanted to live in the West, by the ocean, in a house he would build and design. Armed with the confidence he had gained at Esalen, he fulfilled his dream. The group experience helped him to change his life for the better. But that change was made possible by his economic resources. What would happen to a thirty-five-year-old auto worker, with four children, who decided he no longer wanted to work on an assembly line? On this subject, it is interesting to note that Rogers, in *On Encounter Groups,* admits that there is little interest among less affluent people in the encounter group phenomenon. Rogers believes this is due to the fact that poorer people simply do not have time to worry about expanding their emotional horizons. Perhaps another reason why the encounter group has not attracted working-class Americans is that encounter groups do not deal with the problems a poorer citizen would have in realizing changes suggested during the group experience.

The failure to deal with people's social situations is one of many dangers a lonely person seeking solace may find in the HPM. Other dangers include lack of control over who runs groups, lack of follow-up contact after an encounter group, and finally the confusion one often finds among encounter group clients and leaders concerning the function of the experience—whether its goal is simply growth or whether it has also therapeutic intentions.

No controls regulate who can lead encounter groups. Almost anyone can put up a shingle, charge a fee, and become a "professional" encounter group leader. Bad guidance is, of course, a problem in any helping profession. But the total lack of any sort of controls is more prevalent in the HPM. The results of such bad leadership are a major problem.

In a recent controlled study that attempted to determine the effects of encounter groups on their clients, Morton A. Lieberman, Irvin D. Yalom and Mathew B. Miles tried to evaluate the effects of encounter groups. The authors point out in their book, *Encounter Groups: First Facts,* that critics of the encounter movement often refuse to recognize that any good can come from such groups, while encounter apologists and leaders see nothing but the positive aspects of encounter groups:

At the other extreme, there is a tendency to ignore, or to disregard rather compelling evidence of adverse consequences of the encounter group experience. Many group leaders and growth centers are hardly aware of their casualties. Their contact with their clients is intense but brief; generally the format of the group does not include follow-up, and knowledge of untoward responses to the experience is, therefore, unavailable. Furthermore, some group leaders reject the medical or psychiatric definition of adverse effects. They assert that stressing members to the point of such discomfort that they require professional help is an accomplishment, not a danger of the encounter group. (pp. 6–7)

Because there is so little follow-up contact, then, a group leader sees only what happens inside the group, rarely discovering what goes on when a person leaves the group and returns to "normal life."

In follow-up studies of encounter groups held on the Stanford campus Lieberman and his coauthors discovered that the "risk factor in several of the groups was considerable." They also determined that there were a significant number of clients who were "casualties" of the group experience:

We defined casualty as a member whose group experience was destructive. During and/or following the group he was more uncomfortable and/or utilized maladaptive defenses and this negative change was relatively enduring. Finally, in our opinion the encounter group could be impugned as the responsible agent. (p. 174)

Encounter group leaders seldom experience firsthand knowledge of such casualties. Many of the nationally known encounter group leaders travel around the country directing groups at various growth centers. Mobile leaders, they deal with mobile participants who have come to a center from far and wide. An individual's reaction to the group experience is his or her problem once the group is over. The psychiatrist or psychologist from whom the encounter participant subsequently seeks counseling may be the only one to know about it.

This lack of follow-up concern is to some extent rationalized by the doctrine of responsibility to which many encounter leaders subscribe. According to this theory, the encounter group is supposed to teach an individual to take responsibility for him- or herself. There is no particular determined outcome of the group experience. You get out of it what you want or what you need. If you have an upsetting experience in the group, that isn't the responsibility of the group leader. Everyone but the facilitator is responsible for his actions. But as Paul Baum, a group leader and psychologist in Berkeley, California, says, encounter groups are supposed to teach caring, not lack of concern:

Part of the pitch of many of these encounter groups is a disclaimer, at the beginning, of the leader's responsibility for anybody in the group. They say that you have to take the responsibility for everything that happens here. And that's not a bad idea, the idea of taking responsibility for yourself, but it ignores one important thing on the part of the leader and that is a sense of compassion and caring for what happens to other people.

The problem of responsibility for what goes on inside the encounter group and for the future effects of that experience is aggravated by a confusion concerning the group's therapeutic function and audience. Many encounter groups state that they are not therapy groups and that they are geared to handle only the problems of the "normal" person. Others say that encounter groups are therapeutic and can adequately deal with "neurotics." The problem with the former type of group is that the ordinary individual may not be equipped to apply to him- or herself such psychological categories.

At a meeting of the Topanga Growth Center in Los Angeles in which I participated this confusion concerning the therapeutic value of the group was evident. The group was comprised mainly of single and divorced men and women who had either been through the singles route or who couldn't stomach trying the singles bar solution. They came to Topanga to spend a nice evening in the hope that they might meet companions. There were, however, several people who had severe problems that the group was simply not equipped to handle. One woman said that she had recently gotten out of the hospital after a year's stay. She had been in a car accident in which she was responsible for the deaths of two people and which had almost caused her own death. In fact, she had been admitted to the hospital as DOA (dead on arrival). The group members responded with concern, but neither they nor the leaders were able to deal with her implicit cry for help. She was quickly passed over in favor of more tractable problems.

Another person in the group, a young man, was very tight and withdrawn. He appeared to be fearful of his own emotions and frustrations; he broke into conversations, and complained that no matter how hard he tried, he couldn't feel comfortable in the group. A young woman berated him and accused him of feeling sorry for himself. He rubbed his hands together nervously and looked as though someone had struck him. He was trying, in his way, to get out his feelings and be open. He just didn't feel at ease, he said, and he wanted to very much. Well, she retorted, what was the matter with him? He could say what he wanted in the group, but he was just looking for the group's sympathy. Why didn't he cut out the self-pity and realize that he had a lot going for himself? Why didn't he stop looking at things so negatively? Looking at the man, I thought it odd that anyone could think he had a lot going for him, and equally odd that this stranger knew so much about him. The young man was effectively silenced, and the group went on to the next basic encounter. The group leader never tried to find out what the man's problem was. How could such an encounter group help this young man grow?

Encounter groups do not generally ask their applicants to fill out extensive questionnaires concerning their mental health. It is true that some centers, such as the Topanga Growth Center, will refer people who seem to need therapy to a therapist. But how can such a limited knowledge of someone else reveal what it is that he or she may need? If someone on the brink of a psychotic episode came to an encounter group, only a skilled leader could diagnose the problem. And the lack of such skilled leaders is a problem throughout the movement.

Carl Rogers has noted that although the encounter movement has enormous potential for helping people make personal changes, it can be misused:

In the first place, I must acknowledge that it [the development of groups] may all too easily fall more and more into the hands of exploiters, those who have come onto the group scene primarily for their own personal benefit, financial or psychological. The faddists, the cultists, the nudists, the manipulators, those whose needs are for power or recognition, may come to dominate the encounter group horizon.*

Rogers believes that the possible misuses of encounter ideas come from self-serving people who wish to exploit rather than help others. This may certainly be part of the problem. Equally, if encounter leaders do not effectively deal with the loneliness of

* *On Encounter Groups*, p. 172.

their clients, it may be because they are more interested in profit than in cure. The fact is, however, that there are basic flaws in the encounter philosophy itself.

To determine whether the HPM is a cure for the loneliness epidemic, we must ask two key questions: Does the encounter movement fulfill its stated aims of really putting people in touch with their feelings, fostering trust, enabling people to have close relationships with others, and creating a sense of community? Does it deal with the social aspects of loneliness?

The HPM believes that the key to ending loneliness is a relationship with another person, and the key to a relationship with another person is self-awareness. In reaction to a society in which feelings are suppressed in the interests of reason and work, the encounter movement argues that unlocking and expressing feelings will lead to mental health. The direct and open person who knows what she or he wants, is aware of expectations, and can trust others is the healthy, self-actualizing person.

To help others achieve self-awareness and to aid them in the expression of emotion is certainly a laudable aim. The question is, do encounter techniques actually lead to self-understanding? Is an awareness of feelings an adequate base for dealing with emotional problems? These questions must be considered in light of the encounter movement's track record and of psychoanalytic theory, on which so much of the movement's ideology and technique (despite hearty disclaimers to the contrary) is based.

Freud's analysis of emotional problems is founded on a theory of the unconscious. The material essential to an understanding of the self is locked away in a part of the mind that is impenetrable by conscious thought. Memories are repressed, buried in the unconscious because of the unacceptable feelings and impulses that are attached to them. It is not enough, Freud said, simply to want to know of the existence of these memories and desires, nor is it enough simply to want to be rid of one's problems. To get "better" one must unlock the closet of repression, examine its contents in a conscious light, and construct a new self that is capable of mediating between desire and reality.

The first step in this process is to learn the language of the unconscious as it appears in dreams, slips of the tongue, jokes, and other phenomena. Analysis of this language in the therapeutic process yields true self-awareness and self-understanding. The process is extremely complex, for the superego and ego make use of various tricks to elude conscious efforts at revelation of unconscious secrets.

Without such analysis the expression of feeling is mere impulse release, which is a relief because it permits the discharging of pent-up emotion, but which does not, of and by itself, dispose of the unpleasant emotion. One can describe one's feelings and experience their reality, but that neither explains—nor changes—the problem.

The analytic process is one in which the patient can feel things, and then work them through. Encouraged by the therapist, the patient re-experiences the anxieties caused by early conflicts. What has been repressed begins to work itself into the conscious mind. The patient transfers archaic feelings and ideas about the world onto the therapist, and he or she not only verbalizes early conflicts but actually experiences the original emotions relating to those conflicts. The transference relationship enables the patient and analyst to interpret the unconscious—to make, as Freud said, what was unconscious conscious, and permit the patient to get rid of a great deal of emotional baggage along the way. But all this, according to Freud and his followers, takes time—sometimes a year, and often more.

The encounter movement and many of its leaders insist that psychoanalysis—the intellectual approach—is "elephant shit" or "bullshit." Analysis is not a way to discover feelings but a way to hide them. Freudian techniques lead one to concentrate only on the past, thus again giving the patient a tool with which he or she can avoid the present. Perls, Hefferline, and Goodman, in *Gestalt Therapy*, dismiss analysis of the past:

Let us here conclude by considering the here and now procedure in comparison to the approaches of Freud and Adler.

These two men, each expressing what was characteristic of his own personality, laid stress, respectively, on past and future. In their work with neurotics they indulged, each in his own way, the patient's wish to dig into the past or to safeguard the future. Delving into the past serves the purpose of finding "causes"—and thus excuses for the present situation. That the present is an outgrowth of the past no one will deny, but it does not, for instance, solve present problems to blame one's parents for the way they brought one up. (p. 38)

The oversimplification expressed here is most astonishing—especially considering Perls's own analytic training. The idea that a search for causes is necessarily indulgent or even peripheral seems, on the face of it, absurd. Freud believed that the origin of neuroses lay in childhood and infancy and that any thorough attempt to resolve such problems necessarily meant a re-examination of the early years. To suggest that the aim of this process is simply to blame one's parents for one's situation in the present is assuredly an incorrect formulation of Freud's theories.*

While Perls accuses Freud of trying to indulge the patient's wish to live in the past, Freud, on the contrary, found his patients highly resistant to such investigation. A patient may wish to live in a false vision of the past, but the job of analysis is to dismiss that false vision and reveal what really was.

The aim of much of the left wing of the encounter movement is to get people to express their feelings. The discharge of feeling is the cure to people's problems, *synonymous* with self-awareness. A client in a successful encounter group is brought to the point where psychological defenses are eroded so that repressed memories and their concomitant emotions surface. Once this happens the goal of the open encounter is fulfilled. The client is not guided through a tour of the meaning of the released emotions, nor is he or she helped to work through those emotions. The group must encourage the next discharge of emotion in the next client.

---

* It is an interesting fact that Karen Horney accused Freud of just the opposite—that is, of having too much sympathy for parents and not enough for the patient as he or she was in childhood.

Thus the open encounter ends at precisely the point at which analysis begins. Of course it is much easier to know what one is feeling than to understand the cause of that feeling. Many people know how they feel. Although they are often ashamed to admit their feelings to others, confession leads only to the knowledge that one's feelings are acceptable. Thus a client may feel a temporary "high" at having confided in others, but personal problems are still unresolved. At this point one might level Perls's criticism of indulgence at the open encounter itself. The group can be set up as a sort of fantasy parent, or society, to tell the group member exactly what he or she wants to hear. As one young woman who went through several encounter group experiences commented: "We were asked to tell our partner what we would most like to hear about ourselves, like that we like to hear that we are pretty, or intelligent. We had to go on about what we like to hear about ourselves for two minutes. But what good does it do me for someone to tell me I'm pretty when I feel shitty? I don't need to hear those things. I want to feel them."

Encounter group leaders who circle the country often report that people who have gone through dramatic catharsis in one group will show up at groups again and again just to repeat the same performance. In such cases one may say that not only did the group experience not solve the problem but it has actually become part of the problem.

The encounter group also ends at the point where transference in analysis begins. Freud believed that the psychic energy released when powerful emotions are experienced is concentrated, or *cathected,* onto people or things. In analysis, energy is cathected onto the therapist, and this is the beginning of transference. In an encounter group that stresses emotional release, however, this release of psychic energy is considered an end point rather than a point of departure. If one accepts the idea of cathexis, a client is left hanging. He or she has expressed powerful emotions and has concentrated psychic energy on group members and a group leader whom the client will no longer see when the group is terminated. Added to the fact that problems are expressed rather than worked through, this can have grave results, such as psychotic breaks, or a desire to find some stable, real-life figure upon whom to direct the energy that could not be invested in the group leader.

In those encounter groups that concentrate on exercises and techniques for gaining interpersonal skills—that is, in the right wing of the HPM—the development of self-awareness and growth is even less likely than in those groups that concentrate on emotional release. Such techniques as "pairing," or Allen and Martin's "intimacy," or other strictly human-relations exercises, pay only lip service to the idea of an unconscious mind. In groups influenced by such techniques there is a functional denial of the unconscious process. People are urged merely to think about their problems, or to exercise their problems away. You can achieve trust by merely looking in someone's eyes, or closing your eyes and following someone's lead, or telling someone else that he or she is attractive. You can drop masks by willing them away. Unanswered, however, are the questions of why you have masks in the first place, why you are unable to trust and take risks even when you are in an environment in which all are trustworthy. When you deny the unconscious you cannot answer such questions.

If we accept the fact that the answer to purely personal problems lies at least in part in the unconscious, then we cannot achieve self-awareness through mechanical exercises whose thrust is to deny such a hidden realm. Such techniques do not recognize the phenomenon of resistance—that the mind has powerful mechanisms that defy all but very specific efforts to reveal its secrets.

The neglect of deeper psychological problems also undercuts the notion that encounter groups facilitate caring relationships between people who appreciate one another's uniqueness. Everyone, we're told, shares certain emotional problems—the inability to trust, the fear of rejection, the need for love, and so on. Yet what makes people who have the same problems unique is not only the form of the problem but its content—that is, its origins and unfolding through a particular life. How we got the way we are, our often buried personal history, is what makes us us. In brief encounter groups people often express their similarities— how lonely or depressed they feel—but not their uniqueness—the how and why of their problems. By ignoring complicated personal problems, their origins and interpretations, many encounter groups not only neglect the processes necessary for the "cure" of such problems but also the means through which people really get to know and understand one another. Despite its pretensions of achieving emotional depth, much of the encounter movement presents an image of a unidimensional individual, through which the self, human nature, is narrowly defined. In so doing, the encounter movement offers superficial concepts of trust, risk-taking, intimacy, community, the relationship of the self and others, and the relationship of the self to the world. Because of the superficiality of these concepts, their application in the world outside the encounter group is unlikely to bring the anticipated results for many people.

Carl Rogers promises that the encounter group will provide the authentically intimate relationships one may lack:

But what is the psychological need that draws people into encounter groups? I believe it is a hunger for something the person does not find in his work environment, in his church, certainly not in his school or college and, sadly enough, not even in modern family life. It is a hunger for relationships which are close and real; in which feelings and emotions can be spontaneously expressed without first being carefully censored or bottled up; where deep experiences—disappointments and joys—can be shared; where new ways of behavior can be risked and tried out; where, in a word, he approaches the state where all is known and accepted and thus further growth becomes possible.*

Trusting others and taking risks brings closeness. If you learn to tell people what you think of them, if you learn to express

* *On Encounter Groups,* pp. 11–12.

your feelings about another person in the encounter group when you feel them, you will see that such expressions of emotion are accepted. The world will not end because you have said something negative. This will, theoretically, help you take risks outside the encounter group—with friends, parents, lovers, co-workers, and employers. The problem is, of course, that the risks in "real" life are very different from the risks in an encounter group.

Those who attend encounter groups are usually strangers. They haven't known each other before, and they may not meet afterward. If you tell a stranger something negative, all you risk is some temporary displeasure; we don't invest a great deal of emotion in people we do not know. It's another matter with people with whom we have close relations. Telling your wife or husband that something is wrong with your relationship doesn't bear any resemblance to telling a stranger in an encounter group that you are angry because of something that happened in the group. In the former case a deep relationship may be threatened; in an encounter group there is no real threat of serious loss.

In many encounter groups, furthermore, the risk of saying negative things to another member of the group is mediated by an implicit agreement among group members and group leaders to say only complimentary things. One young man who attended several drop-in encounter groups given by Esalen, advertising new ways to meet new people, noted:

I found the experience highly alienating because there were so many limitations imposed on how you could communicate with other people. You know—only make direct statements, and that sort of thing. But how can you get to know someone by only saying what you think of them? Also, I found that some groups encourage dishonesty because you're only supposed to say complimentary things to people. Like I had a terrible experience. At the end of the group we were supposed to walk around and bump into people and then touch their hands and head and hug them and tell them what we thought about touching them and hugging them. By the time this came around I was so alienated that I refused to pick anyone to be a partner to. So I and another girl were the only ones in the room without partners. So we had to be partners. Only she was a hunchback. So what was I supposed to do, tell her how nice it was to be touching her hump?

Risk-taking is supposed to lead to trust. Yet the notion of trust espoused by many encounter groups seems quite shallow. Trust is something that develops in a relationship over time. It is one thing to trust someone in the artificial environment of an encounter group where there are leaders and other members who will serve as buffers should something go wrong, and quite another to trust someone at work or at home when no one is there to cushion a possible rebuff or betrayal.

The encounter group notion of trust, furthermore, seems to assume that everyone is inherently trustworthy. It is certainly desirable to have a more trusting and trustworthy population, and one can see that encounter leaders are reacting to a tradition that held that no one should trust anyone. It is difficult to understand, however, why people should be arbitrarily trusting, believing in people who have not earned their trust. Again, encounter techniques may be appropriate to the controlled atmosphere of the group, but not appropriate to the world outside the group.

The quality of the intimate relationships created in many encounter groups also presents difficulties. Encounter groups promise that people will be able to be intimate with others, and that in the process of sharing personal feelings they will be appreciated as unique individuals, cared for by other unique individuals. The advantage of the encounter group is that this intimacy is created almost instantaneously. You avoid having to wait a long time for someone to really get to know you.

The atmosphere of the encounter group, group leaders say, encourages people to drop their masks and defenses. Yet, if caring and intimacy are instant goods, and if people are strangers when they begin an encounter group, how does one distinguish the mask from reality? How do you know that one defense has not merely been substituted for another? It takes an incredible amount of experience to penetrate the façade with which an individual covers his or her feelings. And although encounter leaders assure us that their techniques penetrate masks, one must wonder how leaders with no previous experience of their clients know they have broken through defensive masks. We all know from our own experiences how difficult it is to discover what is façade and what is real in another person.

To people who are in a tremendous hurry to really know someone else and really be known, it is very tempting to believe that such knowledge is possible in a very brief time. There are many pitfalls, however, in this idea of instant intimacy. "Even an idiot has more than forty-eight hours' worth of numbers to run," noted Lloyd Linford, a San Francisco writer and psychologist. And this is often borne out by the experience of people who "fall in love" in encounter groups. Prompted by the leader and the warm environment, and often the beautiful scenery, people form romantic relationships, only to find that things are very different when they leave the group.

A young woman in California began to live with a man she had met at a weekend encounter group. In the encounter group environment, with warm nude baths and fires and a group leader and other group members, all interested for their various financial and emotional reasons in creating intimacy, she felt incredible closeness to her new lover. After knowing her for only a few hours he told her he wanted to grow old with her, and she reciprocated with similar sentiments. The two began to live together, inspired by their initial encounter glow. Reality, however, soon hit, and the relationship degenerated into suspicion and resentment. Things were not like the encounter group on the outside, and the fine feelings that were shared were simply not carried over when real-life problems occurred. When the effects of reality had eroded the confidences of the encounter group, the group leader had gone on to other groups, and there was no supportive atmosphere from which the couple could get help. After all, they, not the group leader, were responsible for what had gone on in the group. If they had had false expectations, that was their problem.

The words "instant" and "intimacy" are almost antithetical. To be intimate with a person means that one has had some experience with that person. To care about a person involves more than temporary knowledge of that person. How can you care about someone whom you do not know? Yet such encounter leaders as Leonard Zunin suggest that giving evidence of caring will help you meet people with whom you can have further contact:

Following are a number of items to help you apply your built-in, do-it-yourself introduction kit:
   1) Talk. Period. It is the most important rule of self-introduction.
   2) Show genuine concern about others in a way that indicates something special about them. (*Contact*, p. 58)

The version of caring and closeness taught in many encounter groups thus seems to totally ignore the person whom one is caring for. It seems that there is no way to be available to care and be cared for without being totally available and completely unselective.

This lack of selectivity can undercut the experience of intimacy in the group. "Going around hugging people in the encounter groups I went to didn't make me feel any less lonely," said one twenty-five-year-old woman in Los Angeles. "I suppose there are some people who can't hug anyone and it's good for them to go around getting practice hugging people, but that isn't my problem. I can hug people, but I like to hug selectively. In encounter groups, I've been told, you're supposed to enjoy hugging anyone, people for whom you have no feeling. It's just unselective hugging, and it doesn't make me feel very good."

It seems that in the encounter movement, as in the singles bar, the only way to find a mate is to be open to anyone and everyone. People seem to be asked to adjust to a dehumanizing environment in which they submerge their individual needs and wants in the interests of the smooth functioning of an anonymous, mobile society.

Indeed, the version of closeness and caring presented in many encounter groups is one that Karen Horney, in the *Neurotic Personality of Our Time*, has characterized as typical of neurotics:

One of the predominant trends of neurotics of our time is their excessive dependence on the approval and affection of others. We all want to be liked and to feel appreciated, but in neurotic persons the dependence on affection or approval is disproportionate to the real significance which other persons have for their lives. Although we all wish to be liked by persons of whom we are fond, in neurotics there is an indiscriminate hunger for appreciation or affection, regardless of whether they care for the person concerned or whether the judgment of that person has any meaning for them. (pp. 35–36)

Will affection and approval from strangers satisfy the cravings of lonely people, or do they suffer rather from the lack of stable relationships?

Rather than establishing truly close relationships between people, many encounter groups substitute "as if" relationships for the real thing. This "as if" quality, as Jules Henry has pointed out, deludes people into believing that they are getting whatever it is they need. In fact, what they have is just a fake, but the whole tenor of our society, he argues, is to make people accept the fake for the real. Thus the encounter group, if it encourages this "as if" quality, is following a traditional path.

If encounter groups provide stable relationships, perhaps they can ease loneliness. But the typical encounter group provides only temporary relationships. As Fred said, it was great to be close to people for forty-eight hours, but he never saw those people again. What he and many others get in encounter groups is a "feeling substitute," similar to the pregnancy substitutes Aldous Huxley described in *Brave New World*. Biological needs could not be totally controlled by the new society in that novel, so women would go through a surrogate experience meant to satisfy their need for experiencing the real thing. When the substitute episode was over, women would return to society until biological needs again surfaced and the process was repeated. The encounter group offers a similar feeling substitute. People need to be loved, and for a weekend or several hours they are loved and feel good. Then they return to an unloving society.

The "do your own thing" ethic promulgated by many of the leaders of the HPM also makes intimacy difficult. Perls's Gestalt precept, for example, suggests intimacy without involvement. People just roll with the punches. If it works, it works, and if it doesn't, it doesn't. Clearly, people wish to avoid entanglements that demand total self-sacrifice. Yet it is hard to imagine the ideal relationships proposed by many encounter leaders, in which people are totally free and yet still trusting and open.

The definition of community used by many encounter leaders is as contradictory as their definition of intimacy. The encounter group posits a community of feeling. All people are neighbors, even if they live at opposite ends of the earth, because they all feel the same emotions. We live in the global village popularized by McLuhan, and so we don't have to feel lonely. People may indeed share the same emotions, but the abstract notion of a global village in which people can theoretically connect with anyone anywhere does not create the kind of community that modern industrial society has destroyed. And the lonely person's sense of emptiness is not eased by the knowledge that there are people in France who are lonely too. Nor is it necessarily alleviated by meeting people in an encounter group whom they will never see again.

In a society that offers mostly brief encounters, what one may get in an encounter group is more of the same. And people may feel more lonely when they leave the group than they were when they came. If their experiences were successful, they may have discharged painful emotions and shared their thoughts with others, yet each has to go home alone to an empty house, and they have not been taught any methods through which they can realistically reproduce their experiences outside the encounter group.

The HPM believes that its growth ethic will lead to harmonious relations between the self and others, and between the self and the world. This harmony will banish the dissonance of loneliness. Yet the definition of the self reflected in the writings and groups run by many members of the HPM appears to project a reduced version of the self rather than a self that is expansive and growing. We can see the narrowness of this definition of the self when we consider the HPM's model of the relation of self and other, and the relation of the self to social change.

Self-revelation, according to the theories of the HPM, is not only what assures the continued success of relationships, it alone can create relationships. If you are open, people will be attracted to you and open with you. If you trust others, others will trust you. If you take risks, others will do the same. George Bach and his coauthors write in *Pairing:*

Underneath, usually hidden even from himself the lover is resentful and feels trapped because he cannot express what he authentically is.

The pairing system deals with the same fears, but by confronting and resolving them. Once these fears are dealt with the bars to intimate love are down. If one can handle the fears, one need not hide from them or from the realities that produce them. If one can then be genuine, so usually can one's partner. For genuineness creates trust and confidence. (pp. 27–28)

Similarly, Jack Crickmore and Emily Coleman believe that acquiring the skills of human relations—stating what one wants —means that one will get what one wants from another person. These ideas seem to totally ignore the nature and wishes of the other.

This vision of the self in relation to the other shows the influence of the psychiatrist Wilhelm Reich, who believed that awareness and satisfaction of sexual desire were the path to mental and social health. In his book *Wilhelm Reich,* Charles Rycroft criticizes Reich's vision of sexual satisfaction because of, among other things, Reich's neglect of the wishes of the other:

I must confess, however, that personally I think that there is something chilling about the way in which he [Reich] explains sexual desire solely by reference to the subject's mounting internal tensions without regard to the desirability—or desires—of the object—and about his emphasis on cosmic longing for union with the "beyond" and his failure to say much about longing for the person of the loved one. (p. 91)

Nowhere, Rycroft claims, does Reich consider the wishes of the other involved. This criticism is equally applicable to much of the philosophy of the HPM. Although the HPM suggests that intimacy will occur between two willing partners, what in fact is implied is not a relationship between two subjects but rather a subject and an object. The other is seen as an extension of the self. If I want I will get; if I trust, I will be trusted; if I risk, others will risk; if I am meetable, I will be met. Like the infant who believes that the mothering figure is an extension of his or her wants, many encounter advocates seem to think that the other does not exist outside the wishes of the self. Equating wanting with getting without considering the subjective needs of the other reduces the other to a mere object whose function is the satisfaction of the wishes and whims of the self. Of course, encounter leaders get around this problem by saying that all people have the same needs. But true as this may be, their needs do not all coincide at the same time and at the same place. The equation of the wishes of the self with the wishes of the other creates a narcissistic vision of the world of the self. There is the self and its reflection, this time in the eyes of the other rather than in the eyes of a shimmering pool.

We can see the same narrow definition of the self when we look at the HPM's definition of the self in relation to social change. If you are at peace with yourself the world will be at peace. Again, influenced by Reich's idea of the consciousness revolution, the HPM believes that people need only think and feel correct things in order for all to be well. We can see this philosophy of change in a passage from Reich's *Listen, Little Man:*

Don't be afraid. It's not so bad to be the mainstay of society.
"What then must I do in order to be the mainstay of society?"

Nothing new or unusual. Just go on doing what you're already doing; till your field, wield your hammer, examine your patient, take your children out playing or to school. . . . Just go on doing what you've been doing and wanting to do all along; work, let your children grow up happily, love your wife at night. *If you stick to this program knowingly and single-mindedly there would be no more war.* . . . If the Huns of any nation attack you, you've got to pick up your gun. But what you fail to see is that the "Huns" of all nations are simply millions of little men like yourself who persist in shouting hurrah, hurrah when Prince Blowhard (who doesn't work) calls them to the colors . . . instead of laying their national consciousness at the feet of their Prince Blowhard, or their marshal of the world proletariat. (pp. 117–118)

Reich's philosophy is the precursor of the suggestion that one should make love, not war. As Rycroft again comments, this idea of change ignores social and political reality:

It [the "make love, not war" philosophy] appeals immediately to all that is warm, generous and spontaneous in human nature. It assumes an extraordinarily direct and simple connection between orgastic deprivation and destructiveness—according to Reich, even genital characters become sadists if confronted with a sudden obstacle to their accustomed gratification. . . . The Make Love Not War philosophy completely ignores the psychology of power—and in practical terms such complications as the fact that those who decide to make wars are not, under modern conditions, the people who fight in them and that there is no evidence that the majority of those who do fight get any sadistic gratification out of it. (*Reich,* p. 30)

The project of self-awareness is limited by the vision of the self in the HPM. For the self is narrowly defined as the sum of its own peculiarities. If you learn to know what you feel you will have accomplished the purpose of your journey. You will also help to bring about social change. You do not have to know about the workings of economic and political systems under which you live. You need only express anger; you do not have to do anything with that anger, nor do you have to analyze what specific social forces cause it. Change means changing your peculiarities.

Emotional change undoubtedly has political importance, but to believe that it is the all of social change is to ignore the dynamic of political and economic reality. It is also to overlook one of the principal barriers to change in our time: political and economic reality. It is interesting, for example, that many encounter advocates, because of their reduced vision of the self in the world, see economic reality as static. Rogers, writing in 1970, prophesied that more and more people will join encounter groups because of the increasingly affluent nature of our society. But five or six years later it has become all too easy to see that the economy has its own dynamic and that we are, for the present at least, getting less, not more affluent.

The task of investigating social reality is one that involves the intellect, and much of the HPM has branded the intellect as anti-feeling and antihuman. People in our culture, HPM enthusiasts believe, think too much. Feeling is good and reason is bad. If those who controlled the wealth and political apparatus of our society would only think less and feel more, perhaps then, many seem to believe, they would give up their power and possessions and share their wealth equally with all.

A truly "person-oriented" society must be based on a fuller definition of the self than that offered by the HPM. The self must be considered not only as a collection of particular emotions but as it exists in social reality. The intellect must be considered not only as a device that objectifies and neutralizes but as something to which one can wed feeling and which can then be applied to understanding both the self and social reality. Growth means not only expansion of feeling but expansion of thought as well; and in seeing the self as divorced from the intellect, from social reality, and from the other, what the HPM presents is not a full view of the self but a very restricted one. If the causes of loneliness are partly a result of social conditions—and they certainly are partly social—the HPM's "cure" is only a specious and ineffective one.

Encounter groups can provide relationships with which to assuage loneliness if the group is a long-term one or if a person returns again and again to group after group. This takes money —and the encounter experience can become as expensive as the psychotherapy it is intended to replace. Even so, a sustaining community may not result. The encounter group is not geared to permanence.* It is a transitory experience, with transient members and transient leaders. Ultimately one must find a community outside the boundaries of the group.

But the creation of such a community is hampered by social conditions, which much of the encounter movement seems to ignore. A person is told that once he or she becomes "meetable, intimate, et cetera" he or she can find a mate. Yet because of dehumanizing social conditions this is not so easy. Faced with this contradictory dilemma, a person may feel that he or she cannot find a companion because of some deep flaw in character—a flaw so deep that even encounter groups cannot erase it. Thus people can feel more and more depressed about themselves.

Many people go on to seek other solutions. Through encounter groups they have tried listening to themselves and their own inner voices, and that hasn't worked. So they may go on and decide to listen to others for a change. To people who will tell them what to do and who to be. And so we have the birth of new gods—gurus whose mystical charisma promises a magical union and an escape from one's loneliness.

---

* The only permanent group to make use of encounter techniques is Synanon, which does provide a constant communal identity for its members.

Chapter Thirteen
The Magic Business

Domination differs from rational exercise of authority. The latter, which is inherent in any societal division of labor, is derived from knowledge and confined to the administration of functions and arrangements necessary for the advancement of the whole. In contrast, domination is exercised by a particular group or individual in order to sustain and enhance itself in a privileged position. Such domination does not exclude technical, material and intellectual progress, but only as an unavoidable by-product, while preserving irrational scarcity, want and constraint.

HERBERT MARCUSE, *Eros and Civilization*

After you've tried everything else—the singles bars, endless series of encounter groups, even some psychotherapy—this is the last resort. Listen to me, do what I say, they tell you, I have the prescription for happiness, the panacea that will not only end loneliness but make all kinds of emotional pain unnecessary. Just come to my group, pay the fee (ridiculously low for this kind of knowledge), and you will reach not only personal awareness but cosmic awareness and the full experience of your own hitherto undiscovered inner harmony.

Ladies and gentlemen, the guru business.

There are any number to choose from in America today—the Guru Maharaj Ji, the Jews for Jesus, the Hare Krishnas, Werner Erhard of est—who give faith to the masses. A variety of less well known and smaller-time local gurus provide "families" for the young and confused who only want a purpose and a prescription to deaden pain.

So much for freedom, so much for doing our own thing by ourselves, and so much for the liberal dream of free expression in the marketplace of ideas. The guru business does away with all this; there is, after all, only one way. The path to salvation may travel through self-sacrifice and humiliation. It may require obedience to an authoritarian father figure (for most of the gurus are men) or it may posit a vision of social well-being in which all do as they are told. But the goal is always salvation—the acquisition of a new identity through submersion in a group whose internal relations are defined by the savior.

Although there are many brands of salvation for sale in contemporary America, one can divide the different gurus and their new religions into two categories. There are those who preach to a mass audience. They are the gods and god's helpers whom one sees mainly from afar, and who ask that while believing truly and completely you stay in the world, make money with which to pay for "knowledge," and proselytize. And then there are those who offer closer contact. With their followers, they form not only communities but actual families. You do as you are told, you forsake the world, maintaining only a commercial relationship to the "uninitiated," and you proselytize, but only to a select few. Both styles of guruing are characterized by a great deal of financial and emotional exploitation.

There are an infinite number of small-time gurus who offer a "cure" for loneliness. In Los Angeles a well-known guru has established a large "family" composed mostly of young people in their twenties, who renounce their blood families and accept him as their "spiritual Father." The former Jim Baker, who runs the Brotherhood of the Source, is the guru whom everyone follows. His family is totally obedient to his word. And there is a unity of purpose and an identity that he grants his followers, who work for nothing at the health food restaurant The Source on Sunset Boulevard. The family is closed to outsiders, whom it considers with a good deal of disdain. Baker and his followers believe in a great apocalypse that will come and wipe out the nonbelievers—an apocalypse from which the faithful only will be saved. Not a very charitable attitude.

The same withdrawal from the outside world is evident in a small family in New York whose twenty members live in a large mansion with their guru, a Middle Eastern mystic who lives on the premises, where he meditates and hands down decrees through which the family solves its day-to-day problems. The group of parents and children live totally divorced from their community. They do not allow their children to play with others after school, nor do they have anything to do with their neighbors. Only those who will join the group, turning over all assets to the family, are welcomed.

Similarly, in Atlanta, a small family gathers around a guru who teaches salvation through listening to music. In a flat painted black the neophytes live with their master, working in order to pay for the privilege of listening to his knowledge. People sit rigidly for hours listening to his discourse and classical music, through which they are supposed to reach a state of body liberation. The group recruits followers very selectively and will not permit members to communicate with those outside the group—except commercially.

Another rapidly growing, larger "religious" group, whose leader promises generalized salvation from the ills of the modern universe, is that formed by the followers of the Guru Maharaj Ji, the Perfect Master—the Satguru (living god)—and new messiah. The Maharaj Ji has attracted thousands of devotees in the United States.

Through belief in his word, the word of the living god—as the guru fancies himself—come peace and unity. If only (through a revolution of consciousness) the world would follow his dictates and partake of his knowledge, all would be well. His successes are already remarkable. The guru and his followers point to the cures that they have worked on drug addicts, alcoholics, lonely young men and women, and former radicals. If the guru made Rennie Davis into a humble servant, he can do anything, say the faithful.

The guru teaches in a special way. Through an inner light, an inner sound of music, an inner taste of nectar, and an inner trembling, "knowledge sessions" convince people that the guru's path is in fact bliss. "After you receive knowledge you just realize how beautiful everything is," said one San Francisco Premie (or lover of God). "It's a time of constant growth. That's what's so beautiful about it—it never ends. And it's all inside you. We've all got that place inside us, but the Guru Maharaj Ji lets you reach it. If you get in touch with that place inside all of us you'll feel that sense of purpose that we're supposed to have. You experience love."

Love banishes the separations between people which so seriously plague modern youth (for the guru's followers are mainly young people). "We have a community of people who gather daily to hear *satsang,* and there are ashrams where we live. The community we have is getting to be more and more of a family. Whatever we experience inside manifests itself outside in our family and we experience love."

One of the main differences between this brand of love and other traditional Vedantist Indian religions is that the guru puts his followers at the service of western industrial society, as Francine du Plessix Gray writes in the *New York Review of Books:**

His [the Guru Maharaj Ji's] teaching is not vastly different from that of the Vedantists I listened to when doing comparative religion at Columbia. The rational everyday mind is the obstacle, the great demon that stands in the way of understanding; suffering is created by the duality which that mind posits; Enlightenment is the resolution of that duality and the merging into the One Consciousness. The Mahatma's principal departure from rigorous Vedanta doctrine is that Maharaj Ji does not want his devotees to leave the world. Quite the contrary, we must keep our jobs and enjoy our meals, the only thing we must renounce is *mind,* and much of what we *previously* considered to be "knowledge." As a matter of fact, the new Divine Maharaj Ji will give us increased concentration and will make us *better* businessmen, musicians, writers.

* "Blissing Out in Houston," p. 36.

Receiving knowledge allows you to do the commercial thing you are doing—and do it better. (Thus one of the guru's followers, whom Gray quotes, is a tennis pro, Tim Gallowy, who finds that his tennis game has improved enormously because of the guru's meditation techniques. To praise the guru Gallowy has just written a book called *Inner Tennis*.) Although this knowledge is initially free, the guru collects extraordinary sums of money from his devotees, many of whom become so rooted in the organization that it becomes their life. The Maharaj Ji is noted for what he does with that money: he buys electric appliances, motorcycles, cars, and mansions. True, the organization does social service work, establishing food cooperatives, missions, and various programs through which they provide services and spread the word; but much of this can be taken off taxes.

Nonetheless people do see the light, they insist, and their lives are changed for the better, they say, through their connection with the Maharaj Ji. There is an end to loneliness through life as members of a great following. People are told what to believe and what to do and how to live. They are promised not only instant intimacy, instant self-realization, and an instant community but an instant earthly and spiritual revolution. Their lives take on a cosmic meaning that makes insignificant problems such as loneliness and anonymity disappear. It is no surprise, then, that such revolutionaries of the sixties as Rennie Davis and others are turned on to the Maharaj Ji, for he offers what the sixties failed to bring about—instant unity and harmony. A new world revolution. Loneliness is absorbed in this vast dream, again at the price of the individual and his or her autonomous self, and at the expense of a solution for plaguing social problems.

Another such instant cure is promised by a new arrival on the American scene, the Reverend Sun Myung Moon, the Korean anticommunist who has established the Christian Unification Church. The 15 million-dollar organization has amassed a following in Europe and is beginning to become popular in America. Like the Maharaj Ji, Moon is seen as a sort of messiah, and it does not seem to perturb his followers that he upholds the Korean dictatorship and has significant financial interest in a vast Korean munitions company. All this is overlooked because Moon's organization gives its young followers a secure life and identity. Relations with others outside the elite are unnecessary and scorned, and one is not lonely, because all one's needs and thoughts are taken care of. An ex-"Moonie," Stephen Yafa, who lived in a San Francisco area Moonie house, is quoted in the *San Francisco Chronicle* concerning his experiences as a devotee:

> If you're in the Unification Church, you're allowed no close human attachments. You're woken up after a few hours sleep and are made to go on long fasts—body pain is supposed to free the spirit.
> Once you leave you're considered "dead." It's very hard to get out. And if you fall in love before the Church is ready to give you its marriage blessing, you're physically separated from each other. . . . When you join you can stop searching. You don't have to worry about responsibilities.*

Again loneliness ends through self-sacrifice and absorption in a group that denies the unpleasantness of the world outside. The new religion is rather like the movies made during the Depression, in the 1930s. One is confronted with a fiction or a joke: watch the Maharaj Ji ride around on a motorcycle as he promises eternal bliss. His group absorbs followers into a fantasy as alluring as that provided by Hollywood.

True, you pay a price for your fantasy, but what a small price to pay for salvation! And since that salvation is internal, you don't have to worry at all about the reality around you.

The number of such groups is great. The solution to loneliness is, with such organizations, submersion in the group. The differences, however, are in the degree of withdrawal from the world and the degree to which the group encompasses the lives of its members. In the smaller groups the degree of contact is much

---

* "Moon's Rise in the World," *San Francisco Chronicle*, December 11, 1974.

greater, but so is the degree of freedom one gives up. The gurus maintain total, immediate, and intimate control over their followers. They provide the path and the decisions to life problems, and the followers give up their freedom in return. It is one solution to loneliness—but it is a solution that denies the individual the determination of his or her own development. Many people say that the guru solution works and that they no longer feel lonely. In fact, these people have made a decision that no self is better than a lonely self. This decision is an exercise of the freedom to choose among the different solutions our society has found to loneliness. The problem is that there are so few viable alternatives available to us.

Erhard Seminars Training (est) is the best example of effective mass psychological manipulation in the guru business today. And est pulls together what happens in most authoritarian groups. Perhaps the most obvious thing about est is mystification. There seems no way to describe it. When asked to do so, followers echo stock phrases: "We don't know how it works—it just does." "It's like electricity, we don't ask where it comes from, we just know how to use it." "It's something you can't describe, you have to experience it." Est-ers insist that words not only cannot capture reality in this case but they actually undermine it. The only way to find out what est is all about is to pay the $200 (soon to be $250) admission fee, and with 250 other neophytes, suffer through 60 hours of instruction on how to reach bliss.

And people in droves pay this price. There are now over 20,000 graduates, and what began in San Francisco, in 1971, has spread to Los Angeles, San Jose, New York, Washington, Colorado, and Hawaii.

Est is a combination of everything: encounter, attack, scientology, Gestalt, Dale Carnegie, behavior modification, general semantics, and transactional analysis, and most of all the charisma and hustle of Werner Erhard (né Jack Rosenberg), the ex–used-car salesman who founded and leads est. Dissatisfied with existing techniques for growth, Erhard put together what he considers to be an unbeatable package (both spiritually and financially). A total experience whose originality lies not so much in the ideas it incorporates as in the browbeating style through which the est experience unfolds.

Est draws its participants through word of mouth. Graduates—those who have gone through the two-weekend training—are encouraged to tell their friends about the transformations worked by est. And because no one can sell est like Werner Erhard himself, several times a year the organization rents a large local hall where Erhard gives a free rap telling you why you too should join the growing ranks of est graduates.

The house at San Francisco's Civic Auditorium is full. Erhard's name over the last couple of years has become synonymous with magic. "Why, at one training," a black secretary in the audience whispers to her white girlfriend whom she is trying to recruit, "some man was talking about his problems. The trainer just came over to him and began yelling 'You're full of shit, you're an asshole, all your problems are your fault.' The man looked afraid for a minute and then began smiling. When he left he said he felt better than he'd ever felt before."

"At first," one graduate tells me in a hushed voice, "I thought it was bunk. I didn't like Erhard and I didn't like his manner; he was too slick, a snake-oil salesman type. But I just came anyway, and I've never been so glad." "But how does it work?" somebody asks. "You can't explain that," the young man retorts, echoing thousands of other voices around him, "you just have to experience it yourself."

When Erhard comes onstage the audience applauds, then the graduates rise to their feet, and after them the potential followers. The enthusiasm generated by the graduates who attend (obviously those for whom est has worked its magic) is infectious. Erhard waits a few minutes and then silences the crowd.

He's a clever man—an accomplished showman. Nothing like the guru figure I and many others in the audience had expected. He looks more like Joey Bishop than a spiritually glowing master. His dark hair is neatly cut and combed, his conservative blazer and gray pants are well cut and expensive. He moves with obvious ease onstage. This guru who appeals to a hushed audience of housewives, businessmen, secretaries, and "average" folks resembles more than anything else a nightclub comedian who has just come from a long run in Vegas.

Onstage Erhard begins his monologue.

"I know why you're here," he tells us. "It's because life isn't working for you. Don't bullshit me, don't tell me your life is working the way you want it to work. You have not been happy getting what you want out of life. You've gotten things and that's fine. It's a good game. But est is about being happy and getting what you want.

"I don't think you're very different from me—for instance, I know some very intimate things about you. I know you want to be loved."

The audience stirs.

"Most people don't know what they want out of life, and that's all right. You can experience yourself without knowing what you want.

"You haven't got the remotest idea of who you are. Not the remotest. You could come out and tell me who you are. You know who you think you are. Some people even feel themselves. But that's different from experiencing yourself directly. At est you experience yourself directly. After est you get to have what life is really about without doing anything.

"What is the training?" Erhard asks the audience.

"You want to know what happens. The training is fully unreasonable, fully nonsensible. All I can tell you is that it works. You don't have to do anything. You don't take any notes. There is nothing you can do to do it right. As long as you work within the bounds of the instructions. You can't go to the bathroom during the training and you can't eat. Most people think life is about eating and going to the bathroom. If you get anything out of the training, at least you'll learn you're not a tube."

Erhard looks intently at the audience, most of whom seem mesmerized by his approach.

"The fulfillment of est will be determined by you. I don't know what will fulfill you. I can just promise that est works. That after the training you will be able to really experience life. That every institution you're part of will really work for you. There's nothing to understand; understanding is the boobie prize. It's what you do when you don't experience something."

"What about the price?" a man asks from the audience. "Why does it cost so much?"

"I'm glad you asked that," Erhard answers "It costs that much because that's how much it costs. You might want to know what we do with the money. Why, we spend it of course—what else do you do with money?

"But I've said enough," he says. "What you want to know is how it worked for other people. Go out into the lobby and you will see people with their names written on labels with blue borders. Those people are graduates. Go out and ask them your questions."

People applaud, and Erhard disappears.

Out in the hall several thousand people are searching out people with blue-bordered name tags. The graduates are all friendly and all ecstatic about their experience at est. "Est changed my life," one suburban housewife explained. "I used to think everything was so important. So now I don't worry. A few weeks ago my son and some friends were in a car accident and several of them were hurt. Before est I would have thought it was very important and worried. But I didn't worry about it at all."

Another woman explained that she had tried everything—years of therapy, encounter groups. But nothing had worked for her. She always felt unhappy. Now she feels open to the world. She got her daughter into est, and the girl lost fifty pounds right away. "You have to experience est," she said, "you can't just talk about it. If you experience it, then you'll discover how wonderful it is. If you don't like it—well, you're just trying to prove that you're right and est is wrong."

Despite the fact that people object to the bossy style of Erhard and other trainers, all this is appealing. "Nobody likes the trainers' style at first," an est volunteer told me. "They give orders all the time. I used not to like it when people gave me orders. But then I did the training and really experienced my resentment at being ordered around. And now I don't mind doing what people tell me."

Some people sign up then and there, and others go home armed with an est pamphlet in which Werner also speaks from the page.

"The purpose of the est training is to transform your ability to experience living so that the situations you have been trying to change or have been putting up with clear up just in the process of life itself.

"Sometimes people get the notion that the purpose of est is to make you better. It is not. I happen to think you are perfect the way you are. The problem is that people get stuck being the way they were, instead of the way they are."

It is an exciting message. You can change without doing anything except listening to Werner Erhard or one of his trainers. You are perfect, though you may need instruction to see the perfection. Things will work for you and you will find love. If you do sign up, there's a long wait—people are standing in line to pay their $250. Inside the training you begin to find out where your perfection gets you.

For about 60 hours, spanning two consecutive weekends, you are told how you've mismanaged your life. You have been playing right-wrong games. You have been avoiding life. You are full of bullshit. You are an asshole. Everything that has happened to you has been your own doing. If you are lonely, it's because you want to be lonely. You have established patterns, and they must be broken.

To break these patterns, est believes it is necessary to break you, the client. You can't eat or go to the bathroom during the training. And you can't take drugs, drink, or medication (unless it is essential to your health and prescribed by a doctor). You sit in your folding chair and you listen. You can't be late from a break. If you are, you are either harshly reprimanded by the trainer or prohibited from entering the room. "Est functions through intimidation," says Steve Schoen, a psychiatrist in San

Francisco who went through the training. "I was thirty seconds late from a break. I was stopped from entering the room, and the trainer told me I would have to admit that my being thirty seconds late was proof of how I had fucked up my entire life. If I did not admit that that was the meaning of my being thirty seconds late I could not come back into the room."

The actual training consists of listening to men like Erhard (who rarely gives training sessions now) talk. They give lectures and teach various techniques—such as psychodrama, fantasy work, meditation, and attack—through which you will presumably experience yourself more fully. People can either share their feelings with others or remain silent. But once you open up to the group, you are subject to attack. In which case you may find that the experience leaves you a quivering mass. In Los Angeles, for instance, a noted singer went to the microphone and began talking. After the trainer had finished with her, she was left crying on the floor in the middle of the room while everyone else went for a break. It was assumed that what had happened to her was her responsibility, and that if there were any problems because of the training, they were due to her hangups and not to the experience to which she had been subjected.

Much of the training consists of experiencing the various processes that are supposed to help you deal with life. Here is the "fear process," for instance, as Esther Bourg, a Bay Area psychologist describes it:

We were asked to lie down on the floor and imagine that we were afraid of the people next to us. Then both people on either side of us —people began to moan and cry. Then we were asked to imagine we were afraid of people in our own section of the room. At first I was not afraid. I'm not the kind of person to be afraid of other people. But as the process went on and on, I began to be afraid of the people in the room—they were people who were so incredibly suggestible they had become a mob.

The est processes are essentially prescriptive techniques in which you are urged to think about your problem in a specific way. Actually what you do isn't thinking, because thinking is out in est; you don't think about things, you "experience" them. This narrow distinction is characteristic of est language in which old things are given new names. (Erhard's publicity man, for instance, is called a "communicator" rather than a press agent.)

Est people are taught not to play right-wrong games—that is, making yourself right at the expense of others. This helps establish the closed-thought system that is typical of the est organization. There is no way to pass a negative judgment on what is being experienced. A biologist who went to est, for example, raised his hand while Erhard was giving a monologue on biology. The man pointed out that what Erhard was saying was scientifically incorrect. To which Erhard retorted in an accusing, classical analytic put-off, "You always have to be right, don't you?" Those who experience est and don't like it are accused of the cardinal sin of playing right-wrong games. There can be no doubt, and no doubters, in est. There is no way to argue. If Werner says you don't know who you are, and you answer that you do know, he insists that you don't know. You respond that you certainly do, and he argues that you don't; you may not know it, but *he* knows it. You agree, or you walk out and Erhard wins by default.

The ability to draw people into the closed est system is dependent on Erhard's correct reading of his followers. Most people who come to est are indeed unhappy. They don't feel they know themselves or their world. Why else would they spend $200 for a rather uncomfortable 60 hours? Esther Bourg says, "You must remember that Werner is very skillful. He's very skillful at intuiting things about people and he's very skillful verbally. I think he's the most skillful hustler I've ever met."

Erhard is the model of the successful est experience. And to train your intuition to match his, you do personality profiles. Everyone takes a card and writes down the name of somebody he or she knows who is not in the room. You write down the marital status and age of the person. Then you write down three things and how that person responds to them, and you write down three people and how that person responds to them. Then the class hands in their cards.

A very ethereal-looking young lady came into the room to demonstrate the personality profile at the pretraining seminar I attended. She picked a card, and a bearded gentleman in his forties, the author of that particular card, came onto the stage. The woman was to guess what was on the card—presumably to prove that est can free your psychic powers. Of the six statements, she guessed three correctly. The man on the card was married, would respond negatively to the idea of divorce, and was a friend of the man who authored the card. On other subjects the "psychic" guessed wrong. The man in question didn't like jazz, as she said he did. And a man whom she said he hated was in fact his best friend. Nonetheless everyone in the room seemed awed at her "skill."

"How did you do it?" one man asked.

"I took est," she responded.

"Anyone with any intuition could do that personality profile," Esther Bourg explained, "yet all these people fall for it and feel so good because they're psychic."

Est presents itself as a total experience that will totally transform its graduates. It is not something you think about, because following the lead of the encounter movement, understanding is an act that degrades feeling. In fact, est is not even something you feel; it is something you experience—a step higher, we are to believe, than feeling. Furthermore, est offers no specific outcome. It's all individual. You get what you want out of it, and if you get nothing, that's not est's problem. Remember: everything that happens to you is your fault. Besides, life is just a game, and est is the greatest game of all.

After sitting for 60 hours and paying $200, that is the message: est is a game. There is no point to it at all; there is nothing to get. Esther Bourg describes the end of her experience:

At the end of the training the trainer asks if people "got it." One group of people say they got it; they are applauded. Then another group says they weren't sure they got it; the trainer talks to them, and they all say they got it. One group says they definitely didn't get it. He talks to all but one, and finally this last person says he didn't get it, and the trainer says, "Well, you got it, 'cause there's nothing to get." And they turn the whole thing into a joke.

The end of the training is not, however, the end of the est experience. The game goes on. There are post-training seminars that members can attend once or twice weekly for fees ranging from $3 to $35. There are est get-togethers, and graduates can re-enroll in training seminars for nothing. If people are totally turned on to est they can become volunteers, of whom there are currently 3500, who work for nothing in various capacities for the multimillion-dollar organization. And then there is the retinue of select trainers, valets, communicators, chauffeurs, cooks, and fellow travelers close to Erhard himself.

Those who aren't disillusioned by their est experience tend to become evangelical about the organization. It worked for them, and it will work for you. Never mind how—you can't go wrong. Est even has classes for young children so that they will learn the est philosophy early and thus not fall into erroneous ways of thinking.

The main argument in favor of est is based on traditional American pragmatism: it works. Est graduates, therapists, and people in the helping professions are somewhat awed by its "success rate." These admirers, however, neglect to investigate the mechanisms through which est achieves its success and the vision of the world it posits while working its magic.

Much of est's success is due to two factors: a prodigious amount of doublethink; and the authoritarian atmosphere in which it is transmitted and which it in turn encourages. Erhard, for instance, in a classic example of doublethink, says that you are perfect the way you are. But the trouble is, you aren't the way you are, you're the way you were. You are the way you are, except that you are not the way you are, you are the way you were; so if you are perfect the way you are, but aren't the way you are but the way you were, are you perfect the way you were? Or what were you? It is no wonder that est asks people to suspend critical thought.

There are other contradictions. You are perfect, yet you are not perfect, so you need to come to est. You are great, yet once inside est you are bombarded with how terrible you are. The aim is freedom, but you must be totally obedient to get your freedom (rather like arming for war in order to make peace). You determine the outcome of the experience, yet est trainers let you go for the day or weekend only when they think what is supposed to happen has happened. You can't understand est, nor feel it, nor can you describe it, you experience it; but what is the difference between feeling and experiencing and thinking?

Est uses contradictions to convince people that there is a quick, relatively painless solution to life and its problems, of which one of the biggest and most prevalent is loneliness. The denial of the unconscious and the assertion of a unidimensional view of the mind that is obvious resembles the cognitive style of the encounter movement, except that with est the problems are magnified many times over. There is almost no personal contact here. People are supposed to strip away their defenses and clear away past problems simply by osmosis—by being a part of the believing crowd. The "experience" will not only straighten out your personal life, it will make society stop bothering you too.

Yet people insist that est works. So how does it work?

Given that est is a combination of many different techniques all of which are available, either in combination or alone, from different sources, part of est's success would seem to be due to the authoritarian atmosphere in which the "cure" is applied. Est functions through the encouragement of obedience to very strong authority figures who have all the answers and who can, by rather dubious means, silence all questions. To many people beset by personal anxieties, and plagued by the loneliness and insecurity in the world in which they live, such certainty and power is appealing. As Erich Fromm writes in *Escape from Freedom* of Martin Luther's age (and our own):

The compulsive quest for certainty, as we find it with Luther, is not the expression of genuine faith, but is rooted in the need to conquer the unbearable doubt. Luther's solution is one we find present in many individuals today, who do not think in theological terms: namely to find certainty by the elimination of the isolated individual self, by becoming an instrument in the hands of an overwhelmingly strong power outside of the individual. (p. 97)

Powerless people are fulfilled in some way by associating with power. It is as though they get vicariously from a strong leader what they cannot get from themselves. Werner Erhard is this kind of leader. He offers freedom through obedience. It makes people feel better about being enslaved, and it makes them fly even more quickly into the arms of their pseudosavior.

Erhard's program appeals to people's dissatisfaction with themselves and their desire to be different without actually changing their way of life. Est offers the trappings of change, which permit people to feel different because they are told they will be different. "Est," said a former est trainer, "is training in desensitization." A direct retreat from the sixties, est protects the "system," which the sixties threatened. It asks people to stay in the institutions that the sixties attacked, and cherish the material ethic of America. All est asks is that people follow a leader who will give definite instructions as to what to do and what to think (experience). It undercuts the individual freedom that is its stated aim.

Like Calvin and Luther, Werner Erhard speaks to a middle class caught in a particularly confusing period during which security and safety become more important than satisfaction. And as Fromm says in *Escape from Freedom*, the appeal to security through self-humiliation and abnegation is still operant today:

To this [conservative middle class] Calvinism had the same psychological appeal that we have already discussed in connection with Lutheranism. It expressed the feeling of freedom but also of insignificance and powerlessness of the individual. It offered a solution by teaching the individual that by complete submission and self-humiliation he could hope to find a new security. (pp. 106–107)

In the mailings sent out to its graduates after trainings, est clearly plays up to this need for security. The price of this sense of security is the submergence of the self in a group over which the individual has no control. The highest evolutionary state described in those brochures is to serve those in power.

There is absolutely no certainty outside yourself. There is no certainty in a picture. And a decision is nothing more than a creation of a picture which you've decided to make stick. And you get stuck with them. The minute you realize that, you're willing to choose all the time. There's another word for that—absolute and total surrender. It's exactly the same thing. Please do not think I just said "succumb." I said surrender, that has absolutely nothing to do with succumbing. The way to serve is to serve one who serves. This is the PATH . . . making that which makes you and others able more able. By serving one who serves, which means making the source of power more powerful, you move out of detriment. You find you are no longer serving, you *are*.

Est's philosophy of power—who has control over whom—is riddled with contradictions. It insists that everyone is responsible for his or her own life and what happens to him or her: "You are the only one to blame for your problems; if you are lonely you have made yourself lonely." What this total acceptance and responsibility encourages, however, isn't the ability to control one's own life but rather a false sense of control.

A seventeen-year-old runaway who was an est graduate explained that she had caused everything that had happened to her—including her parents' divorce, her mother's alcoholism, and the fact that neither her parents nor the juvenile system wanted to deal with her and shunted her into jails and honor farms, from which she ran away. A classic example of a person who's been buffeted about by the system and is powerless to control it, the girl was attracted by est's ability to give her the sense that she was totally in control. It was all her fault; she was no longer powerless but all-powerful.

Because this idea of total control ignores much of reality, it encourages neglect of how one is being controlled and manipulated by others—including est. If you are in total control, est seems to say, how can we be controlling you? Another tempting aspect of this distorted idea of control is that it tends to vitiate one's sense of guilt for whatever ill one has done to others. If people are responsible for what happens to them, no one is responsible for what he or she does to others. If something bad happens to you, it's your fault. You asked for it. If you are lonely, est says you want to be lonely. It's neither the fault of society nor anyone else. If you are ill treated, you must want to be ill treated. A woman who had been raped was accused of having taken on the rape victim as her identity: she was embracing the pose of being everybody's victim.

Many people feel a diffuse sense of guilt. And the idea that they are responsible for their own lives, while others are responsible for what happens to them, is attractive. If I do something bad to someone it's because the other person asked for it. A convenient side effect is that anything that happens to a person inside an est training is the individual's fault, not est's. One man who had gone to est with his girl friend said that she had tried to commit suicide the week after the training, and having failed, she joined the army. It was perfectly all right, the man said, that that had happened. It was neither his responsibility nor est's, because she must have wanted it to happen.

Est's doctrine of total responsibility also appeals because it is no threat to the social system. A denial of forces outside the person—or merely outside the person's consciousness—which may have created individual problems implies that social problems do not exist. Any institution can be made to work for you if you just have the est attitude. There is nothing wrong with institutions and the way they are run except in your head. This philosophy speaks to middle-class people facing frustrating and alienating social and economic situations in which the question of responsibility seems simply unanswerable. The frustration of loneliness is absorbed into a community of guilt.

Est may "work," but it works through mind-boggling techniques intended to break down not only the defenses but the wills of its clients. It is interesting that almost all the people with whom I spoke insisted that they did not like Werner Er-

hard initially or the other trainers whose lead they were to follow. Yet they put their futures, as it were, in the hands of men
whom they neither trusted nor respected. What this implies is
that most clients are people who will follow any leader who
promises salvation through security. The whole thrust of the
marathon training is to break down the will and encourage such
obedience. By the end of a long, torturous period of being
forced to sit in place, not eat, and refrain from going to the
bathroom, people have become pliable and meek, willing to
believe what they are told.

What's perhaps most interesting about est is its combination
of various group psychologies—notably transactional analysis
and Gestalt—into a psychology of the mass. Est works by imposing regression on the audience—by taking control of the
group's oral needs (eating and smoking), its posture, even its
bowels. While Erhard says, "If there's one thing you'll learn
here it's that you're not a tube," in fact the lesson is just the
opposite. You *are* a tube; you're an infant. You're too little even
to think for yourself. Don't think, experience (which Erhard
says is superior to feeling). I assume control over your body and
its functions, you are what I tell you you are. As a by-product of
this regression the audience develops first a sense of infantile
omnipotence, which is then subsumed into a sense of the
omnipotence of the leader, Papa Werner.

While est is not a foot-stomping, fascist organization, some
totalitarian parallels suggest themselves. Est posits not only a
personal solution through which the self is obedient and
thoughtless, it posits a world view as well. Order is obedience to
a strong authority figure, believing what you are told unques-
tioningly and imposing your view on others. Change equals
continuing to serve powerful people and institutions, and anything outside the chosen path is unacceptable.

The fact is est "works" for many people. Unfortunately, however, authoritarian solutions, although they may make people
feel temporarily less lonely, tend to defeat both the individual
and the society. If est banishes the loneliness of its clients, it

does so by negating the autonomous self: you are not alone because you no longer exist outside the group. You are not to complain because everything, including your loneliness, is your fault. There is no external cause for your problems. If this illusion can be maintained, loneliness can indeed dissolve into a sort of group psychosis. But should anything threaten the solidarity of this profound mystification, loneliness will reappear along with a sense of reality.

The solution to loneliness offered by the loneliness business— the singles industry, much of the human-potential movement, and the guru or new religious movements—often exacerbates and exploits people's sense of alienation and depression rather than resolving it. The primary aim of most of the loneliness business is profit and power over others. If a cure results from that profit and domination, as Marcuse so eloquently stated, it is generally only a side benefit and that occasional result insures the life of the myth that happiness can be found in a reduced vision of the individual and his or her world.

The dangers and failures of the loneliness business are far more numerous than its successes. On both the social and personal levels the boundaries of the self are either reduced or totally eliminated. In the name of privacy and individual freedom, people's personal lives, their emotions, and their human needs are transformed into commodities whose price tags can be prohibitive. Human-relations skills replace relationships, and private emotions are manipulated in the service of industrial profit. As Marcuse writes in *One Dimensional Man:*

In this society, the productive apparatus tends to become totalitarian to the extent to which it determines not only the socially needed occupations, skills and attitudes, but also individual needs and aspirations. It thus obliterates the opposition between private and public existence, between individual and social needs. (p. xv)

Because the manipulative techniques of the loneliness business are more subtle, the kind of domination they impose is less apparent than, say, that of a large, heavy industry. But the ill effects of the loneliness business can be just as severe. The most intimate interchanges, such as sex and affection, are standardized so that personal uniqueness is surrendered to technique and exercise. People feel less and less like unique and worthwhile individuals. They feel that the distinctions between themselves and others fade. After they lose the sense that they are unique in and of themselves, even if they do find a relationship, they still feel lonely. They perform only a function that countless others could do equally well.

The relationships initiated by participation in one or another aspect of the loneliness business are usually brief or based on a denial of individual freedom. The person accepts that this is the best thing available. Second or third best is all he or she is entitled to. Obviously such relationships can't fill up the well of loneliness, and the person often feels lonelier and desperate for anything at all. A slow detachment from the self and others can occur, with loss of both self-respect and respect for others. A feeling of apathy sets in about the future and its promises. Believing that unsatisfactory relationships are the only possible kind of relationships, the individual comes to accept the very conditions that eroded his or her potential for personal and social life. There is nothing to attach oneself to other than the constant search for attachment and success.

The loneliness business is both the symbol and locus of this endless search—a search that brings not personal plenty but scarcity.

Conclusion

Some popular thinkers feel that loneliness today is really a positive rather than a negative thing. Such poets of loneliness as Clark Moustakis and Anne Morrow Lindbergh insist that experiencing the pain of loneliness opens one's social and personal horizons. They see loneliness as a vitalizing experience—a voyage of self-discovery whose ending will usher in better and better relationships. Another common view is that loneliness is a matter of personal choice. Subconsciously or consciously people are lonely because they choose to be lonely. And in so choosing, people get *something*—an odd sort of satisfaction, perhaps, or the affirmation of a world view. Nobody is responsible for the lonely person's dilemma, and he or she can be ignored, because anyone who desires to live in isolation really doesn't want help. Loneliness becomes a fate to which people abandon themselves.

Other popular philosophers—futurologist Alvin Toffler, for one—admit that loneliness is most frequently a negative experience that tends to snowball. Yet this school, no less than the others, is mystified when it claims that loneliness is an inevitable part of modern life, brought about by an uncontrollable rate of technological growth. We must adapt to this state of affairs by quickening the formation of interpersonal relationships, moving people in and out of our lives as swiftly as the times demand.

These popular thinkers would have us either resign ourselves to living in a world in which the disruption of our significant relationships is everyday fare, with loneliness an irrevocable by-product, or they would have us sanctify loneliness, leading us to believe that the solution to the problem is the problem itself.

Our experience with loneliness is that it tends to spiral. We believe the answer to it is an exclusive relationship, and so we give up community, friends, and family in the name of that alliance, only to find that in so doing we have harmed the very relationship we meant to fortify. And then we find that we have neither community nor family nor friends to support us should close relationships falter.

To be caught in such a spiral is often agonizing. Men and women are social creatures, dependent upon intercommunication with one another. Without such intercommunication people begin not only to feel strange but to act strangely. Their very humanity is called into question. In the best of all possible worlds such a situation would be hard to bear. In our society, dominated as it is by concern for success and profit, loneliness is particularly difficult to deal with both because mechanisms used to combat its effects in the past are no longer available and because our expectations concerning the potential of personal relationships are so high.

Ours is the age of the RELATIONSHIP. The new psychological awareness that has grown in our century has helped us to gain greater insights into our personal and social lives. While giving us tools with which to comprehend the mind, the social sciences have also, presumably, allowed us to rid ourselves of the kinds of problems that lead to emotional and social isolation. We can, we believe, finally control our personal and social lives.

This new comprehension of our humanity gives personal relationships a hitherto unheard-of potential. We can indeed become closer to others, we believe, because we understand the barriers we build against closeness; and we can do something about removing those barriers. If we can't do it ourselves, we can get help from the experts. We can also increase the number of our relationships, because psychological awareness allows us to see that an exclusive relationship with only one other person isn't sound. It is motivated by neurotic needs, which we can now overcome. The promise of the latter half of this century, then, is the creation of more and better relationships through which we can fulfill our lives in a way that our parents were unable to do.

To realize this potential seems crucial, since traditional means of achieving satisfaction and self-affirmation have failed. We've been taught to think that "work" is the answer to the question, "What is the meaning of life?" Up until quite recently, in fact, work had dominated our search for significance, often to our loss. Today, however, the tables seem to be turning, and for many, work has little or no meaning. When people feel that they can get no satisfaction out of their work, it becomes important for them to seek fulfillment elsewhere. Interpersonal relationships, then, may appear to be the only place where self-esteem can be affirmed.

And yet the social conditions conducive to the development of human relationships seem to be disappearing. Today our life-styles both create isolation and make it more difficult to cope with such isolation. Everybody, is seeking the same thing —companionship; and everyone seems to be having trouble finding it. The search for companionship becomes a competitive and desperate undertaking. Relationships have become scarce, like a precious commodity, and when scarcity occurs in this country, there's usually somebody around to exploit it. Relationships have been turned into commodities by a service industry that covers its exploitative intentions with psychological jargon.

Armed with the right lingo, the loneliness business tempts us with an array of relational possibilities to fulfill our interpersonal needs. We can be free, close, trusting, sexy, uninhibited, risk-taking, swinging, intimate, open (inside or outside marriage). We can have any kind of relationship we may desire. The only thing we don't seem to be able to become is unlonely.

People today seem to lack the means to make the shadow of "the self" take on substance. In our do-your-own-thing culture the other has become an obstacle whose reality cannot be penetrated, or a transparent image with no reality at all. We seem to have progressed past the world in which the potential of personal life was limited by consideration for others. But perhaps we have entered a world in which the self is paralyzed because nobody else seems to care.

Selected Bibliography

Allen, Gina, and Clement G. Martin. *Intimacy: Sensitivity, Sex and the Art of Love*. New York: Pocket Books, Simon and Schuster, 1971.

Alvarez, A. *The Savage God: A Study of Suicide*. New York: Random House, 1972.

Bach, Dr. George R., and Ronald M. Deutsch. *Pairing*. New York: Avon Books, 1970.

Bartell, Gilbert D. *Group Sex: A Scientist's Eyewitness Report on the American Way of Swinging*. New York: Peter H. Wyden, 1971.

de Beauvoir, Simone. *The Coming of Age: The Study of the Aging Process*. New York: G. P. Putnam's Sons, 1972.

Berezin, Martin A., M.D. "Psychodynamic Considerations of Aging and the Aged . . . An Overview," *American Journal of Psychiatry*, Vol. 128:12 (June 1972), 1483–91.

———— and Donald J. Fern, M.D. "Persistence of Early Emotional Problems in a Seventy Year Old Woman," *Journal of Geriatric Psychiatry*, I, No. 1 (Fall 1967), 45–60.

Bowlby, John. *Attachment and Loss. Vol I. Attachment*. London: Penguin Books, 1969.

————. *Attachment and Loss. Vol. II. Separation: Anxiety and Anger*. London: Hogarth Press, 1973; New York: Basic Books, 1973.

Brown, Norman O. *Life Against Death: The Psychoanalytical Meaning of History*. Middletown, Conn.: Wesleyan University Press, 1959.

————. *Love's Body*. New York: Vintage Books, Random House, 1966.

Budson, Richard D., M.D. "The Psychiatric Halfway House," a *Psychiatric Annals* reprint (June 1973), Insight Communications Inc.

Caine, Lynn. *Widow*. New York: William Morrow and Co., Inc., 1974.

Cameron, Charles, ed. *Who Is Guru Maharaj Ji?* New York: Bantam Books, 1973.

Chopin, Kate. *The Awakening.* New York: Avon Books, 1972.

Cox, Harvey. *The Seduction of the Spirit: The Use and Misuse of People's Religion.* New York: Simon and Schuster, 1973.

Drabble, Margaret. *The Needle's Eye.* Middlesex, Eng.: Penguin Books, 1972; New York: Knopf, 1972.

Durkheim, Emile. *Suicide: A Study in Sociology.* New York: Free Press Paperback, Macmillan, 1951.

Eliade, Mircea. *Rites and Symbols of Initiation: The Mysteries of Birth and Rebirth.* New York: Harper Torchbooks, Harper and Row, 1958.

Eliot, T. S. *The Complete Poems and Plays, 1909–1950.* New York: Harcourt, Brace and World, 1952.

Epstein, Joseph. *Divorced in America: Marriage in an Age of Possibility.* New York: E. P. Dutton, 1974.

Fisher, Esther Oshiver. *Help for Today's Troubled Marriages.* New York: Award Books, 1970.

Freud, Sigmund. *Civilization and Its Discontents.* Translated by Joan Riviere. New York: Anchor Books, Doubleday, 1958.

———. *A General Introduction to Psychoanalysis.* Translated by Joan Riviere. New York: Doubleday Permabooks, 1935.

———. *The Interpretation of Dreams.* Translated and edited by James J. Strachey. New York: Basic Books, 1954.

Fromm, Erich. *The Anatomy of Human Destructiveness.* New York: Holt, Rinehart and Winston, 1973.

———. *The Crisis of Psychoanalysis: Essays on Freud, Marx and Social Psychology.* New York: Holt, Rinehart and Winston, 1970.

———. *Escape from Freedom.* New York: Avon Books, 1942.

Giammattei, Helen, and Katherine Slaughter. *Help Your Family Make a Better Move.* New York: Dolphin Books, Doubleday, 1968.

Godwin, John. *The Mating Trade.* New York: Doubleday, 1973.

Goffman, Erving. *The Presentation of Self in Everyday Life.* New York: Anchor Books, Doubleday, 1959.

———. *Relations in Public.* New York: Harper Colophon books, Harper and Row, 1971.

Goodman, Paul. *Growing Up Absurd.* New York: Vintage Books, Random House, 1960.

——— and Percival Goodman. *Communitas: Means of Livelihood and Ways of Life.* New York: Vintage Books, Random House, 1960.

Greenburg, Dan. *Scoring: A Sexual Memoir.* New York: Dell Publishing, 1972.

Harris, Thomas A., M.D. *I'm OK—You're OK: A Practical Guide to Transactional Analysis*. New York: Harper and Row, 1969.

Henry, Jules. *Culture Against Man*. New York: Vintage Books, Random House, 1965.

————. *Jungle People*. New York: Vintage Books, Caravelle Editions, Alfred A. Knopf, 1964.

————. *Pathways to Madness*. New York: Vintage Books, 1973.

————. *On Sham, Vulnerability and Other Forms of Self-Destruction*. New York: Vintage Books, Random House, 1973.

Horney, Karen. *Feminine Psychology*. Edited and with an introduction by Harold Kelman, M.D. New York: W. W. Norton, 1967.

————. *The Neurotic Personality of Our Time*. New York: W. W. Norton, 1937.

————. *New Ways in Psychoanalysis*. New York: W. W. Norton, 1939.

————. *Our Inner Conflicts: A Constructive Theory of Neurosis*. New York: W. W. Norton, 1945.

Howard, Jane. *A Different Woman*. New York: E. P. Dutton, 1973.

————. *Please Touch: A Guided Tour of the Human Potential Movement*. New York: Dell Publishing, 1971.

Hunt, Morton. *Sexual Behavior in the Seventies*. Chicago: Playboy Press, 1974.

Huxley, Aldous. *Island*. New York: Bantam Books, 1962.

Jacobs, Jane. *The Death and Life of Great American Cities*. New York: Random House, 1961.

Jacoby, Susan. "Forty-nine Million Singles Can't All Be Right," *New York Times Magazine*, Feb. 17, 1974, pp. 13, 41–49.

Jerome, Judson. *Families of Eden: Communes and the New Anarchism*. New York: Seabury Press, 1974.

Johnson, Sheila K. "Growing Alone Together," *New York Times Magazine*, Nov. 11, 1973, pp. 40–54, 59.

Josephson, Eric and Mary, eds. *Man Alone: Alienation in Modern Society*. New York: Dell Publishing, 1962.

Jung, C. G. *Memories, Dreams, Reflections*. Recorded and edited by Aniela Jaffe; translated by Richard and Clara Winston. New York: Vintage Books, Random House, 1965.

————. *Modern Man in Search of a Soul*. Translated by W. S. Dell and Cary F. Baynes. New York: Harvest Books, Harcourt, Brace and World, 1955.

————. *Psychological Reflections*. Edited by Jolande Jacobi. New York: Harper Torchbooks, Harper and Row, 1953.

Kanter, Rosabeth Moss. *Commitment and Community: Communes*

and Utopias in Sociological Perspective. Cambridge, Mass.: Harvard University Press, 1972.

Katz, Leo. "Meeting Opportunities for Adult Singles." A report to the task force on Marriage and Divorce Commission on Synagogue Relations, Federation of Jewish Philanthropies (April 1973).

Keniston, Kenneth. *The Uncommitted: Alienated Youth in American Society.* New York: Harcourt, Brace and World, 1960.

Keyes, Ralph. *We, the Lonely People: Searching for Community.* New York: Harper and Row, 1973.

Kierkegaard, Sören. *Fear and Trembling and The Sickness unto Death.* Translated by Walter Lowie. Princeton, N.J.: Princeton University Press, 1941.

Klein, Judith. "Hello in There . . . Another Perspective on Nursing Homes." Unpublished article, Baltimore, Md., 1973.

Krantzler, Mel. *Creative Divorce: A New Opportunity for Personal Growth.* New York: M. Evans, 1973.

Kubler-Ross, Elisabeth. *Questions and Answers on Death and Dying.* New York: Macmillan, 1969.

Laing, R. D. *The Divided Self: An Existential Study in Sanity and Madness.* Middlesex, Eng.: Penguin Books, 1960; New York: Pantheon, 1969.

————. *The Politics of Experience.* New York: Ballantine Books, 1967.

————. *The Politics of the Family and Other Essays.* New York: Vintage Books, Random House, 1969.

————. *The Self and Others.* Middlesex, Eng.: Penguin Books, 1961; New York: Pantheon, 1970.

———— and D. G. Cooper. *Reason and Violence: A Decade of Sartre's Philosophy 1950–1960.* New York: Vintage Books, Random House, 1971.

———— and A. Esterson. *Sanity, Madness and the Family: Families of Schizophrenics.* Middlesex, Eng.: Penguin Books, 1964.

Lessing, Doris. *The Golden Notebook.* New York: Simon and Schuster, 1962; Ballantine Books, 1962.

————. *The Grass is Singing.* New York: Thomas Y. Crowell, 1972.

————. *The Summer Before the Dark.* New York: Alfred A. Knopf, 1973.

————. *The Temptation of Jack Orkney and Other Stories.* New York: Alfred A. Knopf, 1972.

Lieberman, Morton A., Irvin D. Yalom, and Mathew B. Miles. *Encounter Groups: First Facts.* New York: Basic Books, 1973.

Lifton, Robert Jay. *Home from the War: Vietnam Veterans: Neither Victims nor Executioners.* New York: Simon and Schuster, 1973.

Lindbergh, Anne Morrow. *Bring Me a Unicorn: Diaries and Letters of Anne Morrow Lindbergh, 1922–1928.* New York: Harcourt, Brace and Jovanovich, 1971.

————. *Earth Shine.* New York: Harcourt, Brace and World, 1966.

————. *A Gift from the Sea: An Answer to the Conflicts of Our Lives.* New York: Pantheon Books, 1955.

————. *Hour of Gold, Hour of Lead: Diaries and Letters, 1929–1932.* New York: Harcourt Brace Jovanovich, 1973.

McGrady, Patrick M., Jr. *The Youth Doctors.* New York: Coward, McCann, 1968.

MacWilliams, Wilson Carey. *The Idea of Fraternity in America.* Berkeley, Cal.: University of California Press, 1973.

Mailer, Norman. *The Naked and the Dead.* New York: Signet Books, New American Library, 1948.

Marcuse, Herbert. *Eros and Civilization: A Philosophical Inquiry into Freud.* New York: Vintage Books, Random House, 1962.

————. *One Dimensional Man: Studies in the Ideology of Advanced Industrial Society.* Boston: Beacon Press, 1964.

Maslow, Abraham. *Toward a Psychology of Being.* New York: Van Nostrand Reinhold, 1968.

May, Rollo. *Love and Will.* New York: Dell Publishing, 1969.

————. *Man's Search for Himself.* New York: W. W. Norton, 1953.

Meltzer, Robert. "Street People . . . A Challenge for our Social Institutions," *New York University Education Quarterly,* IV, No. 3 (Spring 1973), 7–13.

Merton, Thomas. *Contemplation in a World of Action.* New York: Image Books, Doubleday, 1973.

————. *The Seven Storey Mountain.* New York: Signet Books, New American Library, 1948.

————. *Thoughts in Solitude: Reflections on the Spiritual Life and Love of Solitude.* New York: Image Books, Doubleday, 1956.

Miller, Arthur. *Death of a Salesman.* New York: Viking, 1949.

Mitchell, Juliet. *Feminism and Psychoanalysis.* New York: Pantheon Books, Random House, 1974.

Moustakis, Clark. *Loneliness.* New York: Spectrum Books, Prentice Hall, 1961.

Mumford, Lewis. *The Culture of Cities.* New York: Harcourt Brace Jovanovich, 1970.

Oates, Joyce Carol. *Marriages and Infidelities.* Greenwich, Conn.: Fawcett Publications, 1968.

Ollman, Bertell. *Alienation: Marx's Concept of Man in Capitalist Society.* London: Cambridge University Press, 1971.

O'Neil, Nena and George. *Open Marriage: A New Life Style for Couples.* New York: Avon Books, 1972.

Packard, Vance. *A Nation of Strangers.* New York: David McKay, 1972.

————. *The Sexual Wilderness: The Contemporary Upheaval in Male-Female Relationships.* New York: David McKay, 1968.

Pappenheim, Fritz. *Alienation and Modern Man: An Interpretation Based on Marx and Tonnies.* New York: Modern Reader Paperbacks, 1959.

Parent, Gail. *Sheila Levine Is Dead and Living in New York.* New York: Bantam Books, 1972.

Perls, Frederick S. *Gestalt Therapy Verbatim.* Compiled and edited by John O. Stevens. Lafayette, Cal.: Real People's Press, 1969.

————, Ralph F. Hefferline, and Paul Goodman. *Gestalt Therapy: Excitement and Growth in the Human Personality.* New York: Julian Press, 1962.

du Plessix Gray, Francine. "Blissing Out in Houston," *New York Review of Books,* XX, No. 20, Dec. 13, 1973, 36–43.

Proulx, Cynthia. "Sex as Athletics in the Singles Complex," *Saturday Review—The Society,* I, No. 4, April 21, 1973, 61–66.

Reich, Wilhelm. *Listen, Little Man.* Translated by Ralph Mannheim. New York: Noonday Press, Farrar, Straus and Giroux, 1974.

————. *The Sexual Revolution: Toward a Self-Regulating Character Structure.* Translated by Therese Pol. New York: Touchstone Books, Simon and Schuster, 1974.

Rettig, Solomon. "Relation of Social Systems to Intergenerational Changes in Moral Attitudes," *Journal of Personality in Social Psychology,* IV, No. 4 (1966), 409–414.

Rhys, Jean. *After Leaving Mr. MacKenzie.* New York: Vintage Books, Random House, 1931.

Riesman, David, with Nathan Glazer and Reuel Denny. *The Lonely Crowd.* New Haven, Conn.: Yale University Press, 1961.

Rogers, Carl. *On Encounter Groups.* New York: Harrow Books, Harper and Row, 1970.

Rosenbaum, Jean and Veryl. *Conquering Loneliness.* New York: Hawthorn Books, 1973.

Roth, Philip. *Goodbye, Columbus.* New York: Bantam Books, 1959.

————. *Letting Go.* New York: Bantam Books, 1961.

————. *Portnoy's Complaint.* New York: Random House, 1967.

Rycroft, Charles. *Wilhelm Reich.* New York: Modern Masters Series, Viking, 1969.

Sarton, May. *Journal of a Solitude.* New York: W. W. Norton, 1973.

Scheer, Robert. "Death of the Salesman: Portrait of Rennie Davis," *Playboy*, XXI, No. 6 (June 1974), 107–112 and 236–240.

Schrag, Peter. *The End of the American Future*. New York: Simon and Schuster, 1974.

Schutz, William C. *Here Comes Everybody: Everyman's Guide to Encounter*. New York: Harrow Books, Harper and Row, 1971.

———. *Joy: Expanding Human Awareness*. New York: Grove Press, 1967.

Seidenberg, Robert. *Corporate Wives, Corporate Casualties?* New York: Amacom, American Management Association, 1973.

Sheehy, Gail. *Hustling: Prostitution in Our Wide Open Society*. New York: Delacorte Press, 1973.

Siroka, Robert W. and Ellen R., and Gilbert A. Schloss, eds. *Sensitivity Training and Group Encounter: An Introduction*. New York: Grosset and Dunlap, 1971.

Slater, Philip. *Pursuit of Loneliness: American Culture at the Breaking Point*. Boston: Beacon Press, 1970.

Smith, James R. and Lynn G., eds. *Beyond Monogamy: Recent Studies of Sexual Alternatives in Marriage*. Baltimore: Johns Hopkins University Press, 1974.

Stein, Maurice R. *The Eclipse of Community: An Interpretation of American Studies*. Princeton, N.J.: Princeton University Press, 1971.

Stern, Richard. *Other Men's Daughters*. New York: E. P. Dutton, 1973.

Sullivan, Harry Stack. *The Interpersonal Theory of Psychiatry*. New York: W. W. Norton, 1953.

Tillich, Paul. *The Eternal Now*. New York: Charles Scribner's Sons, 1963.

de Tocqueville, Alexis. *Democracy in America, Vols. I and II*. New York: Vintage Books, Random House, 1945.

Toffler, Alvin. *Future Shock*. New York: Bantam Books, 1970.

Tonnies, Ferdinand. *Community and Society (Gemeinschaft and Geselschaft)*. Translated and edited by Charles P. Loomis. New York: Harper Torchbooks, Harper and Row, 1957.

Turnbull, Colin M. *The Lonely African*. New York: Touchstone Books, Simon and Schuster, 1962.

Updike, John. *Rabbit Redux*. New York: Alfred A. Knopf, 1971.

———. *Rabbit Run*. New York: Modern Library, Random House, 1960.

United States Government, Department of Health Education and Welfare, National Institute of Mental Health. "Halfway Houses Serving the Mentally Ill and Alcoholics in the U.S. 1969–1970," Series A, No. 9, 1971.

318 : Selected Bibliography

United States Government, Department of Health Education and Welfare, Special Task Force to the Secretary. *Work in America.* Cambridge, Mass.: MIT Press, 1973.

Vecsey, George. "Nassau Elderly Find Only Isolation in Suburbia," *New York Times,* Dec. 4, 1973, pp. 47–73.

Wakefield, Dan. *Starting Over.* New York: Delacorte Press, 1972.

Warner, Lloyd, and James Abegglen. *Big Business Leaders in America.* New York: Atheneum, 1963.

Weiss, Robert S. *Loneliness: The Experience of Emotional and Social Isolation.* Cambridge, Mass.: MIT Press, 1973.

West, Nathanael. *The Day of the Locust* and *Miss Lonelyhearts.* New York: New Directions Paperbooks, 1933.

Whyte, William H., Jr. *The Organization Man.* New York: Anchor Books, Doubleday, 1956.

Wolfe, Linda. "Take Two Aspirins and Masturbate," *Playboy,* XXI, No. 6 (June 1974), 114–116 and 164–171.

Wolfe, Thomas. *The Hills Beyond.* New York: Harper and Bros., 1935.

————. *Look Homeward Angel: A Story of the Buried Life.* New York: Modern Library, Random House, 1929.

Wood, Margaret Mary. *Paths of Loneliness: The Individual Isolated in Modern Society.* New York: Columbia University Press, 1953.

Zunin, Leonard, with Natalie Zunin. *Contact: The First Four Minutes.* New York: Ballantine Books, 1973.

About the Author

Suzanne Gordon received her B.A. from Cornell University and an M.A. in French literature from Johns Hopkins University. She has been a reporter with United Press International, and her writings have appeared in *The Washington Post, Newsweek, Ms.,* and *The Village Voice.* She is the author of *Black Mesa: The Angel of Death.*